The EYPS Handbook

The EYPS Handbook

Jackie Basquill
Liana Beattie
Joanne Ryan

PEARSON

Harlow, England • London • New York • Boston • San Francisco • Toronto • Sydney
Auckland • Singapore • Hong Kong • Tokyo • Seoul • Taipei • New Delhi
Cape Town • São Paulo • Mexico City • Madrid • Amsterdam • Munich • Paris • Milan

Pearson Education Limited
Edinburgh Gate
Harlow
Essex CM20 2JE
England

and Associated Companies throughout the world

Visit us on the World Wide Web at:
www.pearson.com/uk

First published 2012

© Pearson Education Limited 2012

ISBN: 978-1-4082-4189-9

British Library Cataloguing-in-Publication Data
A catalogue record for this book is available from the British Library

Library of Congress Cataloging-in-Publication Data
A catalog record for this book is available from the Library of Congress

10 9 8 7 6 5 4 3 2 1
15 14 13 12 11

Typeset in 10/15 pt Arial Light by 73
Printed in Great Britain by Henry Ling Ltd., at the Dorset Press, Dorchester, Dorset

Brief contents

Contents

Preface

Welcome to *The EYPS Handbook*. The aim of this book is to support early years practitioners and members of the wider children's workforce in understanding and providing evidence of the 39 EYP standards to underpin quality practice. Early years professionals (EYPs) work in a wide range of roles in group settings such as nurseries, children's centres and as home-based child carers. They lead practice, support other practitioners and are central to helping children develop from birth until the age of 5, a crucial time in a child's life. The move to a graduate-led profession is crucial to ensuring the best possible outcome for our children. This is the only book to look at each of the 39 standards on an individual basis, giving examples of leadership and practice for every standard.

In December 2008 the government published the 2020 Children and Young People's Workforce Strategy. This sets out the government's vision that everyone who works with children and young people should be:

- **Ambitious** for every child and young person
- **Excellent** in their practice
- **Committed** to partnership and integrated working
- **Respected** and valued as professionals.

To meet government targets, settings are now training their workforce to higher level qualifications and promoting the skills outlined above. The EYP status was launched in September 2006 as a pilot and has raised the quality of care provided in settings. This book will support practitioners who are now accessing the EYP course and gaining EYP status, and it complements the guidance to the 39 standards produced by the Children's Workforce Development Council (CWDC).

Chapters 1, 2 and 9 address the historical development of early years practice and legislation. The assessment process is prescribed by CWDC and the book aims to give practical examples of how naturally occurring evidence may be gathered to be presented at the end of the course. Practitioners have given personal examples of their journeys and their experiences in undertaking EYPS.

Chapters 3–8 address each of the groups of standards. Each of these chapters starts off with some theoretical underpinning knowledge to give an understanding of the group of standards, each standard is then deconstructed with an example of what it may look like in practice and then an example is given of what this may look like in leadership. We aim to give candidates sufficient understanding of the standard to be able to apply it in practice. Each standard is then followed by some reflection points and comments from the stakeholders.

We hope this book will help you on your journey, not only to achieving EYP status but also in developing your practice and that of others.

Acknowledgements

The authors are indebted to the people who have made this book possible.

We would like to thank the early years professionals who have shared their excellent practice with us, demonstrating the impact that achieving EYPS has had on their provision for young children and babies.

We would also like to show our gratitude to the following colleagues, who committed their time and expertise to deconstruct the standards, enabling future EYPS candidates to understand what each one means and how to evidence them fully, thereby improving their own practice and leading colleagues to do likewise. These colleagues are: Jo Albin-Clark, Karen Boardman, Paddy Burgess, Joanne Chatburn, Denise Corfield, Ian Currie, Dawn Davies, Linda France, Julie Goodman, Marjorie Jack, Jennifer Lee, Louise Masterson, Delyth Mathieson, Andrea Riley, Helen Torr, Elaine Canale, Catherine Curl and Karen Howard.

The publisher would like to thank the following for their kind permission to reproduce their photographs:

(Key: b-bottom; c-centre; l-left; r-right; t-top)

Page 1 Pearson Education Ltd: Jules Selmes; page 13 Fotolia.com: Coka; page 29 Alamy Images: Leila Cutler; page 61 Pearson Education Ltd: Jules Selmes; page 157 Alamy Images: Mira; page 179 Alamy Images: Picture Partners; page 203 Getty Images: Susan Barr; page 225 Alamy Images: Katrina Brown; page 249 Alamy Images: Blend Images.

All other images © Pearson Education

Chapter 1

Introduction to EYPS

Introduction

The first chapter explains the background to EYPS and the government initiatives to achieving this status. It details the EYP process, explaining the different pathways that students can take.

Objectives

By the end of this chapter you should have:

- Gained an understanding of the legislation and government initiatives underpinning the EYPS standards
- Gained an understanding of the different pathways available to achieving EYPS
- Started to consider how legislation underpins your own practice.

Pathways to gaining EYPS

All candidates undertake the same validation process within their course of study; they have to demonstrate that they can meet all 39 standards and provide sufficient evidence of personal practice and leadership in each group of standards as well as showing that they have sufficient experience of working with children in the following age ranges: 0–20 months, 16–36 months and 30–60 months.

From January 2012 there are four pathways to achieving EYPS as outlined below; The two 'practitioner' pathways are part-time and designed for current practitioners. The two 'entry' pathways are full-time and designed for new entrants to the workforce.

The Graduate Practitioner Pathway – a 6 month programme aimed at graduates currently working in the children's workforce who require a small amount of learning or experience before they can demonstrate the EYP Standards. Candidates undertaking this pathway must already hold a degree.

The Undergraduate Practitioner Pathway – a 12 month programme aimed at current practitioners working in the children's workforce with a Level 5 qualification. At the start of this pathway candidates must hold a qualification with a total of at least 240 CAT points, 120 of which must have been obtained at Intermediate Level on the Higher Education Qualifications Framework.

The Graduate Entry Pathway – a 12 month programme aimed at people with a degree in any subject and limited experience of working with children from birth to five but who are looking to pursue a career working in early years. This is a full time programme where candidates will undertake practical placements as part of the course.

The Undergraduate Entry Pathway – a 12 month programme aimed at undergraduates completing a degree in Early Childhood Studies. An equivalent full and relevant degree for this entry onto this pathway would need to reflect EYFS learning outcomes at level 6. Candidates must be studying in the final or penultimate year of a degree in Early Childhood Studies at the start of the pathway.

At the **start** of all EYPS Pathways candidates must have:

- A Criminal Records Bureau enhanced disclosure check which shows that they do not have a criminal background that might prevent them working with children and have not previously been excluded from working with children.
- An equivalent to grade C in GCSE Mathematics
- An equivalent to grade C in GCSE English.

The Pathways below were the previous routes to EYPS:

Long Pathway – candidates accessing the long pathway must have already achieved a level 5 foundation degree and will top up their degree to an ordinary degree or a BA (Hons) degree as part of this programme. Some candidates accessing the long pathway may already hold a degree but need to develop their experience in leadership or with a particular age group of children.

Short Pathway – candidates accessing the short pathway will usually be working towards most of the standards and must have a level 6 degree. They usually need to develop an aspect of knowledge and understanding or experience within one of the age ranges or standards.

Validation Pathway – candidates accessing the validation pathway will need to have a level 6 degree, mathematics and English GCSE grade C or above and must already have sufficient experience of working within the three age groups. The aim of this route is to validate the knowledge, skills and experience practitioners already hold against the 39 standards.

Full Training – candidates accessing full training will already hold a degree, although it may be in an unrelated subject and they will have little or no experience of working with children 0 to 5. Candidates develop their knowledge and understanding of child development and theory through underpinning knowledge sessions and then apply this knowledge in placements that they undertake in at least two settings and consisting of at least 18 weeks.

In some places within this book the stakeholder comments refer to above pathways as these were undertaken by the individual.

The DfE and CWDC have four strategic priorities that they are aiming to achieve within the next round of EYPs. They are:

- To direct activity so that early years professionals are most likely to benefit children at the greatest disadvantage
- For training providers to develop sustainable alternative funding sources for early years professional training
- For training providers to actively engage with, and respond to the needs of, employers in order that there is sufficient supply of high quality early years professionals to meet demand
- For training providers to encourage more applications from under-represented groups (e.g. men and people from minority ethnic groups) to undertake training and enter the workforce.

The first strategic priority of engaging with early years professionals so that children at the greatest disadvantage are most likely to benefit has evolved from The Graham Allen Report (2011), Frank Field Report (2010) and Munro Review (2011). When Graham Allen reviewed Early Intervention he recommended that the government improve the workforce capability by increasing graduate leaders and ensuring all early years settings employ an EYP. He described how the workforce development is critical in early education and how quality impacts upon child outcomes. By creating more early years professionals the government is aiming to support disadvantaged children in particular, as EYPs will be knowledgeable and well qualified practitioners.

At this stage of development in the early years landscape, we also need to consider Dame Clare Tickell's recommendations on the *EYFS framework: Setting the standards for learning, development and care for children from birth to five* (Tickell, 2011).

Dame Clare Tickell emphasised the importance of simplifying the current EYFS to make it even more accessible for parents and practitioners. At present the EYFS contains six areas of learning and development linked to 69 learning goals. The EYFS profile is used to assess children at the age of five against these goals on a 117 point scale. Clare Tickell suggested:

- Reducing the number of early learning from 69 to 17
- Placing more emphasis on three prime areas of learning: personal, social and emotional development; communication and language; and physical development. In addition, developing four areas of learning where these skills are applied: literacy, mathematics, expressive arts and design and understanding the world
- Creating a summary for parents and carers updating them on their child's development alongside the health visitor check at the age of two, which should provide an early warning of any problems
- Freeing the workforce from unnecessary paperwork and procedures, so they can spend more time interacting with children. This recommendation also to be considered in Ofsted inspections
- Ensuring that all early years practitioners have at least a level 3 qualification and the government should consider applying the 'teaching schools' model to the early years.

As a result of the Tickell Review (2011) of the Early Years Foundation Stage, CWDC and the DfE will conduct a full review of the EYP Standards and their supporting documentation. The new EYP Standards must be adopted for all EYPS Pathways that start on or after a date to be specified by CWDC.

There has been a considerable amount of legislation and policy produced over the past 10 years, giving a greater emphasis on the importance of the first 5 years of a child's life. Some of the legislation is outlined below. The legislation and policy that has developed underpins the EYPS standards. Listed below are some of the key early years policies with links to the EYPS standards. All the policies and guidance make direct links to standards 4 and 5.

1996 – Desirable Learning Outcomes – the government introduced a framework for an early years curriculum which set out a number of outcomes for children to achieve by the term after their fourth birthday (St 1, 7, 14).

1978 – The Warnock Report identified that the education of children with disabilities or significant difficulties must start as early as possible without any minimum age limit. In the earliest years, parents, rather than teachers, should be regarded, wherever possible, as the main educators of their children (St 2, 3, 29, 31, 18).

1981 – The Education Act identified the need to provide adequate safeguards, rights and duties for all those concerned with the education of children with special educational needs. It also recognised the recommendations of the Warnock Report, which emphasised the importance of early identification of children with special educational needs and, where possible, provision for their education to be integrated (St 2, 3, 6, 36, 19, 18).

1988 – The National Curriculum developed from The Education Reform Act 1988, which required that all state school students be taught a national curriculum. The aim of the national curriculum was to standardise the content taught across schools in order to enable assessment. The 1988 curriculum consisted of 10 foundation subjects, of which three, English, mathematics and science, were core subjects. The other seven consisted of technology, history, geography, a modern foreign language, music, art and physical education (St 1, 7, 14, 15).

1989 – The Children Act recognised that the welfare of children must be paramount when courts are making decisions about them. The Act gave local authorities duties to identify children in need and to safeguard and promote their welfare (St 20, 19, 18, 27, 25).

1989 – UN Convention on the Rights of the Child – the UN Convention on the rights of the child has been approved by all governments apart from the United States of America and Somalia. The convention sets out the rights of children within 54 articles and its main principles include non-discrimination; devotion to the best interests of the child; the right to life, survival and development; and respect for the views of the child. Article 12 (Respect for the views of the child) links with standard 18 'promote children's rights, equality, inclusion and anti-discriminatory practice in all aspects of their practice'. Many of the other articles could be linked to EYPS standards and the practice within settings (St 12, 18, 25, 26, 27).

1994 – The SEN Code of Practice identified eight areas of special educational needs:

1. Learning difficulties
2. Specific learning difficulties (dyslexia)
3. Emotional and behavioural difficulties
4. Physical disabilities
5. Sensory impairments/hearing
6. Sensory impairments/visual
7. Speech and language difficulties
8. Medical conditions.

In addition, five stages of identification and assessment were highlighted:

1. Differentiation of work
2. Individual education plan in place
3. Involvement of outside agencies
4. Formal assessment
5. Statement produced outlining provision and placement.

The SEN code of practice was revised in 2002, changing the eight areas of special educational needs to four areas.

1. Communication and interaction
2. Cognition and learning
3. Behavioural, emotional and social development
4. Sensory and/or physical,

and the stages of identification and assessment to

- Early years Action
- Early years Action Plus
- Statemented provision.
  (St 6, 36, 2, 3, 7, 8, 9, 10, 12, 13, 17.)

1998 – National Childcare Strategy – the National Childcare Strategy was a complex initiative for the development, expansion, implementation and sustainability of early years and childcare services. It aimed to provide affordable childcare and early years services supporting child development and removing barriers to parental employment and alleviating child poverty (St 24, 18, 20).

2000 – Curriculum guidance for the foundation stage was introduced by the DfEE. The guidance was focused on the development of children aged 3–5 and had been developed by the Qualifications and Curriculum Authority (QCA) working with early years practitioners and experts. The guidance helped practitioners provide learning and teaching, allowing flexibility to the needs of the children and their families. The guidance is broken down into six areas of learning and then early learning goals within each of the six areas (St 1, 7, 8, 9, 10, 11, 12, 13, 14, 15, 16, 17, 21).

2000 – The Care Standards Act reformed the regulation of childminders and daycare provision for young children, transferring the regulatory function from local authorities to Her Majesty's Chief Inspector of Schools for England (HMCIS) under a new arm of Ofsted (St 35, 34, 38, 24).

2002 – Birth to Three Matters Framework aimed to provide support, information and guidance for practitioners with responsibility for the care and education of babies and children from birth to 3 years. It turns its attention to the child, keeping away from specific curriculum headings but bearing in mind the skills that babies and young children are developing and the environment that should be provided for them to achieve these skills. There were four aspects and each aspect was divided into four components. Each component also has several features that professionals should focus on to develop each child's aspect (St 1, 2, 7, 26).

2003 – Lord Laming's report on Victoria Climbié finds that the death of an 8-year-old girl is due to a gross failure of the system of public agencies responsible for protecting vulnerable children from deliberate harm. The report contains 108 recommendations for fundamental changes to the way that social care, healthcare and police child protection services are organised and managed at national and local level, in order to establish a clear line of accountability in the provision of services for vulnerable children and the support of families (St 20, 6, 36, 3, 8, 35).

2003 – National Standards for under-8s Daycare and Childminding are a set of outcomes that providers must achieve. Each standard describes a particular quality outcome and is accompanied by a set of supporting criteria giving information about how that outcome is to be achieved. Ofsted produced further guidance to help daycare providers to meet these national standards. The national standards applied to full daycare, sessional daycare, out-of-school care, crèches and childminders. The full daycare standards were split into 13 sections (St 24, 1, 8, 33, 35).

2003 – Green paper 'Every Child Matters' had four key themes. They consisted of:

- Increasing the focus on supporting families and carers
- Ensuring that interventions were taking place before a critical point for children was reached, and protecting children from not being identified
- Addressing the concerns raised in the Lord Laming report
- Ensuring that practitioners working with children were well trained, valued and rewarded.
  (St 29, 30, 31, 32, 20, 39.)

2004 – The Common Core followed on from the Green Paper 'Every Child Matters', recognising that practitioners working with children should have a common set of skills. The common core splits the knowledge and skills into six areas:

1. Effective communication and engagement
2. Child and young person development
3. Safeguarding and promoting the welfare of the child
4. Supporting transitions
5. Multi-agency working
6. Sharing information.
   (St 33, 34, 35, 36, 37, 38, 39.)

2004 – The effective provision of preschool education (EPPE) project was the first major European longitudinal study of a national sample of young children's development between the ages of 3 and 7 years. It aimed to investigate the effects of preschool education. The EPPE team collected a wide range of information on 3000 children and found that the impact of attending a preschool meant that disadvantaged children benefit significantly from good quality experiences, especially where they are with a mixture of children from different social backgrounds. The effects of quality and specific practices in preschool showed that high quality preschooling is related to better intellectual and social/behavioural development for children. The importance of home learning identified that the quality of the home learning environment is more important for intellectual and social development than parental occupation, education or income. What parents do is more important than who parents are (St 29, 30, 31, 32, 17).

2004 – The 10-year Strategy for Children, 'Choice for parents, the best start for children', identified the government's long-term vision which aims to ensure that every child has the best start in life and gives parents more choice. It aimed to provide affordable, flexible, high-quality childcare places for families with children aged up to 14 years. The provision was to be of high quality with a highly skilled early years workforce driving the quality (St 29, 30, 31, 34, 38, 37).

2004 – The Children Act 2004 aimed to improve multidisciplinary working and remove duplication. It placed a new duty on local authorities to listen to children and their families in the planning of services and to promote the education of children who were being looked after (St 6, 36, 27, 18, 29).

2005 – The Children's Workforce and Development Council was set up to support the development of qualifications and skills for practitioners working within the children's workforce. The CWDC support 2.6 million people working with children and young people across education, welfare, social work and social care (St 33, 34, 37, 38, 39).

2005 – 'Key Elements of Effective Practice' is a key document which emphasises that effective learning depends on a high quality environment appropriate to the child's needs and stresses the importance of secure relationships with caring and understanding individuals. The importance of working with parents and a range of professionals is also highlighted (St 24, 30, 8, 19, 25).

2005 – The Disability Discrimination Act gave people with disability new rights. Settings are required under the Act to make reasonable adjustments to their premises. Early years settings have to consider how they can improve access to early years education (St 13, 18, 12, 2, 3, 7).

2006 – The Childcare Act was the first ever exclusively concerned with early years and childcare. The act required authorities to improve the five Every Child Matters Outcomes for all preschool children, secure sufficient childcare for working parents and provide better parental information. The Act simplified the early years regulation and inspection procedures, offering an integrated care and education framework (St 30, 31, 32, 3).

2006 – The first early years professionals cohort. Phase one was offered from September 2006 as a validation-only route for practitioners who were already meeting the standards and just needed to validate the work they undertook. In January 2007 the first 338 EYPs were given the status.

2007 – The Children's Plan: Building Brighter Futures aims to build on the existing support for all families. It plans to involve parents in their children's learning and give young children opportunities that are interesting and exciting whilst being safe. The plan includes a set of objectives:

- To secure the health and wellbeing of children and young people
- Safeguard the young and vulnerable
- Achieve world class standards.

2008 – Early Years Foundation Stage (EYFS) brings together the principles from the Birth to Three Matters with the curriculum guidance for the foundation stage along with elements of the national standards for under-8s daycare and childminding. The EYFS aims to ensure consistency in provision for children from birth to 5 in any type of setting.

2010 – The government aims to have an EYP in every children's centre offering early years provision.

2015 – The government aims to have an EYP in every full daycare setting.

The recognition that the government has given to how young children's learning will impact on the rest of their life identified above has led to the introduction of the EYP whose role is to raise the quality of provision in early years settings. Having an EYP in a setting benefits a range of stakeholders. Children in the setting should be exposed to a higher quality learning environment that caters for their individual needs as the practitioners caring for them are led by a highly qualified and knowledgeable EYP. The parents will be viewed as the child's first carer and the EYP will work with the staff to identify how the setting can demonstrate to parents that their contribution is essential to the child's development and establish ways in which effective partnerships can be built. Practitioners in a setting where an EYP is based have a person with whom they can share ideas and who will support them to become reflective practitioners identifying how improvements can be made and contributing to a culture of collaboration and mutual respect. Many local authorities work with the EYPs in the form of a network group to share good practice and identify developments. This can then be taken back to the setting and disseminated among the team, again enhancing the experiences with which the children engage and contributing to improving the overall aim of the Every Child Matters five outcomes. EYPs will work across a wide variety of roles and across a range of different centres, but ultimately all trying to achieve the same goal.

Conclusion

There are various routes into EYPS to suit candidates' individual needs and to give recognition to personal development that needs to take place over the duration of the course. The various routes identify candidates' individual needs and build upon their existing skills, ensuring by completion of the programme that they can demonstrate personal practice and leadership across each group of standards and have sufficient experience within each of the age ranges.

There have been considerable changes in policy and legislation over the past few decades and a number of research projects have been carried out. This research and change in legislation has given recognition to early childhood development. These changes have reformed the services on offer for children and their families and have played a key role in tackling poverty.

Reference

Tickell, D.C. (2011) *The Early Years: Foundations for life, health and learning. An Independent Report on the Early Years Foundation Stage to Her Majesty's Government.* Online. Available from http://www.education.gov.uk/tickellreview

The assessment process

Introduction

This chapter gives on overview of the assessment process, and describes the requirements of the setting visit.

Objectives

By the end of this chapter you should have:

- Gained an overview of the EYPS formative and summative assessment process
- Reflected on your current role and started to consider the evidence that you can collect to demonstrate your personal practice and leadership within the 39 standards
- Reflected on your current experience and started to consider how you can demonstrate evidence for each of the three age ranges: 0–20 months, 16–36 months and 30–60 months.

The **written tasks** and the **setting visit** form the summative part of the assessment process, and this is the same for all candidates regardless of which pathway they are taking. Candidates submit seven written tasks prior to the setting visit which must cover all 39 standards. By the end of the setting visit candidates must have demonstrated that they have met all 39 standards and have sufficient experience within each age range (0–20 months, 16–36 months and 30–60 months). The 39 standards are split into six groups and candidates must show that they have demonstrated personal practice and leadership within each group of standards.

As part of their course candidates undertake a half-day **Gateway Review** considering three key skills: decision-making, leadership and communication. This forms the formative part of the assessment process and is fundamental to achieving EYPS.

Mid-point Review

Each candidate will undertake a 'development & progress review'. The review will take place before the final assessment, at a point during the candidate's EYPS Pathway which allows them reasonable time to take action in response to the feedback.

The development and progress review will:
- Determine the candidate's understanding of the EYP Standards
- Determine the candidate's progress in evidencing the EYP Standards
- Determine the candidate's understanding of implementing and/or ability to implement change in a setting
- Determine the candidate's ability to lead and support others
- Provide the opportunity for candidate's to receive interim feedback on their progress
- Review and support the candidate's progress towards achieving a successful EYPS outcome.

At the end of the process an action plan/progress review statement will be developed for each candidate to support their progress towards achieving a successful assessment outcome.

The setting visit

Before candidates write the tasks it is important that they have started to deconstruct the standards, as generally each standard refers to more than one aspect of early years practice. It is only when candidates fully understand the requirements of the standards that they can link their experiences to the tasks. The amplifications in the guidance to the standards (CWDC) are particularly useful in helping candidates to do this.

Reflection points

Consider each of the age ranges

- 0–20 months
- 16–36 months
- 30–60 months

and reflect on the following points:

- What personal practice have you carried out within each age range in the past 3 years?
- What activities/projects have you led within each of the age ranges in the past 3 years?
- Reflect on your current experience and put together a professional development plan to extend your experience with each of the age ranges.

Tasks 1, 2 and 3 have an emphasis on leading and supporting other practitioners, and each has a recommended word count of between 1500 and 2000 words. The tasks can cover any activities that candidates have engaged with in the past 3 years.

The tasks are written on pre-set forms which will be provided to the candidate by the training provider. Tasks 1, 2 and 3 require a reflective account and analysis of experiences in which the candidate has led other practitioners across the full age group. The candidate writes their tasks under the following headings:

1.1 Nature of the activity
1.2 Age range, in months, of the children directly or indirectly affected by this activity
1.3 What you planned to do and why
1.4 What happened when you carried out the work
1.5 Your assessment of the effectiveness of the activity
1.6 Your personal learning.

Examples of written tasks

Examples of Task 1
Lead and support other practitioners in implementing aspects of the Early Years Foundation Stage (EYFS) for babies (0–20 months)

Case A

A candidate has observed practice in the baby room and the observations identified that the use of treasure baskets is limited. The candidate researched the benefits of treasure baskets to the youngest children and produced an information leaflet for parents and staff. The candidate then led a meeting held with the baby room staff to discuss the leaflet and how the practice could be developed. The staff views and opinions were sought and then some treasure basket activities were role-modelled. The improved practice was observed and shared with parents and recorded in the children's learning journeys.

Case B

In a children's centre, the provision for the children aged 0–2 years was offered in one room. The candidate reflected on the planning and asked the staff how they felt the planning was working. As a team they looked at the EYFS and how this linked into their planning and observations. They discovered through the reflection that the planned activities that were offered came from the Development Matters statements and that the same activities were accessible to all the children. However, the planning and observations required development to include the children's interests and differentiation. The candidate worked with the children's centre teacher to develop new forms and then shared them with the staff. As the staff used the new forms they identified further improvements, including adding a section to include parents. The candidate listened to the staff's ideas and amended the form again. The new planning and observation system showed how individual children were progressing and gave key workers an opportunity to build supportive and constructive relationships with their key children.

Reflection point
- Write down some ideas that you could use for Task 1.

Examples of Task 2
Lead and support other practitioners in implementing aspects of the EYFS for toddlers (16–36 months)

Case A

A candidate noticed during story time that the children are becoming bored and uninterested in the session. She used the EYFS 'Linking Sounds and Letters' and 'Reading' 16–26 months and 22–36 months to work with the practitioners to identify how they could make the story time more interesting. In consultation with the practitioners she liaised with the parents to find out what the children's favourite stories were and used this as a starting point. They then developed the story time by using puppets and other props to support the session and developed the children's interaction in the session. The candidate then took photographs of the session and displayed these for the parents to share the experience.

Case B

After attending a training session on outdoor provision, the candidate recognised that there were improvements that could be made within her setting. She asked the practitioners to observe each other in the outdoor area and the peer observations identified that practitioners were mainly providing physical activities outdoors and supervising children as opposed to interacting with them. The candidate arranged for the practitioners to visit the early excellence centre to give them further ideas on how they could develop their outdoor provision. There was no access to allow free flow provision so the practitioners decided that they would each develop a box for outdoor provision based on the children's interests and which covered the six areas of learning. The candidate ordered the resources that the practitioners needed and because of budget restrictions made some of the resources from other materials. Each practitioner then used their box in the outdoor area, scaffolding the children's learning.

Reflection point

● Write down some ideas that you could use for Task 2.

Examples of Task 3
Lead and support other practitioners in implementing aspects of the EYFS for young children (30–60 months)

Case A

The candidate was the preschool leader and, after accessing training on 'A Unique Child', she analysed the observations and planning used in her room. This identified that they did not recognise and support changes in children's personal circumstances in enough detail. The candidate held a meeting with the staff in her room and each key worker considered their own key children and the individual needs. The discussion highlighted the varied backgrounds of the children, including a child whose mother was pregnant and a child whose parents were going through divorce. The candidate supported the key worker in having a meeting with the parent of the first child to see if any discussions or activities with the child had taken place about the body. The parent said that the child did not want the baby to come and would throw around the toys that had been bought for the baby at home. So the candidate, key worker and parent decided how to deal with the situation to create a consistent approach. In the setting the key worker spoke with all the children about babies and they decided as a group to set up a role play area as a baby clinic. The children looked at some catalogues and chose how they would like the area to be set up. The children and key worker, with the support of the room leader, made some of the resources out of materials in the creative area. The role play area then created lots of opportunities for the child to express his feelings and the key worker observed the child's play and engaged in discussions to support the child's emotions. The candidate then supported the practitioner in recording this in the child's learning journey and continuing to build a constructive relationship with the child and family.

Case B

This candidate was the setting manager of a playgroup caring for children aged 2–5 years. This role incorporated responsibilities for safeguarding. The candidate wanted to ensure that the practitioners were fully aware of their responsibilities with regard to recognising when a child may be at risk of harm and that they knew how to act to protect the child. The candidate gave all the practitioners a copy of the child protection policy and asked them to read it before the next team meeting. At the next meeting the candidate created a range of potential scenarios and held discussions with the practitioners surrounding the issues that the scenarios presented and what the appropriate action would be in each case. She used the scenarios to identify when and how it might be appropriate to use a common assessment framework (CAF) and how the procedures in the setting linked to local and national policies.

Reflection point

● Write down some ideas that you could use for Task 3.

Examples of Task 4
An account of your personal practice with a young child or children

Case A

One of the children in the candidate's key group had a hearing impairment. The candidate liaised with the teacher for the deaf and the child's parents to develop an individual educational plan (IEP). She worked with the child, implementing an agreed programme and interventions on a regular basis. She adapted aspects of the provision to ensure that it was accessible and inclusive for all the children. A communication book was developed to share achievements and daily events between the parents and the setting. The child also contributed to the communication book and was consulted on the actions in the IEP to give priority to the rights of the child. The candidate then supported the other practitioners to understand how to manage the equipment for the child. When the child moved to school the candidate met with the parent and school teacher and passed on all the records the setting had and supported the child on visits to ensure a smooth transition.

Case B

A 3-year-old child regularly had outbursts where he became violent towards other children. The candidate sensitively spoke with the parents about the behaviour within the setting and also emphasised all the good aspects of behaviour the child showed throughout the day. The candidate agreed with the parent that she would observe the child to try to identify what was causing the behaviour, what happened during the outburst and what happened afterwards. She kept a copy of all the observations so she could compare the time of day, area in the room, amount of children/practitioners present, and shared these on each occasion with the parent. The parent had said that the child did not display this behaviour at home. The observations identified that the negative behaviour was usually displayed in the afternoon and it was at a time when three or four children were involved in an activity with the child. The practitioner consulted with all the children on how they thought they should behave in the setting and they devised a list of positive expectations which they displayed on the wall and then praised the children throughout the day when the behaviour was being displayed and reminded them of the rules if negative behaviour was happening. The cause of the negative behaviour for this individual child appeared to be around sharing with his peers. The candidate, in consultation with the parents and the child, identified a range of strategies to support the child's development. Over a period of time the behaviour improved and the candidate and child built a trusting and supportive relationship.

Reflection point

● Write down some ideas that you could use for Task 4.

Examples of Task 5a
The first activity, event or situation

Case A

The candidate was responsible for the development of the EYFS and, as part of evaluating the provision, she reviewed each area of the continuous provision. The aim was to identify what opportunities for each of the six areas of learning were available in each continuous provision area. She gave each member of staff an area in the room and asked them to take one area of learning at a time and identify the opportunities in that area. The evaluation identified that there were lots of missed opportunities for problem-solving, reasoning and numeracy. The candidate then used the EYFS with the staff to improve the resources in the area and the adult support to create new opportunities for the children to engage with based on their interests.

Case B

When the EYFS was introduced, the candidate identified that there was a need to share the content with the parents and carers. He set up an open event where parents could come along and have a look at the EYFS. The candidate and other practitioners set up a range of activities with links to the EYFS so the parents could see the benefits of the activities on offer. The candidate gave a talk on the EYFS and showed a DVD of the children playing in the setting. The parents/carers then split into groups and spent some time with their child's key worker talking about their child's interests and ability in relation to the EYFS.

Reflection point

● Write down some ideas that you could use for Task 5a.

Examples of Task 5b
The second activity, event or situation

Case A

A group of children had become particularly interested in boats. The candidate developed opportunities within the provision to extend the children's interest. She obtained some books around how boats were made and the names of the different areas on the boats. She provided a range of junk modelling materials and placed in the modelling areas photographs of different types of boats. The children made some fantastic models using a range of materials. The candidate supported the children by extending their thinking and asking open-ended questions. The candidate then provided a range of larger materials outdoors and the children made bigger boats in which they could sit. A trip was then arranged by the candidate to a boat museum where the children could see and feel the boats.

Case B

While a child was playing outside he fell over and cut his arm open. The candidate wore the appropriate protective equipment and reassured and comforted the child, cleaning the wound. She then recorded the accident in the accident book and sensitively informed the parent at the end of the session. The candidate checked the area to see if there was anything that had caused the accident and noticed that it was caused because of a chip in a flagstone. The candidate reported the area to the health and safety officer immediately and carried out a risk assessment.

Reflection point

● Write down some ideas that you could use for Task 5b.

Examples of Task 5c
The third activity, event or situation

Case A

A new member of staff started in the toddler room and it was the candidate's responsibility to carry out their induction. The candidate gave the new member of staff a copy of all the policies and procedures and discussed the key ones, highlighting how the setting's practice linked into the EYFS, Every Child Matters, The Children's Act and the SEN code of practice. She also talked with the practitioner about 'contact point' and the practitioner's responsibilities if she suspected abuse. The candidate shared the planning and observations with the new practitioner, supporting her to understand her role. The candidate then proceeded to show the new member of staff the risk assessments in place and the procedure for reporting an accident or identified risk. A time was then arranged for the candidate and practitioner to meet again when the new member of staff had had some time to read and digest the information given to her.

Case B

One of the candidate's key children was at the stage of development where it was appropriate for them to move up to the next room. The candidate met with the child's new key worker and had a discussion around the child's ability and they shared the learning journey. The candidate then met with the parent and discussed the methods they would use to move the child into the next room. The child's new key worker came to the child's existing room to get to know the child in familiar surroundings. The parent wanted to be involved so she came with the child on the first few short visits to the next room. Then the key worker went with the child on the next few short visits. The child then went for a short visit with her new key worker, and over a period of time the child became confident in the new room, demonstrating that a successful transition had taken place.

Reflection point

● Write down some ideas that you could use for Task 5c.

The tasks are then submitted to the training provider, and the assessor who is going to carry out the setting visit assesses the tasks in relation to each of the 39 standards and also considers the personal practice and leadership within each group of standards and the experience that the candidate has shown within each of the three age groups (0–20 months, 16–36 months and 30–60 months).

Setting visit timetable

The candidate decides the time at which the setting visit is going to start and then the activities throughout the day all have a prescribed length of time, as identified below:

- First candidate interview – 30 minutes
- Scrutiny of documentary file – 75 minutes
- Tour of the setting – 45 minutes
- Assessor writing and reflection time – 30 minutes
- Witness interviews – 75 minutes
- Assessor lunch – 30 minutes
- Assessor writing and reflection time – 30 minutes
- Second candidate interview – 15 minutes.

Candidate interviews

The candidate interviews provide opportunities for the candidates to give examples of their practice in relation to the 39 standards, personal practice and leadership, and the three age groups. The assessor will ask predetermined questions based on the tasks they have read and supplementary questions will be asked as required. It is important that candidates use 'I' instead of 'we' as the assessor is gathering evidence of the candidate's experience. The candidate will need to give examples of his or her experience, describing particular situations and not make assertions.

Reflection points

Look at the standards and identify the range of experience you have had within each of the six groups. Break this experience down into personal practice and leadership.

- Have you experience of both personal practice and leadership in each group of standards?
- Have you an example of experience to cover each standard?
- Can you give examples of the standards in relation to working with the three age groups?

Tour of the setting

The tour allows the assessor to put the candidate's role into context. The candidate needs to be clear about their role in the setting and articulate this to the assessor. The candidate submits a written commentary of the tour to the training provider prior to the setting visit to ensure that they have considered carefully what they would like to show the assessor. The candidate identifies which standards will be shown through the tour of the setting.

What the assessor will see: my contribution	Std	Assessor's notes on the candidate's work
Reception – parent's notice board; I have created this board to keep parents informed. It displays the daily routines and planning. I write a monthly newsletter, which goes on the board and contains information about the EYFS.	31 32	
Preschool room – I work in this room and designed the layout of it, taking into consideration the other practitioners' ideas. I considered safety and inclusion, and the resources are set at children's height so they have the opportunity to choose. The resources I have selected are based on children's interests and backgrounds and represent diversity. Within each continuous provision area I have provided books and mark-making materials to support the development of children's communication skills.	33 8 12 15	
Children's learning journey – I support other practitioners to complete the learning journeys. This includes observations of the children that are used to inform the planning of next steps for individual children.	10 14	

Reflection point

Take a member of staff around your setting and talk about all the practice you have implemented or to which you have contributed. Ask the member of staff to take notes on the way round. Afterwards, analyse the notes and link them to the standards and consider whether there is anything else you need to include or something you could take out.

Scrutiny of documentary evidence

The candidate puts together a file of documentary evidence which stays within the setting and the assessor scrutinises this on the day of the visit. Documents within the file may include observation forms, planning sheets, minutes of meetings, reports and witness testimonies. It is essential that the candidate makes clear their role within the documents and links the documents to the standards. The file should be put together in order of the standards. The candidate submits the list of documents to the training provider prior to the setting visit. The candidate needs to remember that the assessor will scrutinise the file for 75 minutes and therefore needs to give consideration to the range of documentary evidence provided to ensure that the assessor has sufficient time to assess the documents.

Std	Title or description	Doc. no.	What the document shows about my work
1 2	Planning sheet	3, 7 and 12	I have completed the planning form, which shows the links to the EYFS Development Matters. The documents show activities that I have carried out with children from 6 months through to 4 years and how I have planned for individual needs within my key worker planning
3	Witness testimony	1	The witness testimony is from a parent describing how I supported her child moving from one room to the next. The child's parent was unwell, going in and out of hospital, and this was affecting the child's behaviour and development. We used a range of strategies, which I coordinated
4	Photograph of display	6	I put up a display of children carrying out activities in the reception area for parents and staff. I linked the activities to the EYFS and to Every Child Matters with an explanation for parents

Reflection point

Over a period of a week, collect together a range of paperwork that you have been using. Match the paperwork to the standards to ensure that you have a full range of standards covered and then write down your role within each of the documents, making the link to the standards explicit.

Witness interviews

The candidate will select three witnesses to be interviewed; this will usually last for 75 minutes. The assessor will ask questions to gather evidence for the 39 standards, give examples of personal practice and leadership and verification of the candidate's experience within each of the three age groups. The questions will be tailored to the witnesses' role and the witnesses will need to give examples of the candidate's practice.

Outcomes – internal and external moderation

There are three possible outcomes for candidates: met, not met or standards shortfall.

Met – the candidate has provided sufficient evidence of the 39 standards and has demonstrated personal practice and leadership within each of the six groups of standards. The candidate has also shown sufficient experience of working with children in the three different age groups.

Not met – the candidate has not met three or more standards and therefore the shortfall is significant or the candidate has not provided sufficient evidence of personal practice and leadership within each of the six groups of standards and the weaknesses cannot be remedied within 3 months. The candidate has not provided sufficient evidence of working with babies, toddlers and young children and the experience cannot be gained in the next 3 months.

Standards shortfall – the candidate has a small number of standards that have not been met; normally there can be no more than three standards. The candidate has not provided sufficient evidence of personal practice or leadership within each of the six groups of standards. The candidate has not provided sufficient evidence of experience of working with babies, toddlers and young children. The candidate is able to provide further evidence within 3 months to address the deficiency.

The assessor then makes a recommendation for one of the above outcomes. The candidate's full file is presented at internal moderation and a sample of files is moderated. All files that are not met and standards shortfalls will be moderated and a selection of the met files. The results of the internal moderation are then shared with the external moderators and the external moderators select a sample of files. The recommendation made by the assessor can be changed at internal or external moderation. The final decision lies with the external moderators. After internal and external moderation has taken place, candidates are sent a letter informing them of the outcome.

Conclusion

The EYPS assessment process is designed in such a way so as to give candidates every opportunity to demonstrate that they have met the 39 standards. The number of different methods the candidates use gives them a chance to show their range of experiences. The assessment process is stringent and quality–assured to ensure that the assessors' work is of the highest standard and that candidates are being assessed fairly.

References

CWDC. (2008) *Guidance to the Standards for the Award of the Early Years Professional Status.* London: CWDC.

CWDC. (2009) *Handbook for Candidates. A Guide to the Gateway Review and the Assessment Process.* London: CWDC.

Chapter 3

Knowledge and understanding

Introduction

This chapter details current legal requirements, national and local policies, the principles of the Early Years Foundation Stage (EYFS), theories and research on child development.

Objectives

By the end of this chapter you should have:

● Gained an overview of the key theoretical perspectives in relation to the main strands of knowledge and understanding expected of EYPs

● Reflected on how you can promote through your practice the requirements identified in standards 1–6

● Reflected on how you can lead and support others in relation to the requirements identified in standards 1–6.

Theoretical underpinning knowledge for standards 1–6

Innumerable studies have shown that the experiences received by children during their early childhood are crucial to their further development. Given that brain development is taking place at its fastest when children are very young, with 90 per cent of brain development occurring by age 5, these early experiences help with making connections in the brain. The EYFS framework (DCSF, 2008) has been introduced to ensure that all children from birth to 5 years old are provided with the best possible early years experiences to underpin and promote their learning and all-round development and help them to achieve the five outcomes for Every Child Matters: 'stay safe', 'enjoy and achieve', 'make a positive contribution' and 'achieve economic well-being' (DfES, 2003). With this in mind, we have to acknowledge that having a knowledgeable and skilful practitioner leading delivery of the EYFS is essential in the process of providing young children with the highest quality of early years learning opportunities. The dimension of the EYP's role as strategic leaders and agents of change (CWDC, 2008) is firmly linked to their knowledge and understanding of the principles and content of the EYFS and ways of implementing the latter in practice. According to the DCSF (2008):

> the leader of practice should be able to demonstrate . . . sound knowledge and understanding of Early Years pedagogy: the holistic needs of all children from birth to five and competence in planning, implementing and monitoring within the Early Years Foundation Stage framework.

This group of EYP standards embraces not only knowledge and understanding of the EYFS framework, but also of broader aspects of child development. One of these aspects includes knowledge and understanding of the individual and diverse ways in which children develop and learn from birth to the end of the foundation stage and thereafter. 'A Unique Child' is one of the four complementary themes of the EYFS, and highlights the importance of the child as an individual and reinforces the need for all facets of provision to be responsive to the needs of each child. The idea of uniqueness of each child stems from the educational philosophy of Friedrich Froebel (1782–1852), who was one of the pioneers of early years provision. As an idealist, he thought that all children possessed at birth their full educational potential, and that an appropriate educational environment was necessary to encourage each child to grow and develop at their own pace through the developmental stages of the educational process. Froebel did not believe that the child should be placed into society's shape, but should be allowed to form his own nature and grow at his own pace without being rushed or hurried in his development:

> Young animals and plants are given rest, and arbitrary interference with their growth is avoided, because it is known that the opposite practice would disturb their pure unfolding and sound development; but, the young human being is looked upon as a piece of wax or a lump of clay which man can mould into what he pleases.   (Froebel, 1907: 8)

Today this process can be referred to as an educational philosophy that requires practitioners to tailor their teaching and assessment whilst adjusting the framework to the needs of individual children rather than expecting children to fit the existing curriculum (Rogers, 2007; Cole, 2008). Addressing the full range of children's needs involves EYPs using innovation and flexibility across a range of strategies to create learning opportunities and environments that are beneficial to all children, including those with special educational needs (SEN). This requires EYPs to develop their knowledge and understanding of both developmental stages of children's progress and the ways in which children's learning, development and behaviour can be influenced by cultural and environmental factors. A key influence on this area of knowledge is the work of Piaget (1983), who developed the idea of children following linear developmental patterns as they progress from early years to adulthood. In contrast to Piaget's belief, contemporary theories assume that development proceeds in a web of multiple strands, with different children following different pathways (Ayoub and Fischer, 2006), and with the process of learning occurring in 'overlapping waves' (Siegler, 2005). Although average 'Development Matters' indicators have been used throughout the EYFS to indicate a certain chronological outline in the achievement of developmental milestones, children's development is presented in the framework under six overlapping phases. This overlap is intended to emphasise the fact that there can be big differences between the development of children of similar ages. At the same time age can be a cue, when taken with all other factors, to indicate that development may be atypical and that a child may need extra support (DCSF, 2010a).

Within the context of this group of standards, EYPs are also required to consider cultural and environmental influences on children's learning and development. The EYFS framework places emphasis on, firstly, helping children to develop their own sense of identity through the understanding of their 'family culture' and values; and secondly, on helping young children to develop further their understanding of wider communities and other cultures. The importance of social and cultural influences formed the cornerstone of social constructivism, a theoretical perspective, the origins of which are largely attributed to Vygotsky (1978), who stressed the role of the social and cultural context in children's development. Nowadays, the value of social and cultural diversity within the context of the early years environment has been widely acknowledged by both theorists and early years practitioners, who suggest that effective early years practice needs to support cultural and social diversity from the earliest months of children's development and learning (Lindon, 2006; Nutbrown and Clough, 2008).

Considering the effects of sociocultural aspects on children's development requires EYPs to adopt strategies, tools and resources that will promote and shape children's learning with a variety of social and cultural experiences. In view of the advantages that cultural diversity can offer, early years practitioners need also to utilise their own cultural backgrounds and experiences as a way of developing their skills and knowledge in this area. As DSCF (2010b: 125) assures: 'the Government will . . . continue to take steps to support the children's workforce in becoming more diverse and more culturally sensitive, and thus better able to reflect the needs of the families who use services'.

EYPs also need to be aware of other aspects that influence children's learning and development, including the issues of social disadvantages and poverty. Unfortunately, poverty still affects the daily lives of many children. As highlighted in the Child Poverty Act (HMSO, 2010), which became law in March 2010, sustained action must be taken to tackle child poverty by this, and future, governments, by the devolved administrations, and by local government and their partners. The Act requires the Secretary of State to publish a strategy every 3 years showing how the UK government intends to tackle the child poverty targets, using the following 'building blocks':

- Parental employment and skills
- Financial support for children and parents
- Information, advice and assistance to parents and promotion of parenting skills
- Physical and mental health, education and social services
- Housing, the built and natural environment and the promotion of social inclusion.

The building blocks of the strategy are shown on the outer edge of Figure 3.1, illustrating how each work towards reaching the four aspirations of the strategy, as detailed in the central circle (HMSO, 2008: 29).

Within this context, it is imperative that EYPs research, analyse and understand fully the influence of poverty upon children's wellbeing and their capacity to learn and develop.

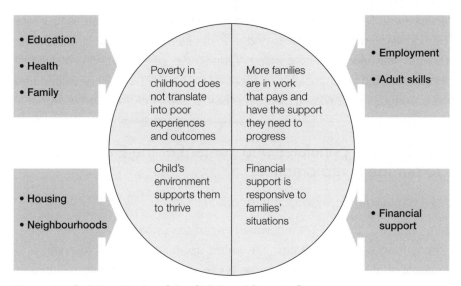

Figure 3.1 **Building blocks of the Childhood Poverty Strategy**

Standards 4, 5 and 6 require EYPs to have knowledge and understanding of the current legal requirements, national policies and frameworks and their implications for early years settings as well as the contribution that other professionals within the setting and beyond can make to children's physical and emotional wellbeing, development and learning. Since these aspects of early years practice are evolving rapidly and are continuously shaping the landscape of early years provision, practitioners' knowledge and understanding of relevant legislation and national policies are considered a high priority, as the latter form the basis for current and future development of early years provision. As CWDC (2008) points out, EYPs are not expected to have a detailed knowledge of all such frameworks, but they must be sufficiently familiar with their content to understand their own responsibilities and the implications for early years settings. Thus informed, they are better able to develop, evaluate and modify their own practice; and they are better able to lead and support colleagues in developing their understanding of statutory and non-statutory frameworks and in introducing changes when necessary. Current research (Baldock *et al.*, 2007; Waller, 2009; Siraj-Blatchford and Siraj-Blatchford, 2009) highlights the idea that coping with scores of changes and working in collaboration with other professionals and agencies might require EYPs and other early years practitioners to move out of their comfort zone and to take some risks, which can be quite demanding and challenging. As Anning (2005) rightly notes, some of those complexities involve, firstly, the challenge for practitioners to create new professional identities in the emergent communities of practice (who I am); and, secondly, the challenge to articulate and share their personal and professional knowledge to create a new version of knowledge (what I know) for new ways of working. Without this 'personal and professional knowledge', it would be impossible to accomplish the EYP's objective to lead and support colleagues in providing the best possible quality of care and education.

Standard 1 – the principles and content of the EYFS and how to put them into practice

Example of standard 1 in personal practice

The introduction of the EYFS framework is seen as a positive and constructive step in ensuring a consistent and integrated approach to care, learning and development of children from birth to the end of the foundation stage. Standard 1 requires EYPs to have a secure knowledge and understanding of the EYFS framework and to use this knowledge to both inform their own practice and lead the practice of others.

First of all, it is crucial that EYPs develop a consistent and clear pedagogical approach to the process of implementing the EYFS into practice if the teaching and learning capacity of the framework is to be effectively utilised. The study of pedagogical effectiveness in early learning (SPEEL) project highlighted the importance for early years practitioners to be able to identify key features of effective pedagogy within the context of early years. The project was based on the belief that excellent practitioners can – and should – be involved in the drive for understanding existing pedagogy and ultimately raising standards for teaching and learning (Moyles *et al.*, 2002).

Along with using strong pedagogical insights, EYPs are expected to have the EYFS framework at the heart of their planning and assessment processes. As the EYFS Principles into Practice Card 3.1 (DCSF, 2008) advises: 'All planning starts with observing children in order to understand and consider their current interests, development and learning.'

Candidates for EYPS are expected to demonstrate through their practice their ability to:

- Plan on a long-term, medium-term and short-term basis with consideration of the four principles of the EYFS along with the five outcomes of Every Child Matters framework
- Use observations of individual children to inform future planning that is based on children's interests

- Track children's learning and development and identify next steps to support and enhance their learning further
- Include children and their parents in the planning and assessment processes
- Be flexible in their planning; allow time to listen to children and make informed judgements on changing certain learning pathways to make them more pertinent to children's immediate interests
- Employ effective intervention strategies for those children who require additional support.

Other examples of personal practice towards meeting standard 1 entail EYPs demonstrating confidence in accomplishing the assessment process which is an integral part of the EYFS. Assessment in the early years should be predominantly based on observations of children's learning and development. According to QCA (2008): 'Observation of children participating in everyday activities is the most reliable way to build up an accurate picture of what children know, understand, feel, are interested in and can do.' EYPs are expected to have a sound knowledge and understanding of the EYFS profile, a statutory assessment tool, which has to be completed for each child during the academic year in which he or she reaches the age of 5. The assessment information will then be used by parents and year 1 teachers to facilitate the planning of an appropriate curriculum that will meet children's needs.

Along with the requirements of the EYFS profile, EYPs also employ effective assessment tactics, such as:

- Using a range of assessment strategies in both structured and child-initiated activities
- Setting targets and planning next steps based on assessment
- Creating and maintaining a consistent and comprehensive system of recording individual children's progress
- Using assessment records for sharing information with children's parents/carers and other involved practitioners.

Example of standard 1 in leadership

According to Moyles *et al.* (2002), quality early years provision is impossible without practitioners who have a sound awareness of the best pedagogical models and values, which ensure that early years practice underpinned by those values has a positive effect on children's learning and development. EYPs as leaders and the 'agents of change' need to consider the complexity of pedagogy and the features that characterise its effectiveness in relation to the principles and content of the EYFS. Moyles *et al.* (ibid.) suggest that, owing to the vastness and complexity of what constitutes effective pedagogy, it has to be viewed as a whole rather than a mixture of different aspects taken in isolation from each other. One of the outcomes of the SPEEL project included the development of the SPEEL wheel (Figure 3.2), a visual picture of key elements of effective early years pedagogy that can be used by EYPs for developing a higher awareness of their leadership opportunities in applying a coherent pedagogical approach to each aspect of early years practice in the process of implementing the EYFS.

Being able to see a bigger picture is a skill that allows EYPs to extend the boundaries of their existing leadership roles. In relation to planning, candidates

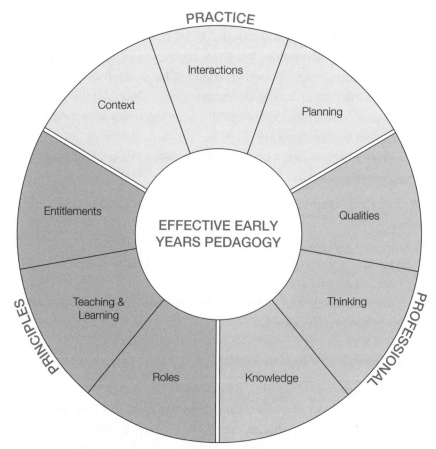

Figure 3.2 **The SPEEL wheel, explaining the contents of the framework of effective pedagogy** (based on Moyles *et al.*, 2002: 4)

need to ensure that the planning is not only flexible enough to follow the children's interests, but that it also contains clear evidence of how the EYFS principles will be put into practice. It is also essential for early years leaders to demonstrate that their differentiated planning is based on the principle of 'uniqueness' of every child, when individual children are regularly observed to identify their interests, preferences and needs, and to ensure that all children make progress towards the early learning goals.

Along with supporting and leading colleagues in terms of developing their knowledge and understanding of the planning requirements for the EYFS the candidates might also consider the following elements of standard 1 in the process of developing and applying their leadership skills:

- Encourage practitioners to make good use of the whole range of resources available in paper and electronic forms that show effective ways of putting into practice the principles and the content of the EYFS
- Identify and collect evidence of effective practice in your own setting, focusing on planning, observations and assessment procedures; share your findings with your colleagues and discuss how these examples benefit children in their learning and development towards the early learning goals
- Consider any staff development events that members of your team have recently attended; use this opportunity to disseminate new information among the team and make explicit links to the EYFS requirements and guidance
- Carefully evaluate all the resources available in your setting; discuss with your team what equipment needs to be updated or replaced to meet the requirements of the EYFS better.

Standard 1 reflection point

The EYFS challenges EYPs to think more deeply about all aspects of children's learning and development, including the practitioners' skills of observation, assessment and planning as well as how the environment is organised.

Consider one particular area of the EYFS and try to find evidence that demonstrates how you apply your skills and knowledge or support others in meeting a specific requirement of the framework for each of the following age groups of children:

- 0–20 months
- 16–36 months
- 30–60 months.

Standard 1 stakeholder comment

Leanne Hailey works as an EYP at one of the children's centres in Lancashire. Here she describes how, in her role as an EYP, she helps her colleagues to deconstruct standard 1.

'As an early years professional I strongly believe that the EYFS is a positive step forward in meeting the learning, development and welfare needs of all children. During our team meetings I try to highlight the point that practitioners need to view the document as a useful tool for "personalising" children's learning and planning activities that will meet individual children's needs. In our setting we see the EYFS as a flexible framework that is not set in stone; I try to promote my colleagues' aspirations in using the document creatively through adapting their planning, resources and environment to meet the needs of individual children. Differentiation is key to any planning within early years and beyond, and that is clearly promoted by the EYFS. I am convinced that all practitioners should have an in-depth knowledge of children's interests and abilities to be able to plan learning opportunities and activities in the ways that interest children.'

'Using assessment based on observations on children is another aspect of the EYFS that requires clear understanding and participation of all team members. At my setting, the observations do not take a long time to complete: each member of staff uses a pad with "Post-it" Notes, which enables them to record short notes on children's progress quickly without taking the practitioners' attention away from interacting with the children.'

'I also encourage all team members, and especially those who are struggling with the understanding of certain aspects of the EYFS, to evaluate their practice and take a further look at the principles and the content of the EYFS. In our setting I try to advocate the idea that any framework or curriculum in itself cannot be effective or ineffective – it is the practitioner's skills, knowledge and understanding that make any curriculum valuable.'

Standard 2 – the individual and diverse ways in which children develop and learn from birth to the end of the foundation stage and thereafter

Example of standard 2 in personal practice

The EYFS places a strong emphasis on the importance of meeting the diverse needs of all children, including those with learning difficulties and additional needs. Achieving this goal is not feasible outside the process of inclusion, which requires early years practitioners to develop policies and practices to include children of all ages and abilities. EYPs need to be aware that nowadays inclusion is not perceived as being relevant just to certain marginalised groups (e.g. children with SEN, children of ethnic minorities, etc.), but it is about including all children, which is closely linked to the ideas of 'personalised learning'. As the EYFS (DCSF, 2008) underlines, practitioners should deliver personalised learning, development and care to help children to achieve the best possible start in life.

EYP candidates need to consider the individual and diverse ways in which children learn and develop through the following aspects of their practice:

- Have a detailed knowledge and understanding of the developmental patterns of children from birth to the end of the EYFS, and use this knowledge to plan learning opportunities that build on and extend children's existing experiences, knowledge and skills
- Personalise children's learning through using differentiated learning and teaching strategies that are responsive to individual children's needs, thereby helping children in reaching their personal goals, developing their self-esteem and promoting confidence in their ability to learn
- Provide play-based, flexible, exciting and stimulating learning experiences that are based on children's interests and needs, with regular observations and consultation with parents. The EYFS (DCSF, 2008) asserts that planning should include all children, and plans need to be flexible enough to adapt to circumstances
- Have high expectations for all children while acknowledging that each child has his/her unique developmental patterns as he/she grows. Plan specific learning opportunities not only for the children who require additional support but also for those whose ability and understanding are in advance of the average developmental norms
- Use a multidisciplinary and multi-agency approach, consulting with other professionals both inside and outside the setting to develop a comprehensive picture of each child's individual needs and abilities
- Adjust communication and instruction techniques to accommodate the needs of children with various cultural backgrounds. Remember that children may have dissimilar patterns of communication styles (e.g. not making eye contact when speaking or pausing for longer before responding) which may be a result of different social conventions and cultural influences
- Make sure that the learning environment is inclusive, supportive and free from discrimination and stereotyping: provide books, toys, displays, props and

other materials that reflect the diversity of our society; respect and value the contribution of all children; remove stereotypical materials from the setting

- Acknowledge that multilingualism and bilingualism are not deficits, but assets, to children's development; foster children's home languages and support bilingual acquisition in all children in your setting
- Include parents in specific activities such as cooking sessions, music and role-play, field trips and creating family stories.

Example of standard 2 in leadership

The EYFS (DCSF, 2008) clearly states that one of the main goals for every early years setting is to ensure that it meets the needs of both boys and girls, children with SEN, children who are more able, children with disabilities, children with complex health needs, children from all social, family, cultural and religious backgrounds, looked-after children, children of all ethnic groups (including traveller communities), refugees and asylum-seekers, and children from diverse linguistic backgrounds. To be able to guide colleagues in the process of achieving this goal, EYPs firstly need to ensure that all practitioners working in the setting have sound knowledge and understanding of the individual and diverse ways of children's learning and development.

One way of accomplishing this objective is through the development of a learning community where, in the process of identifying and articulating one's own experiences and by listening to the experiences of others, one is supported in their pedagogical development (NCSL, 2005). Through the development of the learning community, EYPs as leaders can focus on building a social and learning environment that fosters commitment to effective inclusion through professional discussions, practical support and a variety of opportunities for staff to access training on the issues relevant to the diversity of children's needs and developmental patterns.

Effective leaders should also be able to demonstrate their own knowledge and understanding of child development and model effective practice with confidence and commitment. However, it is important to remember that effective leadership does not only lie with the leader; while the leader should model practice, leadership in this area should also be encouraged in staff, in children and in their parents/carers. This may include: providing more opportunities for staff to plan specific activities for each child and to assess the child's learning; involving children in evaluating their own learning; and listening to parents and carers and allowing them to take ownership of some elements of practice, where appropriate (e.g. involving parents in writing comments on their children's progress in 'learning journals' and 'learning stories').

Other opportunities for leadership in this area may require EYPs to:

- Review on a regular basis policies of the setting related to educational inclusion and diversity; try to involve all team members as well as children and their parents in this process
- Participate in the process of recruiting and supporting practitioners with different ethnic backgrounds and who are better equipped for working with culturally diverse groups
- Provide all team members with an opportunity to receive formal training in one or several aspects of child development (e.g. children with special needs, strategies to encourage parent participation, adapting outdoor environment to suit children's diverse needs, etc.)
- Ensure that the environment of the setting enables staff to provide children with the best possible learning opportunities in all areas of learning and development; monitor the process of adapting the environment for children with learning difficulties, physical disabilities and/or emotional problems. Some of the adaptations may include using sign language for children with hearing impairments, using Braille and large fonts for visually impaired children, and avoiding overstimulating activities to help children with ADHD and ADD
- Ensure that the setting 'reflects diversity considering race, ethnicity, languages, art, gender roles, religious ceremonies, shelter, work, traditions, and customs. The goal is for children to be exposed to the rich diversity of the entire world' (Wardle, 2009). Communicate to the staff the importance of making children's families feel welcome, involved and valued in the setting; support these messages through visual images displayed in the setting to represent the diversity of family structures, job roles, cultural and religious backgrounds and various languages.

Standard 2 reflection point

According to Greenman (2005) early years environments should be:

- – rich in experience
- – rich in play
- – rich in teaching

- rich with people
- significant to children
- places children can call their own.

- Think about your setting and try to relate each of the above points to the question: how does the environment in my setting help children in meeting their individual and diverse needs?
- Now think about one child in your setting, considering his/her unique developmental pattern, individual needs and interests and preferred learning style. How is this child's 'uniqueness' acknowledged and supported by the practitioners in your setting?

Standard 2 stakeholder comment

Jane R. is the parent of a 4-year-old boy who attends one of the private day nurseries in Manchester. Here she describes how she worked together with early years practitioners in the nursery to help them to ensure that all children's individual and diverse needs are met.

'I was always interested to see and understand how practitioners in the nursery manage to take care of 17 children and know what these children need or like. Initially I was getting newsletters from the nursery with an attached sheet for parents' comments asking if there were any activities that my little boy was particularly interested in or whether I would like to discuss with my child and suggest a theme for future planning. I got interested in these ideas and, during one of the "coffee mornings", had a discussion with the EYP at the nursery about how they manage to get all children involved in all activities. The EYP explained to me that the nursery observes children and uses brainstorming sessions with them, and also collects information from their parents, which helps practitioners to plan the activities in a way that all children's needs and interests are met. Following this discussion, the EYP also got me engaged in completing a "learning journey" together with my little boy. I knew that, previously examples of children's work were simply collected together in a folder, which was shown to the parents during parents' meetings. I never felt I was involved in this process as I had no chance to write and share any personal information about my child. It's different with the "learning stories", because now parents can keep practitioners informed about what their children really need and want. I know that one of the parents even suggested including a "parent's story" page into the booklet, which I thought was a marvellous idea!'

Standard 3 – how children's well-being, development, learning and behaviour can be affected by a range of influences and transitions from inside and outside the setting

Example of standard 3 in personal practice

This standard requires candidates to know and understand the influence of specific events on children's development, learning and behaviour, and use this knowledge and understanding to ensure smooth transitions for all children in their setting.

The impact of transitions on a child's overall development has been most explicitly acknowledged in the work of a number of researchers (Fabien and Dunlop, 2002; Sanders *et al.*, 2005; Sharp *et al.*, 2006; White and Sharp, 2007), who stress the importance of understanding the diversity, complexity and uniqueness of each transitional experience for individual children.

EYPs need to acknowledge the value of transitions in children's lives from a developmental perspective. Babies and young children develop rapidly, and the pace of this development is predetermined by the amount of stimulation and new experiences that children receive, which promotes the continual formation of new synaptic connections within their brains. Therefore, transitions from one environment into another or from one stage to the next offer children an excellent developmental opportunity in terms of experiencing new surroundings and forming new relationships.

Starting with the familiar home routines will ensure a smooth transition of each child towards the routines of the setting; however, EYPs need to continue being very sensitive to all children's needs and respect the wishes of individual children who are unable to respond to the setting's time schedules.

Some examples of good practice that candidates might consider employing for smoothing children's home–setting transitions include:

- Using discussions with parents and child observations to inform the changes in the setting's routine to accommodate each child's individual needs. This can be done through creating a 'settling-in journal', where all significant moments of the child's transition can be recorded and shared with parents/carers
- Developing good communication between parents, children and their key workers
- Showing respect for each child's wishes and opinions, providing specific types of care whenever the child needs them

- Making sure that all children develop a sense of belonging within the early years setting, but also keep strong links with their home environment – ask parents to bring children's favourite toys, comfort objects, photos and books to your setting; remind children about their homes and family members throughout the day.

Babies and children whose first language is other than English will appreciate listening throughout the day to the rhymes, songs or just messages from their family members; EYPs might consider providing a tape recorder for parents/ carers to record comforting messages that can be used to comfort children in times of distress.

However, a transition from home to an early years setting is just one of many examples of transitions that children might go through. The candidates need to show their awareness of a variety of transitions that can affect children's learning and development. Just some of these examples include separation from parents, illness of a family member, changing school, moving house, new siblings and bereavement. In addition, some children also go through several transitions throughout each day, such as going from home to a setting, from a setting to a playgroup, from a playgroup to grandparents' house, and, finally, going home at the end of the day. Effective practice in these cases will involve adapting the above-mentioned strategies to particular circumstances and individual children.

Example of standard 3 in leadership

As highlighted in the EYFS 'All about . . . transitions' (DCSF, 2008):

> managers, head teachers and governing bodies need to show that they are aware of the importance of transition by making it a priority. This will have time and cost implications in enabling practitioners to meet children, carers and other settings, make home visits and transfer information, as well as developing a curriculum and ethos that supports the gradual and supported integration of new children. All too often, practitioners are impeded in developing good practice by 'top-down' expectations, routines and procedures, and only minimal recognition of the need to support children in transition.

Unfortunately, the main body of research on transitions seems to be focusing more on the transitions of 3–5-year-old children, while the transitions of babies and younger children remain rather undefined and vague. EYP candidates need to show their knowledge and understanding of the importance of transitions for *all* children, from 0 to 5, and should be able to lead others in supporting babies' and young children's transitions. For example, EYPs might consider explaining to their colleagues that one of the key aspects of transitions of babies and very young children from home into their first early years setting involves working closely with the child's parents and making every effort to establish daily routines that replicate as much as possible the children's home routines. One of the useful strategies involves home visits, which provide practitioners with an excellent opportunity to establish a good communication rapport with parents and to find out about the type of care each child needs throughout their daily activities, such as changing nappies, feeding times, going to sleep and waking up, going for a walk and playing.

Another important aspect of the EYP's role involves developing an effective 'settling-in' policy, a step that is essential for establishing continuous, open, honest two-way communication between parents and early years practitioners. EYP candidates might consider reviewing and updating existing 'settling-in' policy in view of their current knowledge of children's developmental needs, the requirements of the EYFS and the Common Core of Skills and Knowledge as well as recent research findings and government initiatives.

EYPs also need to ensure that a proficient and well organised 'key person system' is in place to support children during their transition periods. The welfare requirements of the EYFS (DCSF, 2008) explain the roles of a key person as a practitioner who helps a baby or child to become familiar with the setting and to feel safe and confident; talks to parents to make sure the needs of the child are being met appropriately and makes sure that records of development and progress are shared with parents and other professionals as necessary. With this in mind, EYP candidates might consider organising training sessions and/or developing training packs for staff to enable them to fulfil the role of a key person in the most efficient way. The focus of these sessions can be, for example, 'roles and responsibilities of the key person', 'theory of attachment', 'impact of separation anxiety on children's behaviour', 'transitional objects', etc.

Successful EYPs appreciate the uniqueness of each child, giving them sufficient time to become used to new people, environments and routines of the setting and involving parents and other practitioners in the process of transition to make it smooth and effective.

Standard 3 reflection point

What strategies will you use to support babies and young children's transitions:

- From home to the early years setting?
- Between room bases?
- From an early years setting to school?
- From one provider to another during the working week?

Standard 3 stakeholder comment

Delyth is a young parent of a 5-year-old boy, Ryan, who was diagnosed with attention-deficit hyperactivity disorder (ADHD) last year. Here she comments on how Ryan was supported in his transition from an early years setting to a reception class.

'I was very upset when I first found out about the diagnosis. My first thought was that it was my fault, but I also tried to comfort myself with the idea that Ryan will grow out of it. Ryan started at Wavertree children's centre when he was 2 years old. Ryan's father, Paul, also thinks that all the early years staff at the centre were really helpful throughout the whole time that Ryan was there. We had the chance to spend time with Ryan in the nursery, so we could see how he was doing. The centre's EYP was especially helpful. She listened to my concerns and reassured me when I was too worried about Ryan's behaviour and his ability to a settle in when he moves to a school environment. She has also shared with me records of observations that other staff completed when they were working with Ryan. This helped me to understand Ryan's behaviour better and to use more appropriate strategies for managing his behaviour at home.'

'Ryan transferred to a reception class at a local primary school after a planned series of meetings between the family, the children's centre and the school. Ryan's transition was supported by the EYP, who was also a part of the inclusion team. The meeting regarding Ryan's transition took place during the summer term, which helped me with managing my time better and easing my worries. The EYP helped both my husband and myself immensely, as she listened to us carefully, wrote down all our concerns and passed them to Ryan's new school. After the meetings, the EYP accompanied us to the school, where we had a chance to look around and meet the staff. Thanks to everybody's efforts the transition went really smoothly for Ryan. Even now, when I have questions about Ryan's behaviour, I can ask the EYP for advice; she has always been friendly and very supportive, which made me feel more comfortable with Ryan's transition.'

Standard 4 – the main provisions of the national and local statutory and non-statutory frameworks within which children's services work and their implications for early years settings

Example of standard 4 in personal practice

Candidates need to consider their day-to-day practice and how this fits in with the bigger picture of the national and local statutory and non-statutory frameworks. Candidates may take photographs of the activities they carry out with children and then link this to the Every Child Matters outcomes, demonstrating how they are improving outcomes for children. This may then be displayed for sharing with children and parents. A candidate showed the assessor the display on their setting visit on the tour as part of their evidence.

When a practitioner is working with children with additional needs they may refer to the SEN code of practice to support their underpinning knowledge of practice and reflect on their current methods.

One practitioner worked with children in the baby room and wished to ensure that she was scaffolding the children's learning. She analysed some of the observations that she had carried out previously and used the EYFS to see what learning intentions she felt the children had achieved and, more importantly, to consider what she might plan for them to do next. She created a file for each child and kept the observations in the file with information about the child's likes and dislikes. She then asked the parents to fill in some of the file to create a holistic view of the child. Based on all the initial information gathered she used the learning and development and initiated a plan for the child to achieve a new skill, ensuring that all the children in her key group are progressing.

As the national and local statutory frameworks are often complex and multi-faceted, candidates need to keep themselves up to date with all the changes. They can do this by accessing training and then disseminating this to the staff or researching on the internet. Candidates can ask their local authority development workers for advice on legislation in a particular area, such as equality of opportunity. It is only when candidates understand the requirements of the frameworks that they can consider how it impacts upon their own and other practitioners' practice.

Candidates need to demonstrate their knowledge and understanding of the frameworks through their written tasks. As they write their accounts of leadership in the age ranges and their account of personal practice they need to demonstrate sufficiently that they understand the frameworks that impact upon their practice and upon the age of the children with whom they work.

Example of standard 4 in leadership

Candidates have demonstrated this standard in a number of ways – one nursery manager used the setting's vision at a team meeting and discussed the purpose of the vision with the staff team, considering how the vision fitted in with the national policy. From this discussion the staff developed their knowledge and understanding of the wider national policy and how it impacted upon their day-to-day work.

The staff members were then able to talk about this experience as part of their witness interview. The candidate followed this through by devising a booklet collaboratively with the staff team; the first page of the booklet set out the vision and the practitioners then worked in pairs and laid out how the frameworks linked to the vision. The candidate collated all the information and developed it into a booklet that was used with new staff as part of their induction and was also given to parents. The candidate included the booklet in her documentary file of evidence.

Another practitioner held a parents' evening for parents/families and she supported the staff by having activities set up in each age-related room that related to the EYFS. The staff explained how the activities benefitted the children and shared experiences with the parents of activities the child engaged in while in the setting. The practitioner encouraged the parents to order themselves a free copy so that they could understand what the setting was working towards. The parent then gave a witness testimony to be included in the candidate's documentary file of evidence. The practitioner then followed up this session by sending out questionnaires to the parents to review the event. The questionnaires showed that the parents who had attended and had received a copy of the EYFS had developed their understanding of how their children developed.

A candidate reviewed the safeguarding policy with the team. She sent all the team members and parents a copy of the policy with an additional sheet for them to complete with comments or amendments. As an attachment she gave them an overview of the common assessment framework (CAF) and the current legislation impacting upon safeguarding. She also attached a brief overview of the Victoria Climbié case and some of the action points from Lord Laming with an explanation of how this linked to the Children Act (2004) to help them to understand the importance of this policy and how it impacted on the practitioner's day-to-day practice. She collated all the responses and amended the policy to reflect the comments raised from the parents/practitioners. Some issues arose from this, including staff wanting to access more continuing professional development (CPD) to extend their knowledge further. The practitioner arranged for this training to take place. They also developed their documentation from the policy and parent suggestions, including an overview of all the policies in the welcome pack which the practitioner followed through. The candidate then put the policy with an explanation in the documentary file of evidence and was able to show the welcome pack in reception on her tour. To demonstrate leadership in standard 4, candidates need to consider how they measure the knowledge and understanding of their colleagues and how they proactively develop this area.

Standard 4 reflection points

- Observe an activity in which a member of staff is engaging with a child/group of children. Use the Every Child Matters outcomes and identify which outcomes the activity has contributed toward
- Look at the setting's policies and procedures – what legislation underpins particular policies and how is this demonstrated to staff in day-to-day practice?
- Use the EYFS to identify an aspect of practice that could be developed in relation to the welfare requirements. Consider how you might bring this change about:

  - Who might you need to consult with?
  - How will you gather other people's ideas?
  - What resources will you need?
  - What are the benefits to the development?
  - What are the potential concerns with the development?
  - How much time will it take?

- Research the current and local statutory and non-statutory frameworks, list areas you are already familiar with and consider how you observe this in practice. What areas of the framework are you least familiar with? Consider how you can develop this area of understanding.

Standard 4 stakeholder comment

A local authority development worker believed that, if candidates could demonstrate their knowledge and understanding of some of the key pieces of legislation that underpinned their work, then the quality of the provision would be higher, as research such as the Effective Provision of Pre-School Education (EPPE) Project demonstrates that the key to high quality provision is a highly skilled workforce. In her experience key people understood pieces of legislation (e.g. the special educational needs coordinator worked and engaged with the SEN code of practice and the safeguarding officer used the CAF), but quite often the wider team did not understand how the legislation applied to them. She reviewed the role of the EYP in developing the knowledge of all practitioners so that they could understand their own responsibilities in working within the frameworks. She had worked with one setting who had bought in bespoke training to develop the practitioner's knowledge and understanding; as part of her role she had monitored quality and there was a clear improvement in the quality owing to this development of the practitioners' understanding.

Standard 5 – the current legal requirements, national policies and guidance on health and safety, safeguarding and promoting the wellbeing of children and their implications for early years settings

Example of standard 5 in personal practice

In line with KEEP (DfES, 2005), which identified that a child's learning was connected to a high quality environment appropriate to the child's needs, a candidate audited their role-play area, considering how the six areas of learning were available continually to children in this area and how this area reflected the needs of the children in her room. The audit demonstrated that the area did not reflect all of the children's backgrounds – there were two Chinese children within the group. The practitioner liaised with the children's families to find out more about their background. One of the children lived a British lifestyle and so all the resources encouraged him to role-play the situations he had seen at home. However, the other child had more of a traditional Chinese background; at home the family very often cooked with a wok and used chopsticks and read Chinese writing. The practitioner introduced these resources into the role-play area, explaining to the children how they were to be used, and placed some books in the area to support the children's understanding. She also included some recipes for Chinese food and placed some Chinese food in the area which was labelled with Chinese writing. During her tour of the setting she showed the assessor the role-play area and explained how it was underpinned by KEEP (2005) and the UN Convention on the Rights of the Child (1989).

Another practitioner worked with the preschool children and, when looking at the accident record book, noticed that a high number of accidents were happening in the outdoor area. The practitioner spent some time each day observing the children in the outdoor area and tried to establish whether there was a pattern to the accidents and any way in which they could be minimised. Her observations showed that the staff were continually asking children to 'stop it' and 'get down', etc. The practitioner worked with the children each day over a period of time, talking about 'what might happen if?' and letting the children respond, therefore allowing the children to recognise the potential consequences. She asked the children 'how will we do this?', 'what will we need to be safe?' The ownership of the play and the risk moved from the adult to the children. Some practitioners found it difficult to let children take risks, saying this would only increase the number of accidents.

Example of standard 5 in leadership

A practitioner accessed a health and safety course. After the course she relayed the information to the team and developed a risk assessment. She asked each room leader to identify the potential risks within their own room and then considered how they might minimise the risks. They then considered the key points from the Health and Safety at Work Act and compiled a setting risk assessment. The candidate then gave all the practitioners a copy and reviewed the risk assessment on a regular basis to ensure that it was up to date.

A practitioner was aware that there were issues arising with staff and often, when the situations were investigated, the issue was caused by the lack of staff knowledge of the setting procedures. The candidate developed a staff induction programme, including:

- Accident procedure
- First aid procedure
- Child protection policy
- Safeguarding policy
- Explanation of the setting's risk assessments
- Health and hygiene policy.

She underpinned each policy or procedure with the legal requirements and the individual staff responsibility. She implemented this induction with existing staff as well as new staff and when reflecting on the process she developed a continuing staff development programme.

Standard 5 reflection points

- Research the procedures used by the local safeguarding children's board in the local authority in which you work or are placed. Consider how these are reflected in the setting's safeguarding policy?
- Reflect on some of your previous experiences in working with children aged 0–20 months, 16–36 months and 30–60 months. How are these experiences underpinned by policies and guidance?

Standard 5 stakeholder comment

One of the students asked her mentor how she could evidence this standard. Her mentor advised that she needed to consider how she kept her own knowledge and understanding of the current requirements up to date and how this then linked to the policies and the practice of the setting. She advised the student to take each section of the amplification:

- Accidents and first aid
- Child protection and bullying
- Promoting equality and combating discrimination
- Safety and risk assessments (including equipment, visits outside the setting, missing children or those not collected)
- Health (such as children with a health condition, medicine policy and infection control, food handling)
- Personal care (such as hygiene and incontinence)
- Staff ratios, staff qualifications and conduct,

and talk with the staff about each section, discussing which legislation fits into each of the above areas, and then consider how that impacts upon the day-to-day practice. Once the candidate has established her own knowledge base and that of the other practitioners she can then put in place a development plan to develop the knowledge in the areas that are needed. The candidate could extend this further by considering how part-time staff and new staff joining the organisation will develop this knowledge and understanding.

Standard 6 – the contribution that other professionals within the setting and beyond can make to children's physical and emotional well-being, development and learning

Examples of standard 6 in personal practice

Recent changes in welfare and education policy and practice have encouraged early years practitioners to stop thinking of themselves as 'just a teacher', 'just a social worker' or 'just an early years worker'. Thus, to be an effective early years practitioner now requires . . . an ability to understand the theoretical constructs of collaborative practice.
(Leeson and Huggins, 2010: 101)

This standard requires the candidate to show that they have a sound knowledge of the range of agencies, both within and outside the setting, that can be called upon to support children's physical and emotional wellbeing, development and learning. In deconstructing this standard, the practitioner should be able to evidence their understanding of the wide range of professionals who address the many areas included in this remit.

They should consider each of the areas mentioned; for instance, the children's physical wellbeing – within the setting, a practitioner may have responsibility for promoting healthy eating or physical development and this may involve working with parents to educate them in how to encourage this. The candidate may have a role similar to this or work with people in these roles, and they need to consider how they support them and when they would ask for their advice or involvement. External agencies may include physiotherapists, occupational health therapists and specialist teachers. The candidate needs to demonstrate knowledge of who these professionals are and how they can support the children's physical wellbeing.

Likewise, the successful candidate will understand that others in their setting will have specific roles to support the children's emotional wellbeing, such as a behaviour management coordinator or a family worker. External agencies involved in this aspect of children's wellbeing may include the children and adolescent mental health service and educational psychologists. When considering children's learning and development, the candidate will provide evidence that they understand who the SEN coordinator (SENCo) within the setting is, and that they know who the local authority SENCo is, as well as how and when they need to be contacted. They will be aware of the wide range of professionals who can contribute to the children's wellbeing and development. Within this they will consider how these services may vary depending on the age of the child. This may vary in different local authorities and the candidate needs to be aware of the provision in their area.

Candidates also need to show evidence of their understanding of the different roles that these professionals have; especially within the setting, they must be aware of the extent of the early years practitioner's role and understand when the child needs to be referred to another agency. A commitment and willingness to work with other agencies is essential for anyone achieving EYPS and the candidate must be able to provide evidence of this by showing an understanding of the roles of other professionals, a willingness to involve them in supporting the children and excellent communication with and support for them. Stacey (2009) discusses how the five outcomes of the Every Child Matters agenda provides a shared vision for all practitioners involved in the wellbeing and development of children. This should enable the different agencies to communicate more efficiently and define their roles and responsibilities clearly. The methods of seeking advice and direct involvement of the appropriate agencies are another important skill that the candidate needs to illustrate and this must be shown in the evidence provided to the assessor.

The successful candidate will also have sound evidence of ensuring parental involvement in any strategies used to contribute to a child's wellbeing and development. Leeson and Huggins (2010) discuss how the EYFS advocates that all parents should be involved with their child's learning and development, and that practitioners must develop an effective partnership by 'showing respect, understanding the role of parents, listening, being flexible, giving time, valuing different perspectives and collaborating in a genuine way' (Leeson and Huggins, 2010: 107). The candidate will also need to communicate and explain the need for involvement to colleagues within the setting. Ensuring that fellow practitioners understand the need for additional interventions will enable them to give the child and parents additional support as well as contributing any relevant information they may have.

Finally, the candidate will be able to show evidence of their contribution to planning or review meetings; this may be by taking an active part within the meetings or contributing reports or observations to the team members regarding the effects of programmes and interventions planned for the child with whom they have been involved.

Examples of standard 6 in leadership

To show leadership in this area, the candidate will have evidence of a sound understanding of the wide variety of needs that children in their setting may have; they will either take on or allocate to other senior members of staff roles that address specific areas that are essential to promote children's wellbeing, learning and development. This will include SEN, behaviour management and healthy eating, amongst others. The candidate will ensure that staff are aware of current legislation and statutory requirements for these areas and will write or contribute to relevant policies and deliver them to all staff to ensure that they understand their role in contributing to that area. The successful candidate will also provide training for all staff to develop their understanding of the variety of agencies that can be involved with children and parents. They will ensure that all staff have an overview of the professionals concerned and their remits. It is important to model effective communication to other members of staff and emphasise how essential this is when working with other professionals. A distributive or transformational approach to leadership is necessary to enable the whole team to take responsibility for efficient collaboration with other agencies (Duffy and Marshall, 2007).

It is important for the candidate to involve and support junior staff in this process to help them to develop a sound understanding of the courses of action. They will ensure that junior members of staff are aware of the procedures to follow if they have a concern about a child and that other members of staff understand the scope of their responsibility and how and when to request further assistance.

In making the decision to involve another professional, either within the setting or externally, the candidate will be proactive in involving the child's parents. This may be directly, role-modelling good practice to more junior members of staff or as a support to colleagues who are developing their own skills in this area. It is vital that the candidate shows an understanding of the rights and roles of parents and works with the '"empowerment" model [in which] professionals actively promote parents' sense of control over decisions affecting their child' (Whalley, 2008: 132). This involves not only informing parents of the setting's concerns for the child, but consulting with them from the very beginning and throughout the whole process, being an advocate for them, ensuring that their voice is heard, and that their feelings, thoughts and opinions are consistently addressed.

The candidate will also take a positive role in contributing to planning and review meetings and be heavily involved in the coordination and implementation of any interventions. They will encourage the involvement of colleagues within the setting and will ensure that relevant staff such as the key person, room leader or SENCo are kept up to date with all developments and have the opportunity to contribute their findings and observations to other professionals. This can be evidenced through witness interviews or statements with colleagues, external agencies or parents as well as in written tasks.

Standard 6 reflection points

- Consider how you can develop your understanding of the roles of different professionals both within and outside the setting
- What are the procedures for involving them with children in your care?
- If you are in a setting which does not have a great deal of involvement with other professionals, could you arrange a visit to a children's centre to meet with them?
- As a leader do you ever invite external professionals into the setting to discuss their role with colleagues?
- Do you encourage colleagues to collaborate with other professionals, rather than take on this role yourself?
- Consider whether colleagues know each other's roles and when and who to involve in supporting a child.

Standard 6 stakeholder comment

Linda Elesedy is a senior childcare practitioner in a foundation stage unit within a school. Her role is to work as part of the team which includes a teacher and teaching assistants (employed by the school) and a childcare assistant who, along with her, is employed by the childcare nursery. They have specific responsibility for the children who require full day 'educare'. It is a complex routine as there are different groups of children accessing the provision in the setting; for example, the full day reception class, the morning nursery group, the afternoon nursery group and the wrap-around childcare group. The staff in the setting have various roles; for example, supporting a child with difficulties. Working in such a setting allows many opportunities for working alongside other professionals and also for supporting people as they gain knowledge and experience during their training within the setting.

The primary reason for undertaking the EYPS training was for her own professional development, to become more qualified in her area of work. Linda felt that, prior to the EYPS, progression for a nursery nurse meant a digression into teaching or nursing. EYPS is the natural progression for a nursery nurse who wants to remain a practitioner, yet have the knowledge and training to lead others in an early years setting.

Linda says 'Undertaking the training has been hugely beneficial to me both personally and professionally. I am delighted to have gained the EYP status.' To provide evidence that she had achieved standard 6, Linda knew that she had worked to support staff to share, develop and implement their ideas. While planning the change in the baby room (up to age 18 months) she was able to discuss with the various members of staff their ideas of utilising a specific corner in the room. This led to some shared discussions about the ideas and the chance for them to reflect on their own reasons for change. Linda was then able to support the staff in considering the options and the possible impact for the children. Finally, she was able to facilitate the change.

Linda also worked with the health visitor to help with a child's physical problem. Prior to the transition of the child from the toddler room to the nursery unit, the child's key person informed her of the child's specific health difficulties. During her discussion with the parents, who explained about the difficulties they faced with their child, she encouraged them to contact their health visitor. At the parents' request she agreed to have direct contact with the health visitor to help the child in the nursery. She became responsible for sharing information within

→

the setting and disseminating information from the nursery to the health visitor and parents. She was able to offer support to the parents and share the child's progress with the other staff. Fortunately, within a few months the problem lessened and was eventually overcome.

Another situation that Linda dealt with involved referring a child for speech therapy. A 3-year-old child who had a speech difficulty was becoming very frustrated because he could not communicate effectively. He was beginning to display some aggressive behaviour. She gained parental permission to make a referral to the speech therapist. She was able to meet the therapist to gain an understanding of the child's difficulties and was given specific instructions on how to help the child. She was able to put this into practice and also to share this information and learning with other staff members.

Linda was able to provide evidence of her leadership skills in this area by supporting a specific staff member in her role supporting a child with a physical disability. She took part in the physiotherapy sessions for this child to learn more about the condition and to enable her to give practical support when required. Together with the supporting staff member, they adapted the planned activities and also the environment so that the child could access all the provision.

Linda had liaised with the family development worker regarding a specific child. The family development worker brought a child from a family who was experiencing some trauma. She was able to offer practical support in caring for this child and so became a point of contact for the development worker, thus supporting her in her role.

Further leadership skills were evidenced by witness interviews regarding supporting a staff member during her training and conducting an appraisal.

Conclusion

The group of standards 'knowledge and understanding' encourages candidates to consider the legislation underpinning their day-to-day work. Candidates are expected to understand how their day-to-day work fits in with local and national frameworks, and to consider the wider impact of their work. Within this group of standards EYPs would support colleagues in developing their knowledge and understanding of the EYFS and wider policies to demonstrate how they can lead and support others.

References

Anning, A. (2005) Investigating the impact of working in multi-agency service delivery settings in the UK on early years practitioners' beliefs and practices. *Journal of Early Childhood Research*, **3**(1), 19–50.

Ayoub, C. and Fischer, K. (2006) Developmental pathways and intersections among domains of development. In: DCSF (2009) *Early Years Learning and Development Literature Review*. Research Report No. DCSF-RR176. University of Oxford: DCSF.

Baldock, P., Fitzgerald, D. and Kay, J. (2007) *Understanding Early Years Policy*. London: Sage.

Children's Workforce Development Council (CWDC). (2008) *Guidance to the Standards for the Award of the Early Years Professional Status*. London: CWDC.

Cole, R. (2008) *Educating Everybody's Children: Diverse Strategies for Diverse Learners*. Alexandria, VA: Association for Supervision and Curriculum Development.

DCSF. (2008) *Statutory Framework for the Early Years Foundation Stage*. Nottingham: DCSF.

DCSF. (2010a) *Children, Families and Child Development. The National Strategies*. Available from http://nationalstrategies.standards.dcsf.gov.uk/node/83951?uc=force_uj (accessed 1 February 2010).

DCSF. (2010b) *Support for all: the Families and Relationships Green Paper*. London: The Stationery Office.

DfES. (2003) *Every Child Matters: Change for Children*. Nottingham: DfES.

DfES. (2005) *Key Elements of Effective Practice*. Nottingham: DfES.

Duffy, B. and Marshall, J. (2007) Leadership in multi-agency work. In: Siraj-Blatchford, I., Clark, K. and Needham, M. *The Team Around the Child: Multi-agency Working in the Early Years*. Stoke-on-Trent: Trentham Books.

Fabian, H. and Dunlop, A. (2002) *Transitions in the Early Years*. London: RoutledgeFalmer.

Froebel, F. (1907) *The Education of Man*. Mineola, NY: Dover Publications Inc.

Greenman, J.T. (2005) *Caring Spaces, Learning Places: Children's Environments that Work*, 2nd edn. Redmont, WA: Exchange Press.

HMSO. (2008) *Ending Child Poverty: Everybody's Business*. HM Treasury, DWP/DCSF.

HMSO. (2010) *Child Poverty Act 2010*. London: HMSO.

Leeson, C. and Huggins, V. (2010) Working with colleagues. In: Parker-Rees, R., Leeson, C., Willan, J. and Savage, J. (eds) *Early Childhood Studies*. Exeter: Learning Matters.

Lindon, J. (2006) *Equality in Early Childhood*. London: Hodder Education.

Moyles, J., Adams, S. and Musgrove, A. (2002). *SPEEL Study of Pedagogical Effectiveness*. Department for Education and Skills, Research Report 363.

National College for School Leadership (NCSL). (2005) *Participants' Guide for National Professional Qualification in Integrated Centre Leadership*. Nottingham: NCSL.

Nutbrown, C. and Clough, P. (2008) *Inclusion in the Early Years*. London: Sage.

Piaget, J. (1983) Piaget's theory. In: Kessen, W. (ed.) *Handbook of Child Psychology*, Vol. 1. New York: Wiley, pp.103–26.

QCA. (2008) *Early Years Foundation Stage Profile Handbook*. London: QCA.

Rogers, C. (2007) Experiencing an inclusive education: parents and their children with special educational needs. *British Journal of Sociology of Education*, **28**(1), 55–68.

Sanders, D., White, G., Burge, B. *et al.* (2005) *A Study of the Transition from the Foundation Stage to Key Stage 1*. London: DfES Publications.

Sharp, C., White, G., Burge, B. and Eames, A. (2006) Trouble-free transition. *Child Education*, **83**(4), 21–2.

Siegler, R.S. (2005) Children's learning. *American Psychologist*, **60,** 769–78.

Siraj-Blatchford, S. and Siraj-Blatchford, J. (2009) *Improving Development Outcomes for Children through Effective Practice in Integrating Early Years Services*. London: C4EO.

Stacey, M. (2009) *Teamwork and Colloboration in Early Years Settings*. Exeter: Learning Matters.

Vygotsky, L.S. (1978) *Mind and Society: The Development of Higher Mental Processes*. Cambridge, MA: Harvard University Press.

Wardle, F. (2009) *Creating Indoor Environments for Young Children. Childcare Education Institute,* vol. 4, Issue 8. Available from http://cceionline.com/newsletters/August_09.html (accessed 16 March 2010).

Whalley, M. (2008) *Leading Practice in Early Years Setting (Achieving EYPS)*. Exeter: Learning Matters.

White, G. and Sharp, C. (2007) It is different . . . because you are getting older and growing up. How children make sense of the transition to Year 1. *European Early Childhood Education Research Journal*, **15**(1), 87–102.

Further reading

DfES. (2006) *Children's Workforce Strategy: the Government's response to the Consultation*. Nottingham: DfES.

Gardner, H. (1993) *Multiple Intelligences. The Theory in Practice*. New York: Basic Books.

Gmitrova, V., Podhajeck, M. and Gmitrov, J. (2009) Children's play preferences: implications for the preschool education. *Early Child Development and Care,* **179**(3), 339–51.

Sylva, K., Siraj-Blatchford, I., Melhuish, E.C., Sammons, P. and Taggart, B. (2004) *The Effective Provision of Pre-School Education (EPPE) Project: Final Report*. London: DfES/Institute of Education, University of London.

Chapter 4

Effective practice

Introduction

This chapter details effective practice with children, using observations to inform planning, to manage children's behaviours, and to promote equality and inclusion.

Objectives

By the end of this chapter you should have:

- Gained an overview of the key theoretical perspectives in relation to effective early years practice
- Reflected on how you can promote through your practice the requirements identified in standards 7–24
- Reflected on how you can lead and support others in relation to the requirements identified in standards 7–24.

Theoretical underpinning knowledge for standards 7– 24

As we have entered an exciting time of development in early years provision, practitioners from a wide variety of settings, bringing a range of strengths, training and experience to the early years, are linked by a common aim – to offer young children learning opportunities and experiences of the highest possible quality, while ensuring that the care and curriculum they receive are appropriate to their needs and stage of development. Standards 7–24 require early years practitioners to be aware of these different facets of early years practice that promote all children's wellbeing, along with providing them with the best learning experiences.

EYPs need to acknowledge the fact that early years provision has always involved much more than the ways of accumulation of academic knowledge. It has been central to the processes by which ideas of childhood have been socially constructed and, therefore, its history has much to tell us about the development of different educational systems in the context of changing ideologies in a changing society. To be able to ensure effective early years practice, EYPs need to be aware that at all times there was a very close connection between beliefs about early childhood and educational provision of the society, within which those beliefs had been held.

Until some time around the twelfth century, European society did not see childhood as a distinct period of development the way that we do now. Children were viewed as miniature adults and participated fully in adult life:

> It is hard to believe that this neglect was due to incompetence or incapacity; it seems more probable that there was no place for childhood in the medieval world.
>
> (Aries, 2002: 33)

Consequently, children were not recognised as having special needs. One of the results of this outlook was the lack of established educational provision for children. The modern conception of childhood began to develop during the sixteenth century with the rise of the middle class and its demand for formalised education for its sons: the education of boys in mathematics and the classics became widespread. This shift reflected an increasing attachment of parents to the child: middle-class parents preferred to keep their children close to them. The change of a social attitude towards children and childhood resulted in the change of a social demand for new educational provision. The number of schools started growing along with the tendency of sending children to school rather than apprenticing them.

At the end of the sixteenth century the first signs of the recognition that the child is a creature distinct from the adult became apparent. People no longer hesitated to acknowledge the diversion which children provided, and delighting in children became fashionable among the upper classes. From the seventeenth century onward this conception of childhood made children a source of amusement for adults. In contrast to this, a second perception of the child arose among groups that stood in opposition: the Church, the moralists and the pedagogues, who felt responsible for the spiritual development of the child. They believed that children needed education and discipline, and simultaneous with the new interest in the psychology of the child, they drafted a demand for an educational system that would satisfy these needs: the child was perceived as 'a delicate creature, who must be protected, educated, and moulded in accordance with the current educational beliefs and goals' (Aries, 2002: 35). However, the idea of early years provision was not yet considered at that time. Early childhood was even then regarded just as a necessary evil on the way to productive adolescence, and in the eighteenth-century Europe still lacked a system of early years provision.

The German educator Friedrich Froebel (1782–1852) was one of the pioneers of early childhood educational provision. As an idealist, he thought that every child possessed, at birth, his full educational potential, and that an appropriate educational environment was necessary to encourage the child to grow and develop in an optimal manner. Froebel did not believe that the child should be placed into society's shape, but should be allowed to form his own nature and grow at his own pace through the developmental stages of the educational process; the child should never be rushed or hurried in his development.

> Young animals and plants are given rest, and arbitrary interference with their growth is avoided, because it is known that the opposite practice would disturb their pure unfolding and sound development; but, the young human being is looked upon as a piece of wax or a lump of clay which man can mould into what he pleases. (Froebel, 1907: 8)

In his study of child-nature one of the most marked characteristics, which attracted Froebel's attention, was the child's inborn desire for activity, which reveals itself in play. According to Froebel, 'play is the freest active manifestation of the child's inner self which springs from the need of that inner living consciousness to realize itself outwardly' (Bowen, 1907: 116). Froebel made a significant contribution to early childhood education by seeing play as a process in which children bring to realisation their inner nature. He recognised that children began to learn as soon as they began to interact with the world, and he reasoned that since the interaction was mostly in the form of play, the way to educate a child was through play, 'as a means of awakening and developing the active side of his nature; wherefore none, not even the simplest gifts from a child, should ever be suffered to be neglected' (Froebel, 1901: 77).

Along with theoretical perspectives on early years provision, EYPs also need to be aware of current international perspectives that will help them to develop a deeper understanding of how they can promote all children's wellbeing, and support their learning and development.

Throughout history, Europe has represented an intense source of many influential educational ideas. In early childhood education, one of the best known approaches with European origin is Reggio Emilia, which is seen as a strong educational alternative to traditional education and as a source of inspiration for progressive educational reform. Research shows that there are many themes and elements regarding children and their development that are common to both Italian and British educational systems. In view of the image of a child in education, the Reggio approach is first and foremost child-centred, based on individual children's needs and interests, and on educators' respect for the differences between individual children. It encompasses the theoretical contributions of Dewey, Piaget, Vygotsky and Bruner, and is similar to the Montessori preschool method. At the centre of the Reggio pedagogy is the child who is competent in building relationships, who holds his own values, who wants to be valued for himself, who respects others and who embodies a curiosity and open-mindedness to all that is possible (Brunton and Thornton, 2005). Similar to the Italian system, the main principles of traditional early childhood education in Britain are child-centred (Bruce, 2004).

In relation to this, EYPs might consider asking themselves the following questions. What are the historical origins and foundational philosophical concepts of the Reggio Emilia approach? How do they compare with the UK system in terms of organisational structures, curriculum and principles? What elements of effective practice can we use in our early years provision?

The modern concept of 'child-centredness' views children as persons in their own right, having purposes and interests of their own. The contemporary sociology of childhood is characterised by the increasing recognition that children must be seen as 'social actors in their own right' (Thomas, 2005: 80). EYPs need to acknowledge that this change in our understanding of children's roles in society led to modification of the child's position from a rights-holder to a citizen, whose opinion has to be considered and whose voice has to be heard. It is important to emphasise that the UN Convention on the Rights of the Child formally acknowledged for the first time in international law that children are the subjects of rights, rather than just recipients of adult protection. Article 12 of the Convention obliges adults as parents and professionals to ensure that children are enabled to and encouraged to contribute their views in all relevant matters and to provide age-appropriate information, which helps them to form their views (Lansdown, 2005).

Since this group of standards (S7–24) covers many interconnected elements of effective practice, EYPs need to be aware of the key historical and current, national and international perspectives on early years care and education to be able to plan and provide appropriate activities and experiences for babies and young children, to create a safe and stimulating environment for them, to practise values and principles that are based on respecting children's rights and to be able to meet children's diverse individual needs.

Standard 7 – have high expectations of all children and commitment to ensuring that they can achieve their full potential

Example of standard 7 in personal practice

The Early Years Foundation Stage (EYFS) places a strong emphasis on the importance of raising children's levels of achievement in their learning and in their development, and to having high expectations of their behaviour. Achieving this is not possible without the inclusion of every child irrespective of ethnicity, culture, religion, home language, family background, learning difficulties or disabilities, gender or ability. This commitment to ensuring that all children reach their potential will be evident in the candidate's observation, planning and assessment – their direct contact with children and their evaluation of their own and their colleagues' practice. As the EYFS (DCSF, 2008) underlines, practitioners should build respectful and caring relationships with children, observing them and listening to what they say so as to focus on their learning and achievement. Candidates will encourage the development of children's positive self-esteem and the achievement of their full potential through these supportive and constructive relationships.

Candidates need to build up good relationships with parents and carers to discover relevant information about children's needs and developmental backgrounds: '. . . working with parents to ensure that each parent is valued and that the knowledge Early Years Practitioners have of each child is as complete as possible should form an integral part of the philosophy of every setting' (Farrelly, 2010: 54).

This information, alongside practitioner and key person observations, will be instrumental in planning children's next steps to support and extend children's learning and development. Candidates need to be aware of children's unique developmental patterns – if a child is in need of extra support to achieve; alternatively, if a child is in advance of the average developmental norms. Consequently, candidates will need to implement additional resources and stimuli to motivate the child to learn and raise their levels of achievement.

The abilities and disabilities of a child with additional needs must be appreciated to support further appropriate development. Candidates need to recognise how vital it is to have a close and supportive relationship with the child's parents and other professionals involved in their care. They need to work collaboratively with both parties to plan for the achievement of the child's full potential.

EYP candidates need to encourage and support children's social and emotional development by having high expectations of children's behaviour towards other children and adults. Positive values and attitudes need to be encouraged, like manners, respect for others, taking turns and resolving their own conflicts.

Successful candidates need to have high expectations for all children while acknowledging that each child is unique. Children's learning should be personalised through differentiated teaching and learning strategies that are responsive to individual children's needs, helping them to reach their personal goals.

This will be achieved by providing motivating, flexible play-based learning that is taken from children's interests and from observations of the children, and providing a broad learning environment that reflects the diversity of our society and is inclusive of each child, providing games, toys, resources, books and a variety of materials to help children to reach their full potential. The EYFS (DCSF, 2008) emphasises that planning should be inclusive and flexible to help children to achieve their full potential.

Example of standard 7 in leadership

'CWDC expects EYPs to be agents of change by improving practice in the settings in which they work' (Colloby, 2008: 13). Candidates need to be able to demonstrate leadership qualities to bring about these changes and improvements within a setting. An effective leader is able to recognise the inevitability of change and to be able to plan and manage the process.

'An EYP is expected to lead practice across the EYFS in a range of settings, modelling skills and behaviour that promote good outcomes for children and supporting other practitioners' (CWDC, 2008: 4). Therefore they need to be inspiring role models, encouraging others to improve their practice by encouraging ongoing professional development; they can advise and guide colleagues on having high expectations of the achievement of all children, irrespective of background, ethnicity, culture, religion, gender or religion by taking account of and minimising the barriers that can prevent a child achieving their full potential.

Candidates need to be able to evaluate their own and their colleagues' practice in the observation of children, planning and assessment to enable all practitioners to have high expectations of all children. An essential leadership skill is the ability to support colleagues in applying their commitment to raising the achievement of all children irrespective of disabilities or learning difficulties.

EYPs need to support colleagues in maintaining high expectations of children's behaviour and role modelling positive values and attitudes.

Standard 7 reflection point

The EYFS challenges EYPs to think more deeply about all aspects of children's learning and development, including the practitioners' skills of raising children's levels of achievement and having high expectations of all children: Consider how you can evidence when you have had high expectations of children and showed commitment to achieving their full potential in the following age ranges:

- 0–20 months
- 16–36 months
- 30–60 months.

Standard 7 stakeholder comment

K is a teacher in an independent nursery class in Bolton. Here she describes how she demonstrates that she has high expectations of all children and consequently ensures that each child achieves their full potential.

'In our setting the ethos of the setting is embedded within the curriculum, staff training, meetings with parents and information given out to parents. We are committed to each and every child in our setting and the individual needs of children – the "unique child" – is at the heart of our planning, observation and assessment, key person system, environment and staff training/ development. Our EYFS ethos is to provide a quality learning environment for all our children. Our children are valued and respected. We display real, honest and purposeful enthusiasm and have clear expectations. Planning is relevant to the children and supports a sense of collaboration and mutual trust. We offer continuous play provision within a positive 'can do' climate, supported by adult-led activities where adults ask open-ended questions: What do you think? How do you think we should sort that? What will happen if/when? Why do you think that happened? Can you think of a way? Adults interact with a positive outcome – sensitively, supportively, extending and enhancing. "That's an interesting idea? How did you think of that?" "I wondered why you had . . ." "I really like what you are doing . . ." "I have never thought about that before . . . What a super idea!" "Have you thought about?" Our nursery ethos is focused on communication, collaboration, creativity, problem-solving – children "learning to learn".'

'We recognise that every child is a competent learner who can be resilient, capable, confident and self-assured. We recognise that children develop in individual ways and at varying rates. Children's attitudes and dispositions to learning are influenced by feedback from others; we use praise and encouragement, as well as celebration/sharing circle times and reward stickers, to encourage children to develop a positive attitude to learning. We value the diversity of individuals within the school and all children and their families. We believe that all children are given every opportunity to achieve their full potential. Account is taken of their range of life experiences when planning for their learning development. We also ensure that each child can achieve their full potential by planning to meet the needs of boys and girls, children with special educational needs, children who are more able, children with disabilities, children from all social and cultural backgrounds, children of different ethnic groups and those from diverse linguistic backgrounds.'

'It is important to us that all children in the nursery are "safe". We aim to educate children on boundaries, rules and limits and to help them understand why they exist. We provide children with choices to help them develop this important life skill. Children are allowed and encouraged to take risks, but are taught how to recognise and avoid hazards and consequences.'

→

'We recognise that children learn to be strong and independent from secure relationships. We aim to develop caring, respectful, professional relationships with the children and their families.'

'Each child is valued unconditionally. Every child is unique, with specific needs and interests, and our planning is based upon meeting every child's individual needs.'

'We acknowledge that the environment plays a key role in supporting and extending the children's development. The EYFS learning environment is organised to allow children to explore and learn securely and safely. There are areas where the children can be active and others where they can be quieter and rest. The environment is set up in learning areas, where children are able to find and locate equipment and resources independently. Space has been imaginatively used so that all our children have varied opportunities for active inquiry and discovery. Experienced adults play a key role in enriching and extending every child's learning potential. The nursery has an attractive, open-ended outdoor area. This has a positive effect on the children's development. Being outdoors offers opportunities for doing things in different ways and on different scales than when indoors. It offers the children the opportunity to explore, use their senses and be physically active and exuberant. We plan activities and resources for the children to access outdoors that help the children to develop in all six areas of learning. The children are encouraged to access all these areas independently and take ownership of their learning.'

Private day-nursery owner of two outstanding settings in the north-west:

'I set very high standards and have high expectations of all children and a strong commitment to ensuring that children can achieve their full potential. As well as achieving in their learning and development, I have high expectations of children's behaviour. Our nursery believes that children flourish best when they know how they are expected to behave. Children gain respect through interaction with caring adults who show them respect and value their individual personalities. Positive, caring and polite behaviour will be encouraged and praised at all times in an environment where children learn to respect themselves, other people and their surroundings.'

'I recognise the individuality of all our children and I encourage and really expect all my staff to keep up to date with legislation and current research and thinking. Staff training and my own commitment to raising children's level of achievement as a nursery owner and manager is a strength that is evident in my Ofsted report.'

Standard 8 – establish and sustain a safe, welcoming, purposeful, stimulating and encouraging environment where children feel confident and secure and are able to develop and learn

Example of standard 8 in personal practice

> The environment plays a key role in supporting and extending children's development and learning.   (DCSF, 2008)

First impressions are extremely important to how a child and parent/carer will initially feel when visiting a setting. A clean and well ordered entrance will convey a strong message that practitioners working here have a very clear vision of the needs of those who attend the setting and how the environment is valued as part of the learning experience. Through personal practice the EYP candidate will recognise the importance of ensuring that all resources and furniture are appropriate for the children and families attending. Signs and messages displayed are clear, visual and will celebrate the many different cultures within the community. Equipment is easily accessible to the child, giving them a sense of ownership. An appropriately well organised environment will in turn encourage children to become independent learners.

The successful EYP candidate will ensure that each child attending the setting has a sense of belonging. It should be common practice for the early years practitioner to greet children and families with a smile and warm welcome. The EYP understands the importance of welcoming the child and family into each session and developing a positive relationship with the parent/carer.

The EYP is a role model to the child, parents and colleagues within the setting. A calm and pleasant approach and manner will reflect a calm organised mind, capable of dealing with many of the issues that may arrive with families at the start of a session. The practitioner who is knowledgeable in child development is the most influential resource within the setting and will have many skills to help children and families through transition times. The EYP will be aware of the need for regular training and support to enable fellow practitioners to become experts within the early years field. As knowledge and understanding of the early years develop between practitioners, so does the shared pedagogical dialogue between staff. The staff move toward becoming a 'community of learners' (Siraj-Blatchford and Manni, 2007).

The EYP candidate will be aware that children learn and develop more effectively within a safe and secure environment. The EYP must also ensure that the environment reflects the community it serves. This will ensure the activities and resources are meaningful to each and every child.

A visual timetable and a selection of pictorial representations of everyday needs demonstrate good practice. Pictures of refreshments, activities, staff members and, of course, a toilet will allow children, especially those with difficulties in communication, to access their needs easily and with a certain level of independence, which will result in the child feeling secure and included. The environment becomes an enabling environment and a safe haven for those children who access it.

A competent EYP will acknowledge the importance of transition to this new environment and will ensure that the family are made to feel comfortable and valued from the first point of contact. A smooth transition will enable the child and family to develop positive relationships with the practitioner. Communication between those concerned will allow the child's interests and needs to be discussed, explained and noted from the beginning. Such information will allow the key person to begin to create opportunities for the child within the setting, which will encourage the child to begin to explore this wonderful new and exciting environment. The EYP will be able to demonstrate how opportunities have been encouraged for the child and family to make regular preparatory visits to the setting or even offered home visits before the child starts.

The EYP will ensure that the environment is clearly arranged into specific areas that will meet the needs of all the children and allow children whenever possible to access the outdoors. The child who arrives in the setting anxious and withdrawn may need the security of a quiet, comfortable area away from noise and distractions. Is there a suitable area for this child to go? The EYP will be aware that children learn and develop more effectively within a safe and secure environment but also one that allows them to explore and experiment. Providing an environment that positively encourages young children to 'look, listen, touch, grab, climb, rest and drop things will be messy from time to time' (Post and Hohmann, 2000: 14). What about the child who arrives and needs to build and construct and explore the endless combinations of block play? Can the child independently choose their activity during the session without the assistance of a nearby member of staff? Are there opportunities for cutting, gluing and creative play? Can the children access equipment to sweep up and clean up if a mess has been made? How is the day structured to ensure that children have the opportunity to visit the many different areas of the setting, including the many various activities outdoors? How do the staff ensure that all children are able to choose activities appropriate to their needs?

The skilled practitioner will observe the children regularly within this environment. Such observations may be in the form of handwritten notes, photographs, dictaphone, video footage, parents' comments, colleagues' comments and the child's comments. Such observations will equip the practitioner with the necessary information to continue to prepare an environment which will allow the child to take the next steps in their development and learning journey.

Examples of standard 8 in leadership

The successful EYP will be aware of the many research programmes that are currently taking place which focus on the early years which may benefit the children within the setting. Such findings should be used to improve the setting and make a positive impact on the children, thus improving outcomes for children.

One example of research having a positive impact on children is Developmental Movement Play (DMP). This is now recognised as an important part of young children's development and is the focus of a research base in the UK, JABADAO, which is a national charity that works in partnership with the education, health, arts and social care sectors to bring about a sea change in the way that people work with the body and movement. DMP is a new approach for early years settings, emphasising two important aspects of movement: first, opportunities for children to indulge in free-flow, child-led, spontaneous movement play; and, second, attention to specific early movement patterns and activities that appear to prompt neurological development. These are innate and occur naturally in all children given good health and appropriate opportunities (Greenland, 2009).

According to Montessori (1988/1912), if teaching is to be effective with young children, it must assist them to advance on the way to independence. It must initiate them into those kinds of activities that they can perform themselves and that keep them from being a burden to others because of their inabilities.

The EYP will ensure that the environment is carefully planned and organised to allow children to access resources and equipment to carry out daily tasks and routines. The staff will be supported to observe the children within the setting both indoors and outdoors. These observations, which may be taken as photographs, in note form or just visually acknowledged, will give the practitioner a good indication of how the children use resources not only for the adult-initiated activities but also the child-initiated activities. It should be common practice to prepare an environment that will encourage opportunities for the next level of learning and sustained shared thinking. The EPPE Report highlights the value of 'sustained shared thinking', where two or more individuals 'work together' in an intellectual way to solve a problem, clarify an activity, extend a narrative, etc. Both parties must contribute to the thinking and it must develop and extend the understanding. It was found that the most effective settings encourage 'sustained shared thinking', which was most likely to occur when the children were interacting on a one-to-one basis with an adult or with a single peer partner. It would appear that periods of 'sustained shared thinking' are a necessary prerequisite for the most effective early years practice (Sylva *et al.*, 2004).

Continual assessment of the environment will allow the practitioner to ensure that the activities interest the children and are appropriate to their level of understanding. The EYP will use observations, discussions with the key person and family and a sound knowledge of understanding of child development to ensure appropriate activities. For example, in a baby room, treasure baskets (Goldschmied and Jackson, 2004) allow very young children to explore objects from their environment using all of their senses. Older children can gain as much from the experience of a 'heuristic play' session using a much larger range of objects (Goldschmied and Hughes, 1992).

The candidate must support colleagues to understand how the environment is used as a continuous learning environment to enhance the child's development, wellbeing and learning. Staff will be encouraged to attend training, staff meetings and hold discussions through planning times as to how the environment should evolve to suit the needs of the group. Good practice will allow all staff to take an active role in developing and using the environment as a tool for learning. The display boards can be a place to inform parents and carers of the day-to-day routines, events and general information, as well as a place to display photographic evidence of learning in progress. It is the learning process that is important, not the end product.

Finally, a successful EYP leader will explore many pedagogical theories and values and look for inspiration in other cultures. Reggio Emilia preschools use the development of communities of learning through a wide range of the expressive arts; for example, Te Whāriki from New Zealand, which embraces curriculum diversity as well as Athey's (1990) research on schematic development and Nutbrown's (2006) research on the development of the curriculum through schematic theory.

Standard 8 reflection points

- What is the first thing the children see when they enter the setting? How welcoming is it from a child's perspective?
- Who is on hand to welcome parents/carers and children?
- Are all of the welfare requirements of the EYFS upheld? Can you see areas in need of development?
- Do activities cover all areas of learning?
- Observe practice to assess how confident staff are when allowing children to take risks and investigate?
- What can be done to support staff who do not feel confident in these areas?
- Are activities differentiated to promote inclusive practice for all ages and abilities?
- How do adults interact with the children and develop sustained shared thinking?

Standard 8 stakeholder comment

Helen, an EYP in a rural setting, recognised the value of home visits after attending a series of 'Birth to Three' workshops held at the local college. She had decided to offer home visits as part of the induction process to new families wanting to attend the setting. A new boy, Joe, age 2, was starting at the setting after the Easter holiday so Helen asked the parents if they would like a home visit from Joe's proposed key person, Fiona. They were pleased to be given this opportunity and welcomed a visit from Fiona, an early years practitioner from the setting. During the visit Fiona not only met Joe and his mother but also his grandparents, who actually spent a great deal of time with Joe during the week. Joe's grandma explained to Fiona that when Joe is upset he loves to sit on her knee and listen to a story. Joe's grandma went on to explain that Joe likes to play with her wedding ring and turns it round and round until he feels completely calm and relaxed. Joe's grandad then went on to show Fiona how good Joe was with a golf club and golf ball as the whole family love playing golf. Joe could use the golf club very proficiently and hit several balls down the garden while Fiona was watching.

Fiona came back to the setting full of news and notes that she had frantically written down after the event.

→

> *Joe arrived in the setting and initially was tearful. Fiona remembered the advice given by his grandma and chose to read Joe a story to settle him. Fiona also showed Joe her own wedding ring and compared it to his grandma's and, as they sat quietly in the reading corner, Joe twiddled Fiona's ring and calmed down. As Joe became more settled in his new surroundings over the following few weeks, the practitioners noticed some quite erratic behaviour. Joe would pick up a random object, for example a skittle, then use this object to hit a smaller object across the room. Fiona recalled his passion for golf. He was mimicking his golf practice and was unaware of the dangers he was causing to those around him. As soon as this was apparent, Fiona spent time developing appropriate activities outside for Joe. Many of these activities and tasks involved Joe aiming to hit various objects towards targets in a relatively safe and controlled environment. The reason behind this particular behaviour would not have been picked up quite as quickly had the home visit not happened. Joe may have been misjudged by many of the staff as a disruptive child who wants to hit other children with small hard objects.*

Standard 9 – provide balanced and flexible daily and weekly routines that meet children's needs and enable them to develop and learn

Example of standard 9 in personal practice

For an EYP, when considering the notion of routines in relation to this standard, it is useful to reflect on the later part of the standard 'to enable them to develop and learn' (CWDC, 2008: 34). An EYP should demonstrate that they have fully understood that any routine is ultimately a tool to support an aspect of a child's development.

Consideration of the 'routine' of the setting as a context for learning has been explored by a range of educationalists. For Reggio Emilia, the routine in the learning environment allows for long-term exploration of children's experiences through access to permanent media, including sculpture, drawing, painting, discussion, mime, movement and dance, as well as exploration of light, dark and colour. Similarly, an EYP may reflect on the principle of Te Whāriki, where the learning routine is of high value with a focus on the physical environment, the inclusion of the wider family alongside the timing and long-term access to personally interesting learning experiences.

Many candidates, when undertaking personal research in relation to the notion of routines, in its widest context, as the mechanism for learning, have reviewed the reported long-term successes of the HighScope approach. They have effectively reviewed their own perception of 'routines' as the regular organisational tools of their day and instead developed their practice to include opportunities for children to plan and review their learning.

This desire to develop routines to support children's development and learning will then need to be incorporated into the organisational framework of their setting. Therefore an EYP will be demonstrating their understanding of 'the individual and diverse ways children learn and develop' (CWDC, 2008: 19) within the context of the routines they establish and facilitate in their setting.

Further analysis of the standard should focus the EYP's attention on the reference to 'children's needs'; therefore it is important that an EYP fully recognises the breadth of potential needs may need to be accommodated within their provision at the setting. For example, does the routine support a child's

- Social or emotional needs?
- Cognitive needs?
- Physical needs?
- Communication needs?
- Physiological needs?

Standard 9 also demands that candidates explore the dichotomy between 'routines', which implies a level of controlled organisation against the requirement for 'flexibility'. Hence, the EYP will need to demonstrate that, while he/she recognises that routines or established patterns of events on any one day are reassuring for a child and a necessary requirement for the smooth running of a busy early years setting, they offer flexibility in the delivery of that routine to support a child's particular need at any given time.

While traditionally a routine is generally acknowledged to be the events in a day to meet a child's physiological needs (for example, feeding, changing or sleeping), a highly skilled EYP will recognise that routines for children are far wider. They should include the opportunity for a balance of playful learning experiences for children, which may include sensory play, imaginary play, constructive play, physical play, social games, stories and songs and periods of quiet reflection and consolidation.

The *Guidance to the Standards* (CWDC, 2008) illustrates clearly what the assessor will be looking for:

- **Plan and implement balanced and flexible daily and weekly schedules that are responsive to each child's needs and enable each child to learn and develop.**

An EYP candidate will therefore need to consider how they can most effectively demonstrate evidence of this standard, drawing on examples from their own practice. Candidates have previously demonstrated evidence of this standard in innovative ways within their written tasks, documents, tour, witness statements and witness interviews.

In practice, within a task a candidate could illustrate how they have observed and understood the needs of a child/children within the setting and, in the short term, responded to that observation with an immediate action or, in the long term, taken time to consider the conflict between the organisation of the routine within the context of the setting against the needs of the child, and taken subsequent action to implement change to the setting's procedures.

Previous candidates have successfully used documentary evidence of an observation of a child which has resulted in a change to the setting's timescale of a routine or an amendment to a policy written by the candidate or an implementation of a change to procedure led by the candidate.

Within the context of a tour, many candidates have shared examples of physical changes to an area of the environment where routines often naturally occur. They have demonstrated their reflective analysis of the effectiveness of the physical space as well as evidence of the improvements they implemented together with an overview of how this was implemented in the setting, with reference to how this is a more effective way of meeting children's needs through the revised provision for the routine.

Example of standard 9 in leadership

The leadership aspect of the standard is intrinsically linked to an EYP's ability to:

- lead and support colleagues to design and implement balanced and flexible daily and weekly schedules that are responsive to children's needs and enable them to learn and develop.

Hence, the EYP is required to demonstrate leadership skills and strategies while working with colleagues in the setting to enhance their provision for routines in the setting.

Highly competent EYPs will draw on a range of formal and informal leadership strategies. In an informal way they may model and demonstrate empathetic and sensitive communication skills with children to listen to, understand and act upon a child's demonstration of conflict within a particular routine. For example, while some children may require close, physical contact as they prepare to fall asleep, others may prefer to fall asleep alone.

However, on other occasions an EYP may demonstrate evidence of this standard using a more formal leadership style, for example through the effective use, with staff colleagues, of a potential range of documents, including SEF (self-evaluation form) documentation, post-Ofsted action plans, local authority early years consultants action plans, quality assurance documentation as well as formal review of setting policy and/or procedures.

Whilst these two leadership styles are very different, an EYP will need to demonstrate their knowledge of an ability to draw on appropriate leadership styles to meet the context at that period of time.

Standard 9 reflection points

- Review your daily timeline/routine to consider whether or not it allows for flexibility in its delivery to meet individual needs?
- Observe the behaviours and practices of colleagues in your setting to evaluate how skilled they are in recognising and responding to children's needs during routines?
- Consider your weekly provision and reflect on whether or not it includes opportunities for children who may attend on specific days of the week to access all aspects of the provision in your setting?

Standard 9 stakeholder comment

A full training pathway student undertaking his final placement was fortunate enough to be offered the opportunity to work alongside and shadow a newly appointed room leader in the preschool area within a sessional voluntary managed setting. The setting had a traditional approach to early years provision where children undertook a full group registration process, then worked in their key worker groups on four half-hour activities in the setting. An opportunity for snack and outdoor play was also included within the routine.

Recognising that although the routine looked orderly and calm, the EYP candidate became interested in the contrast between the provision on offer and the requirements of the EYFS, in particular within the personal social and emotional area of learning, aspect 'Dispositions and Attitudes'. He focused on the Development Matters stages, across the 30–50-month and 40–60-month age groups.

During discussion with his supervising tutor and setting manager in relation to the potential aspects of work he could undertake in relation to EYPS Task 3, he broached the subject of the routines of the setting in direct contrast to a child's ability to demonstrate achievement of some aspects of personal, social and

→

emotional skills as required by the EYFS. He discussed the HighScope approach as a possible technique within the setting and was invited to present his proposal to the voluntary managed committee.

He made a successful presentation to the committee, focusing on the learning potential for children's personal and social skills, and was granted permission to implement the system in the setting on a trial basis. He was able to use recorded minutes of the meeting within his documentary evidence file.

Within Task 3, the candidate was able clearly to claim achievement of his personal practice of standard 9, as he included a commentary of how he had personally worked with a child to support her to make choices within her new learning routine, which met her learning needs and supported her development of personal and social skills.

The candidate also used Task 3 to illustrate his leadership of standard 9, recording how he had engaged with the voluntary management committee, his introduction of this new scheme to staff within a staff meeting and his role in leading the implementation and review of the new routine in the setting. He further supported this in his documentary evidence with the inclusion of the revised setting early years policy, in which he had written an amendment to the policy to reflect the rationale for the learning routine now in place in the setting. Furthermore, during the validation assessment visit, colleagues were able to provide secondary evidence of his leadership and personal practice of standard 9 during a witness interview.

Standard 10 – use close, informed observation and other strategies to monitor children's activity, development and progress systematically and carefully, and use the information to inform, plan and improve practice and provision

Example of standard 10 in personal practice

The EYFS guidance (DCSF, 2008) states the importance and significance of practitioners observing children. The EYFS discusses how observations help practitioners to: understand and gain further insight into a child's development; strengthen relationships with children, families and carers by getting to know a child better; gain a deeper understanding of child development and, very importantly, to identify the next steps in a child's learning and development and therefore inform planning by using these observations 'routinely and systematically'.

Observations can take different forms and are used to develop an under-standing of children's interests, achievements and learning styles. Babies and children need to be regularly observed to identify next steps. Formal observa-tion may be carried out where a written account of a child's actions is recorded. These actions must be put into context for the next steps to be fully identified. Therefore when beginning a formal, written observation, practitioners need to state if, for example, a child is playing alone or in a group. If a child is playing in a group, with whom is he/she playing? In which learning area of the setting is the child playing? Are other adults involved in the activity? Written observations will take different forms depending on the setting, but the overall objective of analys-ing the learning taking place and identifying the next steps is the same.

When a practitioner has carried out an observation it is then necessary to refer to the EYFS guidance to understand and translate the learning that has taken place to plan for further development. If, for example, a child has been building with blocks with another child, there will be a number of aspects of the child's learning that will need to be identified. Good practice is to consider the different aspects, perhaps starting with personal, social and emotional devel-opment (especially for children under the age of 3) and consider which devel-opmental matter the child may have met (or partly met or be working towards). To identify the next steps, practitioners need to consider how the child could meet the developmental matter fully or move on to the next one. Consideration needs to be given to the resources that will need to be made available to the child for the child to progress. The child may also be demonstrating problem-solving, reasoning and numeracy skills whilst building with the blocks. There will also be physical development and perhaps communication, language and literacy skills to be identified (again the latter two are especially significant when observing those children under the age of 3). However, it is important not to identify too many areas of development and next steps as this will make planning difficult. It is therefore good practice to consider the main areas of learning that have taken place and this can be achieved by knowing the child and knowing which areas of development to focus on. It is therefore common for a child's key person to carry out an observation, but this will not be the case in all settings.

The standard also refers to using 'other strategies' as an aid to monitoring children's activity, development and progress. This may involve, for example, photographic evidence of progress being made or short written notes, capturing, for example, a child using a pair of scissors or making a comment or expression.

Example of standard 10 in leadership

The standard is very much about reflecting on and evaluating personal practice to bring about change and lead colleagues so that practice and provision are improved. Planning, whether it be the setting's medium-term, weekly or daily activity plan, is not complete until it has been evaluated and strengths and weaknesses identified to improve practice.

An EYP, for example, may therefore wish to discuss altering the setting's planning proformas to add a section whereby colleagues can add their reflections and evaluations of an activity, resources used, groupings of children, and so on, in order to improve practice.

An EYP may also role model to other practitioners the importance of the observation, assessment and planning cycle and constantly feed back to improve practice. It must be remembered that the overall aim of the EYFS is to ensure that all children are given every opportunity to meet the five outcomes of the Every Child Matters agenda (these being staying safe, being healthy, enjoying and achieving, making a positive contribution and achieving economic wellbeing). Therefore it is the role of the EYP to ensure that observations are looked at in a wider context when identifying next steps, and children and babies are given every opportunity to make choices, test boundaries, understand right and wrong, enjoy physical development and have respect for one another. Practitioners will therefore need to work in partnership with parents, carers and external agencies to ensure that children are given every opportunity to meet these outcomes.

The role of the EYP is also to demonstrate to colleagues the importance of flexibility. Planning may need to be changed in the light of an observation having taken place which has concluded in a child needing different learning experiences than those previously planned. For planning to be truly based on the needs and interests of the child, EYPs must lead in this very important area and demonstrate to colleagues the need to observe children systematically so that personalised learning is taking place. EYPs need to ensure that practitioners know when to observe children. It is important that children are observed in child-initiated play, adult-initiated activities and enhanced provision (this is when resources/activities have been selected by adults but children are free to use them if and how they wish). It is important that observations are carried out in different contexts to truly improve practice. EYPs need to, for example, see what the role-play area is being used for. If it has been set up as a shop and some of the children are using it as a hospital, then a change may need to take place. Anne O'Connor (2009) states how a different way of observing children in role-play challenges what practitioners offer in the learning environment. It is, therefore, important for EYPs to lead planning, based on observation, by consulting the four principles of the EYFS.

Standard 10 reflection points

The manager of a nursery has made the role-play area into a pet shop. She has spent all day Saturday making a beautiful pet shop full of new, shiny resources. You have observed that the children are not using the role-play area as a pet shop and do not seem to have much understanding of what a pet shop is.

- As an EYP how will you approach the nursery manager about your findings?
- What might you suggest the role-play area be made into?
- Who will you consult when deciding on this change?

Whilst the nursery manager is happy for you to change the area and understands that planning should be led by the children, the other practitioners are not as convinced. One practitioner in particular is concerned that the weekly planning sheet is looking messy because of the changes in light of observations that are taking place.

- As an EYP how will you deal with this situation?

The nursery manager asks you to hold a meeting with all members of staff to explain why the way the planning is being done needs to change.

- What issues will you raise at the meeting?
- How will you help and support those practitioners who are unsure about identifying next steps?

One practitioner is concerned that there are 40 children registered at the nursery and states that it would be impossible to have different plans for all these children.

- How will you address this concern?
- How could you involve links with parents/carers to ensure a child's interests, needs, etc. are being met?

Standard 10 stakeholder comment

'When studying for the award of EYPS I carried out regular observations of a 2-year-old who had just started in the nursery. The child was always very distressed when his mother left him despite every effort being made by practitioners working with the child's mother to try and settle him. I observed how the boy would eventually settle when a favourite book was read to him and how he enjoyed seeing this favourite character on a computer programme. However, during times of transition (e.g. going out to play and tidying up or circle time) the boy would become distressed when he could not gain access to his favourite character in some form. I therefore decided (after consulting with the nursery manager and the boy's mother) to put together a themed treasure basket containing the boy's favourite character. I included a book, some laminated cards of the character showing different facial expressions to help the boy express himself, a series of laminated pictures of the character to encourage the boy's language and communication and some dressing up clothes. I had observed how the boy had enjoyed dressing up but, being younger than the majority of other children, had shied away from the role-play area. The basket also contained some trains as the boy had been observed playing with the train set on a number of occasions.'

'My observations led me to plan personally for a young child and in doing so improve practice. The other strategies were talking to the boy's mother informally about his likes and dislikes, and making short notes of the resources that the boy enjoyed discovering and exploring. Some of the resources already existed in the nursery but it was not always easy for the boy to gain access to them. I had therefore considered the role of the environment in planning the resource. The basket contained many elements to help the boy learn and development in the six areas of learning in the EYFS and also promoted positive relationships as I took on a key person role and used my knowledge of child development. I was of course constantly reminded of the uniqueness of children and fully understood the importance and significance of close, informed observations to begin to understand a child's needs.'

Standard 11 – plan and provide appropriate child-led and adult-initiated experiences, activities and play opportunities in indoor, outdoor and in out-of-setting contexts, which enable children to develop and learn

Example of standard 11 in personal practice

The Statutory Framework for EYFS: learning and development requirements (DCSF, 2008) states how all the areas of learning must be delivered through 'planned, purposeful play, with a balance of adult led and child initiated activities'.

Standard 11 very much encompasses all the standards in the effective practice group. For planning to be *appropriate* in every sense, then observation, values and expectations, children's wellbeing, the role of the environment and promoting positive behaviour must all be taken into account.

First it is necessary to determine what child-led and adult-initiated activities are. For an activity to be child-led it is the child who has taken control of the activity with little input from an adult. The role of the EYP is to develop and plan from this so that the child has every opportunity to further develop their learning. Adult-initiated experiences are those experiences that have been started by an adult (for example, the adult will have chosen the appropriate resources), but the child is not directed in their play by the adult. An activity may begin as adult-initiated, then become child-led as the children direct their play. An example may be children being shown how to construct a den (adult-initiated), and then deciding on the type of structure they would like to make and the resources they will need (child-led). It is the role of the EYP to guide and scaffold the children through their den-making, allowing them maximum opportunity to learn and develop.

Mercer (2006) discusses how children learn and develop with the support of those around them. Mercer believes that a teacher has the task of knowing when and how to intervene to maximise a child's learning. Mercer looks at the work of Piaget and discusses how Piaget believes 'each time one prematurely teaches a child something he could have discovered for himself, the child is kept from inventing it and consequently from understanding it completely' (Mercer, 2006: 72). However, Mercer goes on to look at the work of Vygotsky and states that Vygotsky believes 'that the support of a teacher can enable learners to achieve levels of understanding that they never would alone' (Mercer, 2006: 72). An EYP must make the decision when to intervene in a child's play and when to allow the child to discover and delight in new experiences without adult intervention. If adult intervention is inappropriate, then child-led play may become adult-led play, and a different learning outcome will be achieved.

The standard refers to indoor, outdoor and out-of-setting contexts. EYPs have a duty when planning child-led and adult-initiated experiences to ensure that the environment is used to maximise children's learning potential. This can only be achieved if risk assessments and safeguarding procedures are in place, without placing restrictions on a child's development. The planning that takes place must allow for children to be given time to complete tasks or return to them, giving them the opportunity to become sustained and engrossed in their learning experiences.

Example of standard 11 in leadership

The standard is very much about planning appropriate and purposeful activities. The role of the EYP therefore is to lead colleagues in achieving this by understanding children's needs and interests. For an activity to be child-led, EYPs must follow up observations and notes they have made regarding a child's chosen activity or experience and build on these. An example may be adding props to role-play after observing children playing. The props will be carefully chosen so that the child can further learn and develop. Clear objectives will be recorded in the planning using the Development Matters Aims (DCSF, 2008).

EYPs will be responsible for leading practitioners in planning adult-initiated activities. At the heart of the learning experiences will be opportunities for children to develop their personal, social and emotional learning, which is key to children's overall learning and development. If a child's confidence, self-esteem and ability to form relationships are being fostered, then their learning and development will have greater potential.

Carolyn Webster-Stratton (2005: 30) discusses the importance of building relationships for children to maximise their learning potential and states how such relationships help to build trust and act as a tool for behaviour management. Webster-Stratton states

> Building positive relationships with your students is essential. Perhaps the most obvious reason for teachers to develop meaningful relationships with students is because a positive teacher–student relationship built on trust, understanding and caring will foster [the] student's co-operation and motivation and increase their learning and achievement at school.   (Webster-Stratton, 2005: 30)

Webster-Stratton discusses how relationships with children can be developed through parents and carers, and identifies a number of strategies. One particular strategy involves inviting parents into school when appropriate. An EYP, as part of an adult-initiated activity, may plan to invite parents and carers into the setting to be involved in experiences with their children. Building such relationships will help to develop children's self-esteem, leading to an increase in their motivation.

In terms of leadership, an EYP has the overall task of obtaining a balance of child-led and adult-initiated experiences so that a child can achieve their maximum learning potential. It is therefore necessary to know when to intervene in child's play and how to do so. Heaslip (cited in Moyles, 1999: 102) discusses the role of the teacher and states that if an effective learning environment is to exist 'it must be carefully structured, with the adults playing a crucial role in its organisation with selective intervention with the children in their play'.

Standard 11 reflection points

You notice a practitioner observing a group of children playing with some plastic blocks in the construction area. The children take the blocks outside. They put them in the water tray and you can hear the children talking about their play and what they are doing. The children add some plastic figures and some sticks to the water and you are aware of the learning experiences taking place. The practitioner walks over to the children and tells them that they must not add anything to the water and the blocks are for the construction area.

- What advice will you give to the practitioner about child-initiated play?
- How will you direct the practitioner in intervening with the children while they are playing?
- Based on how the children have been playing, how will you plan to develop the learning you have seen taking place.

A practitioner has set up an adult-initiated activity. She has put out a train set and begins putting the track together. A group of children assemble around her and help her to set up the track. One little girl starts sorting out the track pieces into straight and bent sections. You see the practitioner telling the little girl not to mess about with the track pieces as the other children need them to build the track.

- What advice will you give to the practitioner?
- What notes will you make regarding the little girl's learning experience?

Standard 11 stakeholder comment

'I am currently an associate tutor at Edge Hill University and a part-time nursery and reception teacher at a primary school in Liverpool. I gained Early Years Professional Status in 2009. The stakeholders' comments aim to show how an EYP must fully engage in all aspects of the Early Years Foundation Stage (2008) to meet the standards required for the award of EYPS.'

'When studying for the award of EYPS I invited a dental health worker to come and visit the children in the setting as a planned adult-initiated experience. I chose this activity as the children enjoy brushing their teeth after lunch each day so felt this would develop their learning. I fed back to the deputy manager and practitioners regarding the forthcoming visit and compiled a letter for parents informing them of the event. I assured the parents of those children who do not attend the particular session that their child would still receive any information, etc. and that we would be talking about healthy teeth throughout the week in nursery. I also asked parents to send in any books (fiction or non-fiction) about trips to the dentist or any relevant toys.'

'On the day that our visitor was due to arrive I planned an activity about healthy teeth in preparation for our visit. I brought a favourite book of my own from home entitled 'Harry and the Dinosaurs say "Raahh" by Ian Whybrow and the deputy manager had ordered some toothbrushes with the usual supermarket weekly order. I brought out the small world dinosaurs and the books the children had brought in about trips to the dentist. I sat on the carpet and soon a group of children had assembled around me and we enjoyed reading the books together and brushing the dinosaur's teeth. I saw this as a wonderful opportunity to develop the children's language and introduced new vocabulary such as rinse (we used role-play to practise rinsing our mouths), squeeze (again we pretended to squeeze the toothpaste) and brush (we pretended to brush our teeth). I praised the children constantly for sitting beautifully and listening to the different stories and for telling me all about their experiences of going to the dentist. The children's thinking was sustained for some time by this planned activity and their language and counting skills (we counted the dinosaur's teeth) were developed. I used open-ended questions as a strategy for learning and development and to develop sustained shared thinking.'

'Our visitor gave a wonderful talk to the children, which was very interactive. I accepted that the youngest children would not be able to sit still throughout the whole session and at times I was happy to let them play nearby. However, on the

→

> whole all the children, including the youngest (aged 24 months), sat beautifully and listened very attentively to our visitor.'
>
> 'This planned adult-initiated activity was a success. From the activity child-led play became apparent through role-play activities, giving me a greater understanding of the relationship between child-led and adult-initiated play and how children's learning is developed.'

Standard 12 – select, prepare and use a range of resources suitable for children's ages, interests and abilities, taking account of diversity and promoting equality and inclusion

Example of standard 12 in personal practice

For an EYP, when considering this standard it is useful to analyse the breadth of the standard that it requires the EYP to demonstrate:

- Effective selection of resources to meet children's needs
- Effective use of resources to meet children's needs
- Safe use of resources by children and adults.

For an EYP, when reviewing this standard it is valuable to reflect on their provision against the EYFS Principles into Practice card statement 'the environment and resources play a key role in supporting and extending children's development and learning, a rich and varied environment supports children's learning and development' (DCSF, 2008: 3.3). The practitioner is asked to ensure that 'the indoor environment contains resources which are appropriate, well maintained and accessible by children' (DCSF, 2008: 3.3) alongside the EYFS welfare requirements under 'suitable premises, environment and equipment', where it states that 'outdoor and indoor spaces, furniture and equipment and toys must be safe and suitable for their purpose' (DCSF, 2008: 3.3).

The amplification of the standard places a strong emphasis on an EYP's ability to demonstrate effective inclusive practice through the use of a range of carefully selected resources.

Assessors will judge whether the candidate can:

- Provide a range of flexible and interesting resources, suitable for individuals and groups, that reflect diversity and children's ages, interests and abilities

- Select and prepare resources that match each child's age, interests and abilities
- Ensure that resources are safe and are used safely with appropriate levels of supervision.

Whilst children are unique individuals with particular interests, they often hold common interests that are based on their shared culture or local environmental experiences or on key events, which may be impacting on their lives at given times.

Skilled EYPs, when selecting resources, will recognise and utilise a range of key resources, materials or equipment that are generally recognised to be stimulating and interesting to children within a broad developmental stage or within a particular social context. The EYP will then 'enhance' these resources based on aspects of particular interest to a child/children or based on observations of children in order to support a particular schema or aspect of learning and development.

When considering the needs of a particular child who may be experiencing a temporary or long-term physical/sensory impairment, a successful EYP will be able to demonstrate not only their selection and use of specialist resources and materials, but their thoughtful adaptation or manipulation of resources and materials used by other children in the setting so that the particular child feels fully included.

The successful achievement of standard 12 may also require demonstration of partnership with parents/carers and/or other agencies when selecting and preparing resources for a child with SEN or English as an additional language (EAL). Parents and carers will have a unique insight into the physical or communication skills of their child and an effective EYP will build on the knowledge of parents in their selection and use of resources, thus avoiding tendencies to base provision on assumption rather than knowledge. As recommended by the EYFS, the EYP may need to know 'as the parent whether there is a need for any special services and equipment for the children who may require additional support' (DCSF, 2008: 1.2).

A final consideration for an EYP is the avoidance of tokenism in the selection of resources and materials in relation to the notion of 'diversity'. An EYP will support colleagues to avoid the purchase of resources labelled 'culturally diverse', modelling prudent and thoughtful selection and use of resources that positively reflect the ethnic, social, cultural and religious diversity of the environment in which the young children live.

EYP candidates have used Tasks 1–3 particularly well to demonstrate their skills in effective use of resources, including consideration of how the resources are being used; for example, independently/shared use/small groups/focused tasks or in large groups to support children's learning and development. They have made clear reference to how resources were presented or made available to children, the children's interaction with the resource, the candidates' skills in supporting learning and development through the use of the resource, as well as the evaluation of the experience or activity.

EYPS candidates have effectively supported their claim against standard 12, within the context of their documentary evidence, citing the use of Kitemark-approved resources, regular review of resources for wear and tear, as well as regular specialist checks for larger or more specialist pieces of equipment.

Example of standard 12 in leadership

For an EYP to demonstrate leadership skills in relation to standard 12, it is valuable and valid to recognise that on occasion the setting EYP will not have direct control of the purchase of resources and materials. Resources and materials may well be identified and purchased by a setting owner or other member of staff, and one leadership skill of an EYP may be engagement with those responsible for the purchases to demonstrate their knowledge and understanding of suitable and effective resources and materials.

Conversely, when claiming leadership against the standard, a successful EYP may have demonstrated their leadership skills through their informal discussions with colleagues or by modelling the use of resources to support children's learning and development or by presenting more formal training/CPD opportunities to cascade knowledge of effective use of particular resources or materials.

When making a leadership claim against the standard, the assessor will make a judgement as to whether the candidate can:

- lead and support colleagues to select, prepare and use appropriate and safe resources.

An EYP candidate should take time to reflect on how this can be effectively demonstrated. Candidates have used carefully worded witness statements particularly well within their documentary evidence as well as signposting evidence within their written tasks.

Standard 12 reflection points

- Review your continuous provision resources to consider whether or not they reflect the social or cultural make up of your community?
- Observe the behaviours and practices of colleagues in your setting to evaluate how skilled they are in recognising and responding to children's needs whilst selecting and using resources?
- Consider your procedures for safety reviews of the resources and materials to ensure that they are regularly checked and evaluated?

Standard 12 stakeholder comment

Dawn is the owner/manager of a private full daycare setting, providing full daycare for children 0–5 years old. The setting is within a large children's centre, thus providing the daycare element of the children's centre core offer of services. The children's centre works in partnership with the daycare provider and both parties were keen to respond to the local authority priority to further improve the communication, language and literacy achievement of children within their reach area by the end of the foundation stage.

Whilst undertaking the EYPS programme, Dawn recognised the link between the local authority priority area, or outcomes duty, and standard 4 – the main provisions of the national and local statutory and non-statutory frameworks within which children's services work and their implications for early years settings. In response to this and in particular in response to the commitment to actively support the local authority drive to improve the Communication, Language and Literacy Development (CLLD) outcomes for children, Dawn elected to review the practice and provision for children's communication, language and literacy experiences with a focus on the availability of and use of resources and materials. She undertook a self-evaluation review of each area of continuous provision (indoors and outdoors), identifying resources and materials that could potentially support the speaking, listening, mark-making and reading skills for children. She also sourced a range of reading materials from early years publications.

Dawn was able to evidence aspects of her leadership of standard 12 successfully, by demonstrating ways in which she had engaged her staff in the review of current provision, the identification and selection of additional resources and materials to support communication, language and literacy, and her delegation of responsibility

→

→

to members of her staff for the areas of continuous provision. She provided strong evidence of her leadership within the task by her written account of the process with her staff and supplemented this within her documentary evidence by illustrating the staff training sessions she had led in the setting to enhance their knowledge of high quality CLLD experiences further. The standard was also well evidenced at the validation assessment visit. During the 'tour of the setting' the assessor was made aware of the review and range of high quality resources and materials to support communication, language and literacy skills, and Dawn also presented children's learning journals to demonstrate how these resources had been used to support their speaking, listening, mark-making or early reading skills.

Her personal practice was also evidenced well in the written Task 2. She provided a clear account of her personal practice with children during story time sessions. She recorded how she reviewed the current practice during story time and how she further improved this by effective use of all practitioners to join the children and 'story teller' at story time to celebrate and share stories together. She included in the task her own personal use of appropriate age-related texts with familiar and repeating language, interactive texts, large big books, her use of actions and children's participation at key points in the story or with repeating phrases, her use of props and puppets. She recorded how she had selected the story, based on children's current stages of development and interests, how the story and props had been used again to support the learning styles and needs of the children with whom she was sharing the stories. This provided the assessor with clear evidence that she had met all aspects of the standard, i.e. the effective selection and use of a range of resources.

Standard 13 – make effective personalised provision for the children they work with

Example of standard 13 in personal practice

For a practitioner to make effective personalised provision it is good practice for them to use close, informed observations of the children's self-chosen interests as their starting point. Practitioners need to establish a starting point for the child's learning, and experiences from outside the setting need to be considered (Fisher, 2008). Discussions with parents and carers will develop awareness of the child's interests and motivations from outside of the setting and this will also inform practice. Observations, both formal and informal, gathered from other practitioners will also support the planning of personalised provision. Practitioners who are able to ask the child for their views and current interests can plan experiences that utilise these. In practice, plan to work with the interests of the child to access, for example, wider art and craft activity through the children's current preoccupation with Daleks. This engaged them in model-making from planning to completion and required them to draw on their skills in all six areas of learning. It provided personalised provision, particularly for a boy who had little interest in creative activities.

If practitioners consider how children learn they will identify with the need to plan environments that allow children to be active and contextualise their own learning.

The environment should be planned to provide experiences to enable children to interact with others, which will provide the child with the opportunity to use language.

The practitioner will plan a range of activities for all learning styles, whilst ensuring that there is sufficient time and space for the child to become immersed in them.

Practitioners need to take account of the child's gender and abilities, and consider the different ways and rates that children learn and build on experiences (CWDC, 2010).

A child may be observed repeating the same action, such as dropping things or moving things from one place to another or ordering resources. These patterns may be identified as 'schema', patterns of repeated behaviour which will be seen throughout their play. Practitioners can use their understanding of schemas to plan appropriately and build on babies' and young children's preferred way of learning. Observing and recognising individual and current schemas allows practitioners to support and challenge children's thinking and ideas (Featherstone et al., 2008).

Activities and experiences will need to be personalised to accommodate the needs of children with special educational needs, disabilities or for those children learning English as an additional language. For children with eczema, for example, the use of shaving foam in sensory activities will be prohibited as it may irritate their skin. However, the use of an alternative product for the activity such as a suitable cream approved for use on those with eczema enables the activity to be accessed by all children. Children with SEN may need activities lowering to floor level to enable access or equally raising for them to participate. Experiences for EAL children may also need to consider culture or religion as this may impact on the child's ability to engage in self-chosen activity, and further discussion with family to gain an insight into experiences beyond the setting will enable practitioners to plan personalised experiences based on the child's needs and prior experience. Practitioners will recognise that by differentiating activities they are making personalised provision for some children in their care.

Example of standard 13 in leadership

The standard requires the practitioner to demonstrate the ways that they lead practice to ensure effective personalised provision for the children in their care.

Initially, the EYP will take the lead by supporting practitioners to gather appropriate information which will be used to plan for individual experiences. This will establish the starting point for the child's learning and EYPs can support staff to use collective observations of the child in a range of situations to provide interesting and varied activities. These observations should influence what comes next and in some settings the planning for multisensory activities can benefit from the input of a more experienced practitioner. The EYP can support staff to provide for next steps using multisensory activities that will be effective for the children.

Personalised experiences will need to be devised by taking into account the individual ways in which the children learn. The EYP can promote this by discussing, for example, the children's learning styles and schematic behaviour, which may be visible from the observations or discussions with family. The EYPs knowledge of schema or learning styles can provide others with an overview of the theory and the potential impact on practice. Parents and carers may also benefit from the opportunity to understand and support schema play through verbal or written presentation. Similarly, practitioners need to understand the basic, visual, auditory, kinaesthetic learning styles to ensure that play opportunities are holistic and provide for all learning styles. The EYP can develop the knowledge of less experienced practitioners by providing or signposting to supplementary information. The EYFS says that parents should be involved in planning personalised provision for their child's development and learning (DCSF, 2008). Practitioners may need to consider developing this aspect of practice by auditing their communications with parents and looking at how the parents' input can be sought and respected when planning for their child. Upholding children's rights by asking the child to input into planned, personal experiences gives them the opportunity to have their voice heard and interests recognised. The work of the Thomas Coram Research Unit on listening to children can be used by the EYP to promote the development of this aspect of practice.

When children with EAL attend a setting it is important to plan experiences for them that allow them to use their first language whilst learning English. The physical environment should reflect cultural and linguistic identity. In observing the child at play the EYP can identify what interests the child and plan with staff the language to support these activities (DCSF, 2008).

Children with SEN can be subject to individual play or educational plans which are often set up as a result of collaboration between the staff and the SENCo. However, the planning of these interventions can be left to the staff who work directly with the children, as the SENCo may not necessarily produce them. This requires the practitioners to provide for individual needs by differentiating activities. Input and support from an EYP can be of benefit to identify the ways in which this can be achieved. In planning personalised provision, not just for children with SEN or EAL, the EYP may lead and support staff to use visual means of communication through picture representation, signing, props or puppets.

Planning personalised provision is a reflective process that relies on the practitioners' observations and ability to liaise and consider the views of others, including the parents or carers of the child. In order to plan the practitioner needs to be able to evaluate the information and record it so that it may be revisited and re-evaluated. The EYP can role model how to observe the children in all aspects of their play and self-chosen activity and demonstrate how these observations can underpin effective planning for individual children. The EYP may wish to discuss amending the setting's planning proforma to accommodate the collective views and to afford further evaluation.

Standard 13 reflection points

- How do you plan for personalised learning by finding out about each child?
- Do you make learning plans based on information gained from talking to the child, the parents and from colleagues' observations?
- Is each child's learning journey based on their individual interests and needs?
- Do you plan these learning journeys to be suitable for groups and yet flexible enough to cater for individual interests?
- How do you actively engage in working with parents of the children to work together to provide what is needed for each child at a particular time?
- Are your parents involved in the assessment and planning cycle?
- Is there a written policy of listening to children who are non-verbal or who use alternative communication systems or who are learning English as an additional language?
- Could you provide workshops or other sessions for parents to help them understand more about children's learning and development?

Standard 13 stakeholder comment

Joanne Chatburn is a senior lecturer from Edge Hill University with a passion for inclusive education. She explains how she observed full training EYPS students work towards evidencing standard 13.

'In my first year of working as placement coordinator for the EYPS team I have had the challenging task of arranging early years work placement opportunities for students on the full training pathway. I was fortunate enough to have been able to develop new partnerships with some extremely dedicated and supportive early years settings and the numbers continue to increase!'

'An aspect of my role was to observe and support the full training students in placement. It is a challenge for any student to be able to identify and highlight an area pertaining to the EYPS standards, and enable themselves to gain the policy and practice evidence required for validation. The full time students have a particularly difficult job, attending a setting for the first time, being expected to build relationships that will enable them to support the work of a team and develop an area of change or innovation.'

'Many of our partner settings understand this difficulty. They have identified ideas for development that may suit a student with only a limited number of weeks to complete their placement. They then negotiate with the student the role and outcomes they wish the activity to achieve for their service provision. Alternatively, some students identify their own ideas and then successfully negotiate and build relationships which enable them to develop and lead new initiatives.'

'I observed two students provide examples of personalised provision for children who had recently moved from another country. Children with English as an additional language (EAL) can feel very isolated, and communication with the child and their family may be limited.'

'Through observation, one student established that a child with EAL used non-verbal communication signals and certain hand gestures to try to connect with other children and staff. The student developed a personalised approach in the setting by adopting the simple signing technique to encourage interaction. She shared these observations with the other children and staff within the room and encouraged them to embrace a similar practice. In considering the child's individual requirements they began to support the personal provision the child received at the setting effectively.'

→

→ 'In the second case the student spoke the same language as the child and supported the nursery during the child's transition. She communicated with, and supported, the child's family which enabled the collation of personal information to supplement the expertise of the team working with the child. She also developed materials in a simple book to link with key words from the language the child spoke.'

'The two case studies illustrate how encouraging the pedagogical understanding of an EYP trainee can influence their ability to enrich the individual experience of children within an early years setting.'

Standard 14 – respond appropriately to children, informed by how children develop and learn and a clear understanding of possible next steps in their development and learning

Example of standard 14 in personal practice

In providing evidence that they have achieved this standard, candidates need to show a deep understanding of child development and the theories of early years education that underpin every aspect of their practice. Many practitioners change their practice because of local authority guidelines or are told to do so by a superior, but they may never fully understand the reason why. The change in practice will be of little benefit to the children as it is a case of being 'seen to be doing'. The successful candidate will make changes to their practice for reasons they fully understand. They will research new initiatives, such as international approaches, Te Whāriki, forest schools in Denmark and Reggio Emilia, to discover how these changes can benefit the children and what measures need to be implemented to ensure the best results are obtained.

Edgington (2008) discusses how different practice is in the EYFS compared to key stage 1 and 2, and that often practitioners find themselves having to explain their approaches or even stand up and fight to continue practising in this way. Superiors who have little or no experience of EYFS may not understand why children 'just' play and get dirty, and the candidate's knowledge and understanding of underpinning theory will strengthen their argument and enable them to continue in the way they know is best. They may show evidence of this in their written tasks, supporting their actions and methodology.

The successful candidate, while having a strong knowledge of the 'Development Matters' area of the EYFS practice guidance, will understand that this is not prescriptive of how a child will learn and develop. They will embed the principle that 'every child is a competent learner from birth who can be resilient, capable, confident and self-assured' (DCFS, 2008: 5) and use the 'listen, look and note' section to produce informative observations. They will then assess for the child's current level of understanding and interests which they will then use to plan activities to support the child to achieve the next steps in their learning (Fisher, 2008). This will be evident in the candidate's observations, assessments and planning.

Nutbrown and Page (2008: 103) state that 'many researchers and practitioners have followed observational practices in their studies of young children's learning and development because it is *actually* the only way of finding out what young children do'.

This is especially important in very young children, as the less language they have the less they can tell you about what they have been doing. Babies may appear to do little and have few interests and opinions, yet an experienced practitioner will know that this is untrue and that by using regular observations these can soon be discovered and included in future planning.

Within this planning the candidate could show evidence of differentiation. This is an important skill and will demonstrate to the assessor the candidate's flexible approach addressing the individual needs and interests of all the children. Fisher (2008: 56) discusses two basic types of differentiation for EYFS. Firstly she describes 'differentiation by input', where the practitioner knows the child's stage of development and plans an activity to move them on to the next steps of learning. Secondly, 'differentiation by output', where the practitioner provides an open-ended activity and each child's learning will vary depending on the knowledge and understanding they bring to it.

The candidate will need to show an understanding of the procedure to follow when they become concerned about an individual child's progress. They need to demonstrate that they are aware of their own limitations and that they know who to contact for guidance, to enable them to adapt provision to give the child the necessary support they need to develop to their full potential. This will link to standards 6 and 36.

Example of standard 14 in leadership

The leadership aspects of this standard involve the candidate utilising excellent communication skills to ensure that colleagues understand the reasons for working in a certain way. They must ensure that all staff have access to further training to develop their knowledge and understanding of child development and early years education. The candidate may evidence this through delivery of training sessions to staff, encouraging them to access local authority training days or courses in further or higher education.

Once staff have attended such training, the candidate may ask them to cascade the information to other colleagues at a staff meeting. In this way the candidate will be able to gauge the colleagues' level of understanding and any areas for further development. This can be discussed in written tasks, through witness statements or interviews, or evidenced through minutes of the staff meeting in the documentary evidence file.

The candidate must ensure that they are a good role model for colleagues; staff need to see a leader put their ideas into practice. This is especially significant if they are having trouble understanding why they are being asked to do a task. They will be unwilling to carry out observations if they think they are only going to be filed away, but if the candidate can demonstrate the whole observation, assessment and planning process and then devote time to supporting staff in carrying this cycle out and highlighting the benefits to the children, the staff will be much more enthusiastic and confident taking on this role for their group of children. Evidence for this could be through witness statements and interviews and written tasks.

Evidence may also be found through the candidate's support and implementation of the key person approach. The candidate will ensure that each key person has the opportunity and time to carry out the observation, assessment and planning cycle for their children. They will positively encourage staff to contribute to the planning and to see it as a flexible working document which follows the interests they observe their children as having. If interests change then the candidate will support staff to change the planning appropriately.

When staff have difficulties with particular children, the candidate must give staff the support they need to discover how to overcome them. Working with staff they will identify areas that the child needs support in and help to set targets. Staff may need support in understanding how to do this, and the candidate may role model how to create specific, measurable, achievable, relevant, timed (SMART) targets.

They must also show that they understand their limitations and allow staff to see that it is acceptable to do this and look for specialist help. The successful candidate will always look to involve colleagues when contacting other professionals, to help them gain an understanding of the other professional's role, to work with them to ensure that all understand the child's needs and the programme of care to be implemented.

Standard 14 reflection points

- Examine your observations of children and those of colleagues – do they contain relevant information? How can you ensure that colleagues understand how and when to record observations?
- Consider the analysis of observations – do colleagues analyse their own or does one person look at all of them? Could you involve colleagues further?
- Do all colleagues contribute to the planning? If not, can you see benefits to introducing this?
- How confident do you feel about differentiating provision? Do colleagues understand the need to differentiate for individual children? Can you support them in doing this?
- How confident are you at setting SMART targets? Have you supported others in developing this skill?
- Do you understand the procedure for contacting other professionals for specialist support?

Standard 14 stakeholder comment

'I am a teacher supporting a full time EYPS candidate, and I found standard 14 to need a fair amount of consideration and support. The candidate had little experience of observing children, but had studied a module on the theory behind observations and was enthusiastic to put this theory into practice. I ensured the candidate had time to conduct observations during the sessions, then we examined them together once the children had left. Initially the observations were very general and basic. I encouraged him to use the EYFS Development Matters to begin to analyse them. As he looked through his observations, he came to realise that, while he had written a considerable amount, he hadn't actually noted anything significant; for instance, he had commented that the child had painted, but not what was actually done, or that the child had played with others, but nothing about how the child had communicated, or whether they had they played alongside other children or with them.'

'As we continued this over the weeks of his placement, he began to focus more on the particular skills the child was using and then began to understand how this knowledge could support his planning for the child's next steps. He also realised that while he had planned activities he felt the children would enjoy, it did not always work that way. As his relationships with the children developed he began to use his knowledge of their likes and interests to develop more appropriate activities which would encourage them to participate. We worked together to develop his understanding of differentiation, with me role modelling different approaches such as differentiation through adult input, resources and output. We then discussed how successful (or not) these approaches had been. By the last week of the placement the candidate was feeling much more confident in attempting this alone.'

'While at that time there were no children with additional needs, we were able to use the observations to identify a child who would benefit from working towards a particular target with regard to behaviour. I discussed SMART targets and encouraged the candidate to consider how we could develop these for the child in question. The candidate was able to create an appropriate end target and we worked together to break this down into smaller achievable steps, which we were able to involve all other staff and the child's parents in working towards. As there were no opportunities to involve another professional at the time, we recorded a target for the next placement as gaining experience working with other agencies.'

'The candidate was able to use his observations, analysis and subsequent planning, as well as the targets he had contributed to, as documentary evidence towards standard 14.'

Standard 15 – support the development of children's language and communication skills

Example of standard 15 in personal practice

Communication, language and literacy is one of the six areas of learning in the EYFS. Therefore it is essential that all settings support children's development in this area. It is an expectation that an EYP would endeavour to 'support the development of babies', toddlers' and young children's language and communication skills. This applies as much to babies as to older children, as well as to children who have learning and communication difficulties or disabilities and those for whom English is not their first language' (DCSF, 2008: 33).

Children do not usually begin to communicate through speech until their first birthday; however, EYPs recognise that babies start to develop the necessary skills for communication and language development from the day they are born. As soon as babies are born they are striving to communicate with their parents/ carers. From an early age babies communicate through crying; in most cases parents/carers respond to their babies' attempts to communicate by talking to them in a soft voice and through gesture, and this is often referred to as 'mother ease', baby talk or infant-directed speech. EYPs understand that 'adults who are attuned to babies tend to talk to them in quite distinctive ways, using a lot of repetition, with simplified short utterances, raised pitch and exaggerated expression' (Oates *et al.*, 2005: 270).

A successful EYP candidate should recognise that the repetition of language and utterances are essential to the development of language. They have observed how babies repeat utterances when they have entered the babbling stage such as 'abababababa' or 'dadadadadada' and understand that the baby is practising the physical skills needed to perfect sounds that will later make up words. Good early years practitioners will regularly share books with babies; they will understand that 'even if a baby is only two or three months old, a lot can be gained by showing the pictures (in a book) and talking about them' (Crystal, 1986).

Good practice would include encouraging parents/carers to be aware of the Talk to Your Baby Campaign (TTYB) promoted by the National Literacy Trust. This could be achieved by displaying TTYB posters and sharing good practice with parents.

Through personal practice, an EYP would support the development of an older child's language by encouraging the child to become involved in activities that develop early language and communication skills. An EYP may read certain books that explore rhythm, rhyme or the use of alliteration. They will understand that children like to hear familiar stories and songs, and will realise that this is both a comfort and a way for the child to build up a stock of words.

It is good early years practice to use resources available, such as the *Letters and Sounds* phase one teaching programme published by the DCSF (2007), as a tool to increase your knowledge of how children learn language. An enthused practitioner will implement such strategies into the setting understanding that such programmes complement the EYFS. Phase one of the *Letters and Sounds* programme 'relies on providing a broad and rich language experience for children which is the hallmark of good early years practice. In this phase and thereafter children should be enjoyably engaged in worthwhile learning activities that encourage them to talk a lot, to increase their stock of words and to improve their command of dialogue' (DCSF, 2008: 7). Implementing this programme into a setting can be a useful way of supporting less experienced colleagues in understanding the complexities that children face in learning the English language. It will also aid practitioners in adopting sound strategies for supporting the development of language in children.

It should be common practice to use non-verbal communication as a tool for interacting with children but especially when working with 'children who have learning and communication difficulties or disabilities and those for whom English is a second language as they depend upon sign and gestures to aid their understanding' (CWDC, 2008). Consequently, practitioners should use facial expression, eye contact or hand gesture to accompany speech and offer an environment that is rich in both the written word and visual signs, as children of this age will be able to communicate their needs more easily by using pictures.

Finally, when considering how to improve the provision for developing children's communication skills a good practitioner should ensure that the setting takes a holistic approach. Opportunities for good communication should weave in and out of a child's day, beginning with the first welcoming smile from a key worker to the last wave goodbye at the end of their session. In between there should be lots of opportunities to practise skills in all the aspects of communication, language and literacy, through child-led and adult-directed activities.

Example of standard 15 in leadership

One of the roles of an EYP is to lead and support others to raise the quality of early years provision. When working towards EYP status a student must demonstrate leadership in each group of standards. Finding an opportunity to lead others can often seem a daunting task, especially for students on the undergraduate practitioner pathway; however, each placement presents the student with a task that requires them to implement a change within the setting. This exercise requires the students to use their knowledge of good early years provision to identify areas that can be developed or practices that can be improved upon. Students need to be aware that they do not have to make huge changes to demonstrate leadership.

Change is a process, therefore for change to take place the student will need to ensure that their idea becomes practice. To achieve this the student may progress their idea as follows:

- Identify an area for improvement and state their case for improvement
- Liaise with manager, personal tutor or mentor and agree ideas
- Discuss ideas with colleagues, motivating others to be involved in improving provision
- Gather any resources you need depending upon task in hand
- Record changes such as updating policy change with review date, recording practice change with photographs, etc. (as this will all be strong evidence for your assessment file)
- Finally, monitor and assess the outcomes/benefits of change. It is good practice to maintain relationships with the setting to evaluate the benefits of your adaptation to practice continually, as it often takes several weeks or months to see the true benefits of change.

Leading and supporting others in the development of children's language and communication skills could be achieved by auditing the current provision within the setting. During the early years, language skills cannot be taught in isolation, language should develop through close interaction with knowledge-able and supportive practitioners. 'Experts agree that your child will learn language best when you **name** things, **describe** things, **compare** things, **explain** things and **give directions**' (The National Literacy Trust, 2010: 1). To support children's language skills an EYP would assess the environment and current practices against the EYFS requirements for Communication, Language and Literacy.

> Children's learning and competence in communicating, speaking and listening, being read to and beginning to read and write must be supported and extended. They must be provided with opportunity and encouragement to use their skills in a range of situations and for a range of purposes, and be supported in developing the confidence and disposition to do so.
>
> (DCSF, 2008: 41)

Children for whom English is an additional language (EAL) will be supported by the EYP in learning English. However, during this transition an EYP will recognise the importance of celebrating their first language and will naturally seek opportunities to support dual language.

Standard 15 reflection points

Consider the following points and see if you can use them as a basis for improving the provision for developing language and communication skills.

- Do practitioners extend children's language skills by asking open rather than closed questions?
- Do practitioners model appropriate pronunciation of language rather than correcting a child's mistake?
- Are children given time to talk to each other and are these conversations supported by practitioners?
- Are photographs of children engaged in play displayed in the environment, thereby allowing children to reflect and talk about relevant events?
- Is gesture and non-verbal communication used to support communication?
- Are children with EAL or SEN given appropriate support in order for their language and communication to develop?
- Are practitioners fostering a love of books by offering a welcoming well stocked book area?
- Do practitioners share books with small groups of children and on a one-to-one basis?
- Is the setting displaying information for parents regarding the importance of communication with children?

Standard 15 stakeholder comment

Andrea Riley is currently Manager of a preschool which caters for children aged 2–5. She is also an associate tutor for Edge Hill University. In 2007 she followed the EYP full time pathway with a different provider. As part of her training she spent 26 weeks' placement, experiencing childcare provision in a variety of settings.

To evidence standard 15 she carried out an audit of the books and reading practices made available for children in the 0–20-month age range. She spent time observing how children in this age range used the books available to them. She identified three main areas for improvement. Firstly the books available offered little variety in visual stimuli and texture. From her

→

experience she understood that young babies are very tactile and are attracted to a multisensory learning environment; they are also interested in faces' and therefore books on offer should reflect this. Secondly she observed that the books were displayed on a cabinet that was 2-foot high from the ground; consequently the babies were not able to access the books independently and relied on an adult bringing the books down to their level. Thirdly she observed how little time practitioners spent sharing books with the youngest babies and when they did share a book she noticed that there was little communication and a lack of appropriate language.

She approached the room leader, suggesting an alternative approach to sharing books with babies, and explained how her proposed changes reflected the good practice recommended in the Birth to Three Matters document (this preceded the EYFS). The management team were satisfied that her approach would benefit both the children and the setting, and supported her in making the changes.

She purchased some new books for the baby room, including books with babies' faces, as very young children are fascinated by faces. Other books included flap books such as 'Dear Zoo' by Rod Campbell and books that reflect the early lives of babies such as 'Baby Goes' by Verna Wilkins/Derek Brazell. Many of the books she purchased were board books with both visual and tactile opportunities for the babies to explore. With the new books in place she grouped them together in small baskets and stored them on the floor, making them accessible to mobile babies. She also encouraged practitioners to share the books with very young babies, aged 4–8 months, which is something that she had seen little of during her observations. She modelled good practice in book sharing with babies and supported practitioners to become more engaged in language and communication. The outcomes were very promising; babies had more access to a greater variety of books and the practitioners gradually became more confident in sharing books with even the youngest of children.

As can be seen from the above example a great deal can be achieved from making very small changes. As a result of the above process, the student went on to audit the books and reading environments in the toddler and preschool room, and also devised a handout for staff regarding good tips for sharing books with children.

Standard 16 – engage in sustained shared thinking with children

Example of standard 16 in personal practice

Experienced practitioners realise the importance of listening and responding appropriately to children, asking open-ended questions and seizing both planned and unplanned opportunities to develop children's thinking skills.

The EYP assessor is looking for three main requirements of standard 16, which are:

1. Use a range of planned and unplanned opportunities to develop children's thinking skills.
2. Initiate and use topics that interest children to engage in and develop sustained shared thinking with adults and peers.
3. Lead and support colleagues to develop their skills in engaging in sustained shared thinking with children.

The practice guidelines for the EYFS (DCSF, 2008) describe a continually improving setting as one that has qualified and experienced staff who 'are committed to the development of sustained shared thinking'. The guidelines repeatedly link quality with effective communication between the practitioner and the child. The EYFS early learning goals clearly indicate the benefits achieved through close interaction, such as the development of spoken language. There are many examples of effective practice, e.g. 'help children expand on what they say' and 'make suggestions and ask questions to extend children's ideas of what is possible, for example, "I wonder what would happen if . . ."'

Sustained shared thinking strongly links into well established views on childcare and development. Vygotsky (1978: 86) believed that play is developed through social collaboration. He believed that social collaboration helps to raise the 'zone of proximal development' (ZPD) and described the ZPD as 'the distance between the actual developmental level as determined by independent problem solving and the level of potential development as

determined through problem solving under adult guidance or in collaboration with more capable peers'.

Put simply, this means that a child's understanding can be enhanced by
the involvement of others. This is a fundamental element of sustained shared
thinking.

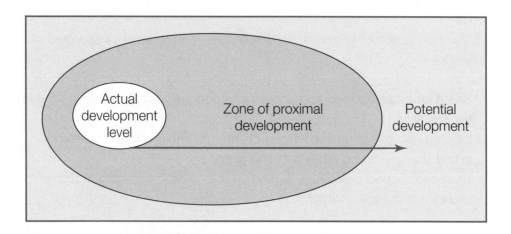

In 1976 Wood, Bruner and Ross used the term 'scaffolding' to describe the
help offered by a parent, teacher or peer to support a child's learning. Vygotsky,
Wood, Bruner and Ross all believed that expanding on a child's understanding
and development requires interaction from adults or peers. This links into sustained shared thinking in practice, since the practitioner must interact with the
child or encourage the child to interact with others as it is through this interaction
that we build the trusting relationships that are necessary for children to have the
confidence to discuss their ideas and for us to help them expand on their thinking.
Practitioners should ask open-ended questions to help expand a child's interest
and understanding; this can be done throughout the day, in both planned and
unplanned activities.

Although verbal communication is vital for sustained shared thinking,
equally important is non-verbal communication, particularly with babies,
where the practitioner has to be more aware of facial expressions and body
language. Activities/opportunities should be provided that can provide long-
lasting play (providing the child is enjoying it). This type of effective interaction helps to develop language and communication and enhances children's

thinking skills: 'What a child can do with assistance today she will be able to do by herself tomorrow' (Vygotsky, 1978: 87).

Example of standard 16 in leadership

Effective engagement in the process of sustained shared thinking requires EYPs to reflect once again on the differences between management and leadership in the early years context. Rodd (2008: 20) offers a useful comparison between the role that managers and leaders fulfil in the table below.

Managers	Leaders
Plan – set objectives, forecast, analyse problems, make decision, formulate policy	**Give direction** – find a way forward, communicate a clear direction, identify new goals, services and structures
Organise – determine what activities are required to meet objectives, classify work, divide it up and assign it (i.e. decide who does what)	**Offer inspiration** – have ideas and articulate thoughts that motivate others
Coordinate – inspire staff to contribute both individually and as a group to the organisation's objectives	**Build teamwork** – use teams as the most effective form of management, spending their time building and encouraging collaboration
Control – check performance against plans; develop people and maximise their potential to achieve agreed outcomes (i.e. they get the work done through and by other people)	**Set an example** – model what leaders are and how they do it
	Gain acceptance – act in ways that arouse acknowledgement of their leadership status in followers

This comparison can help EYPs to develop a clear understanding of their role in the process of leading their colleagues towards successful engagement in sustained shared thinking with children. EYPs should offer direction to help practitioners identify opportunities to support and extend the children's thinking to help the children make connections in learning.

The EYP should offer inspiration, sharing their own experiences on how to engage with children. Plan to improve the communication between the practitioner and the children by using strategies to enhance the individual's own awareness of the child's understanding of an idea (or expression of interest). Most importantly, the EYP needs to help the practitioner understand how to co-construct an idea with the child.

Experienced early years professionals should encourage a collaborative working approach to ensure support is available to those who are less experienced. They should identify training needs and act as a good role model to others. By being a good role model, other staff members will see how to develop children's ideas in an imaginative way, building on the child's interests and working with the child to create a sustainable interesting learning experience. EYPs need to create an environment, where practitioners and children are encouraged to move or adapt resources according to their play; for example, dinosaurs in the sand or small people in the water – this enables the children to use their imagination and explore their environment and gives many more opportunities for adults to offer support to extend the child's learning.

A good leader will encourage the use of observation and assessment to inform practice and to gain an understanding of a child's current level of development. Observations will also enable practitioners to find out what interests the child has. Most of all, a good early years leader will listen to the people they are leading, to the children they are caring for and to the parents of those children. By doing this the EYP will enhance the knowledge of the children, the setting and the requirements of the role of the EYP. 'Every child's learning journey takes a personal path based on their own individual interest, experiences and curriculum on offer' (Foundation Card 3.2 – Enabling Environments – Supporting Every Child).

Standard 16 reflection points

Considering children's different age ranges, reflect on the following points:

- How do you respond to children's conversation to expand on their interests and to encourage problem-solving and critical thinking?
- What activities/resources in your setting encourage the children to ask questions, analyse and evaluate?
- Do you ask children to explain what they or doing, thinking, tasting, hearing, smelling, touching, seeing?
- In what way do you lead and support your colleagues to talk/interact with the children – encouraging open-ended questioning?

Standard 16 stakeholder comment

There are many opportunities for practitioners to incorporate these requirements into their daily practice. Here, an EYPS assessor gives an example of sustained shared thinking observed in practice during her visit to Crossens Nursery School in Southport, where Angela, an EYPS candidate, was on placement.

While the children were playing with a game which involved matching animal shapes to silhouette shapes, they likened them to shadows. Angela discussed shadows with the children and used this conversation to develop an activity using the overhead projector.

Angela demonstrated how to make a shadow with her head and the children quickly joined in. The children noticed how they could make their shadows move around and that sometimes they looked big and at other times small. Angela asked them what made this happen – the children did not know but continued to investigate. Angela encouraged them to experiment, asking open-ended questions to develop their ideas. The children began to look around for other objects with which to make shadows. They used puppets and shapes and continued to discuss the different effects they could make. The group decided that by moving the objects away from the light the shadows became 'bigger' and 'blurry'.

They introduced dinosaurs to the game and Angela asked them about the different types of dinosaurs. The children developed a story and moved the toys closer to and away from the light to make the shadows bigger and scarier to fight the smaller dinosaur shadows.

Angela continued to ask questions at appropriate times to develop the play. The conversation turned to colour and different pieces of cellophane were brought over to see if they would make shadows. The children noticed that they made colours on the screen whereas the toys and puppets were 'silver'. Angela encouraged them to think about where else they would find shadows. This led to a variety of suggestions, one of which being 'outside'.

Angela recorded the conversations and used this as part of her evidence. She also used a digital camera to record the children's investigation as it developed.

→

> Angela has provided good evidence for two of the main requirements by expanding on an unplanned activity to develop the children's thinking skills and extending this by introducing additional resources. She asked open-ended questions, engaged the children's imagination and developed their thinking.
>
> If the candidate had involved colleagues in this activity, role modelling good practice, the candidate could have demonstrated to the assessor her ability to lead and support which is a fundamental role of an EYP.

Standard 17 – promote positive behaviour, self-control and independence through using effective behaviour management strategies and developing children's social, emotional and behavioural skills

Example of standard 17 in personal practice

Behaviour management strategies have always been seen by both theorists and practitioners as an essential part of the educational process, since they aim at establishing children's self-discipline and promoting their achievement and positive behaviour. This allows the suggestion that practitioners' efficiency and children's behaviour are directly linked to the models of effective behaviour management.

When working with babies, one of the most common problems that practitioners have to face involves dealing with repeated incidents of unwanted behaviour, such as aggressive actions towards younger children and tantrums. A child might repeatedly push other children, refuse to talk or accept empathy from adults and show no control over her feelings. According to Kazdin (2009), tantrums can be described as disruptive or undesirable behaviour in response to unmet needs or desires; emotional outbursts when not allowed to do or have something that a child wants; inability to control emotions due to frustration; and difficulty expressing the particular need or desire. Though many sources suggest that temper tantrums are natural during early childhood development, observations show that tantrums and aggressive behaviour present a cause for concern. Firstly, tantrums within an early years setting can be dangerous if they involve self-injurious behaviour such as head-banging, scratching, pulling, or poking, which might result in serious damage. Secondly, tantrums might involve aggressive behaviour toward other children or adults, including biting and scratching, hitting, throwing objects, verbal abuse, screaming, grabbing, so that they present potential danger to the other children around. Finally, non-person-directed tantrums might cause damage to property, as during temper tantrums children do not control their actions and might break toys and other equipment in the room.

When working with children under 3 years old, EYPs have to recognise that very young children are not always able to control their emotions and need sensitive adults to help them learn to do this. The reason that very young children behave in distressing ways towards others lies in the fact that they have not yet developed the biological and cognitive means to manage intense feelings for themselves and, sometimes these feelings overwhelm them.

Behaviour management strategies to support babies and toddlers need to be developmentally appropriate. If children from 0 to 3 years old display inconsiderate or hurtful behaviours, such as tantrums, biting or fighting, EYPs need to be patient and calm, helping children to manage their feelings. EYPs should offer comfort for strong emotions and talk to children about those feelings and help resolve issues and promote understanding.

EYPs need to be aware that there are many different ways to get to know young children well to avoid undesirable behaviour. One of the key strategies that is commonly practised in early years settings is *observation*. All children develop at their own pace. There are genetic and environmental influences, which will affect the rate at which children develop, but they will broadly follow the same sequence. One of the main reasons we observe children, then, is to see if they are following that pattern (Sharman *et al.*, 2007). In observing and studying all areas of child development, EYPs have to recognise a range of differences within what is accepted as normal behaviour and the existence of differences that are considered to go beyond normal. This knowledge will help EYPs to pre-empt inappropriate behaviour and promote young children's self-control and independence successfully. As emphasised in The Common Core of Skills and Knowledge (CWDC, 2010), everyone who works with children and young people is expected to have the following skills related to observation and judgement:

- Observe a child or young person's behaviour, understand its context and notice unexpected changes

- Recognise signs that a child or young person may be engaged in unusual, uncharacteristic, risky or harmful behaviour, including in the online world
- Listen carefully and respond to concerns expressed about developmental or behavioural changes
- Record observations appropriately. Observations should be based on evidence rather than opinion.

EYPs also need to be aware that an over-emphasis on negative behaviour destroys the positive atmosphere in the setting. Learning and development can only take place where positive relationships exist between a practitioner and a child. Therefore, the EYP's role is to develop a healthy climate within which learning will automatically thrive. For this reason, it is essential to use positive behaviour management strategies consistently, such as using verbal praise, providing games and activities that promote cooperation and working together, acknowledging considerate behaviour such as kindness and politeness, helping children to set their own rules for considerate behaviour, and making sure that there are sufficient resources available to avoid unnecessary conflict over waiting for turns and sharing. One of the ways of responding to babies' behaviour is to comfort them through cuddling and holding them. Older children will also calm down in response to cuddling, but they also need to be offered an explanation of their behaviour pitched at their level of understanding. Realising that children's cultural backgrounds, economic conditions and home environments can profoundly affect their behaviour, EYPs find that they can best serve the needs of their children by becoming more family-centred and by improving the ways of sharing information with parents.

One of the examples of the information that can be shared with parents is a record of observations of the child's behaviour. For this purpose a meeting can be arranged by a phone conversation offering a flexible meeting time that would suit both the parent and the practitioner. During the discussion the EYP should exhibit a very polite and positive manner of speaking, ensuring that he/she does not make any conclusions or stereotypical judgements about the child. The EYP might share with the parent the strategies that the setting has used to manage tantrums. The EYP might also consider seeking advice from the parent on the pattern of the child's behaviour at home and the methods used by the parents in such cases. The information obtained from the parent will help EYPs to understand and to explain the child's behaviour, which can be used in future practice for preventing unwanted behaviour.

Some successful strategies that EYPs might consider using to promote positive behaviour, self-control and independence include:

- Acknowledging children's feelings and helping children to resolve disagreements in the ways that are appropriate for the children's age and stage of development
- Helping children to understand and gain control of their feelings through talking to the children and explaining to them what type of behaviour was unacceptable
- Praising children for their efforts in learning a new social skill or resolving a conflict
- Comforting the child who is angry as well as the one who has been affected by the behaviour, without engaging in disciplinary measures, as these will have the opposite effect
- Helping children to recognise their feelings by naming these feelings and helping to express them in a socially acceptable way
- Encouraging young children to empathise with others
- Providing children with repeated experiences in problem-solving, supported by caring and patient adults
- Modelling positive behaviour through activities, such as story telling and drama as well as through developing genuinely close relationships with children.
- Working closely with parents to identify causes of unwanted behaviour and to find a joint solution when behaviour becomes problematic.

Example of standard 17 in leadership

The starting point of a leadership approach to behaviour management is based on the idea that children thrive when their personal, social and emotional needs are met, and where there are consistent, clear and developmentally appropriate expectations for their behaviour. As the EYFS states, children's behaviour must be managed effectively and in a manner appropriate for their stage of development and particular individual needs' (DCSF, 2008).

One of the EYP's main aims should be making sure that all team members who come into contact with children in the setting have a shared understanding of positive behaviour management strategies. It would be useful to involve the team in the process of revising or creating a behaviour management policy, which informs practitioners and parents of the strategies used in the setting as well as the legal requirements by which the setting has to abide.

A good example of leadership in this area might also involve leading a staff development event that would enhance practitioners' knowledge and understanding of some key issues related to behaviour management, such as theoretical perspectives on behaviour problems, screening and assessment of young children's behaviour, the nature and extent of behaviour problems in the early years, etc.

EYPs also need to think of motivating and focused ways of involving all team members in professional discussions and reflections upon their principles and practice in terms of implementing effective behaviour management strategies within their setting.

EYPs might consider choosing a designated person to have overall responsibility for supporting children's personal, social and emotional development, including behaviour issues, as well as keeping the team up to date with relevant legislation and research on promoting positive behaviour. It is also the EYP's role to make sure that all staff have relevant in-service training on behaviour management policies and issues.

Another example of leadership might include leading professional discussions with practitioners on the importance of effective communication with parents to share information on children's behaviour. All staff have to provide a positive model of behaviour by treating children, parents and one another with care and courtesy. Sharing concerns with a parent about their child's behaviour is very important, but EYPs also have to realise that it can evoke an array of responses. The parent may have one or many of the following reactions: become angry with the provider; suddenly remove the child from care; deny a problem; express their appreciation for the information; thoughtfully consider the provider's advice. EYPs need to make sure that their team members are prepared for all of these responses, as it is the best way to cope with a potentially difficult situation. The EYP must be able to speak openly and honestly with the parents, but refrain from describing a child as 'emotionally disturbed', or using any other labels when speaking with the parent. The EYP has to focus on the individual behaviours and avoid making assumptions about what the diagnosis may be. Some of the ways to communicate concerns about the child's behaviour might be: telephoning parents and offering flexible meeting times; expressing a positive caring attitude about the problem; asking for parent input instead of blaming the parent for a problem; agreeing on mutual goals. Widespread support for managing children's behaviour involving parents grows out of convincing evidence suggesting that family involvement has positive effects on children's achievements, social competence and behaviour (Anning and Edwards, 2006).

Standard 17 reflection points

The EYFS challenges EYPs to think more deeply about all aspects of children's learning and development, including the practitioners' skills of promoting positive behaviour, self-control and independence in young children through using effective behaviour management strategies and developing children's social, emotional and behavioural skills.

Consider one strategy of promoting positive behaviour, self-control and independence and try to find evidence that demonstrates how you apply your skills and knowledge or support others in developing children's social, emotional and behavioural skills for each of the following age groups of children:

- 0–20 months
- 16–36 months
- 30–60 months.

Standard 17 Stakeholder comment

Patricia Hughes works as an EYP at one of the children's centres in Manchester. Here she describes how, in her role as an EYP, she helped her colleagues to deconstruct standard 17.

'One of my key concerns as an EYP was to make sure that all our new staff, students and volunteers were familiar with our behaviour management policy. My initial step was to lead a team meeting, where we discussed and revised our behaviour management policy, and where team members had a chance to share their concerns regarding managing children's challenging behaviour. During this meeting we also discussed how we help our children to meet their personal, social and emotional needs through daily activities. As a result of this discussion, it became obvious that children in our setting often engaged in play that was based on aggressive themes, and some practitioners had little understanding of how to handle this type of children's behaviour. I thought it would be useful to introduce a section on rough and tumble play into our behaviour management policy.'

'I prepared a short training session on rough and tumble play, which stressed that young children often engage in play that involves using imaginary weapons and acting as superheroes and "baddies and goodies". I tried to communicate to the team that, though some children can be preoccupied with this type of play, their

→

> behaviour is not necessarily negative and can be contained within acceptable limits if appropriate strategies are used.'
>
> 'During the training session, all team members actively engaged in a professional discussion and came up with a number of useful strategies to help contain children's play within boundaries which are understood by the children and agreed with them.'
>
> 'As a result, all staff recognised that they need to tune in to children's fantasy play to enable the former to make the most of such interaction to encourage empathy in children and to explore alternative scenarios to avoid potential conflicts and disagreements. Our behaviour management policy was updated to provide additional focus on rough and tumble play.'

Standard 18 – promote children's rights, equality, inclusion and anti-discriminatory practice in all aspects of their practice

Example of standard 18 in personal practice

Standard 18 sits within the cluster of standards that relate to effective practice. This indicates the significance of this complex piece of knowledge and understanding being a cornerstone of daily practice. But how can this group of policies and legislation support children's human rights and be understood in terms of what an EYP's daily practice looks like? By understanding the rationale of the policy we begin to see this standard as a value or a belief that EYPs need to hold dear as they ride the rough and tumble of working with young children and their families. As Alderson (2008) notes, the respect for rights improves everyone's wellbeing, including adults. The concept of human rights can be understood through the United Nations Convention on the Rights of the Child (1989). The rights can be broadly defined within three categories: protection rights, participation rights and provision rights. Being alert to children's physical and emotional wellbeing is a fundamental skill that we exercise daily. For example, as we greet children on arrival we attune to their emotional states and observe their play and interaction during the course of the time they are with us. One local authority uses Laevers et al.'s (1997) process-orientated monitoring scale to screen children for their emotional wellbeing. One particular child at 10 months was identified as having a low level of wellbeing. Children (and adults) who are in a state of wellbeing feel like a 'fish in water' (Laevers et al., 1997).

After careful observation, the EYP observed that this child didn't have a close relationship with his key worker. Together they developed opportunities to spend time together using the local children's centre library space to build up the rela-tionship with a practitioner with whom the child had shown an affinity. Effectively the child chose his key worker. Along with tuning into his interests and emotional states, the EYP enabled the key worker to tune into her child. What we now know is that this relationship is fundamental as we learn more about how the brain and children's sense of self is influenced by their closest relationships (Gopnik *et al.*, 1999). The EYP and key person reflected on this aspect along with their manager and since then have reviewed their policies around key person allocation.

Example of standard 18 in leadership

This standard requires EYPs to have a working understanding of the legislation and policy that underpins equality, inclusion and anti-discriminatory practice. Leadership in this context needs knowledge and understanding of the context of the policy and how these are related. 'Policy is important because we have to think about what we are trying to do and why and how we are doing it' (Baldock *et al.*, 2005: 1).

Leadership in this standard can be exemplified through a piece of work that a children's centre teacher undertook when monitoring her assessment policy and procedures. After analysing her assessments in communication, literacy and lan-guage development she found that there were differences between the achieve-ments of genders. After seeking advice from her local authority advisor she developed her outdoor play practice in promoting mark-making. She modelled this aspect of provision with staff and undertook joint observations to track specific learning experiences. Reflecting on the impact of the provision, she was able to explain aspects of the 'equality and inclusion' policy with staff more confidently. The manager of the children's centre incorporated this into the self-evaluation form, an important strategic document in our current political context of external scrutiny.

The context of inclusion has seen changes in its perception. The Warnock Report (1978) was a significant development in how we have moved from the medical model to the social model of inclusion. A 3-year-old boy in one local authority had the opportunity to share his perception of having to use the nappy changing space in the baby room as a result of an action research project. This project was inspired by *Listening to Young Children* (Lancaster and Broadbent, 1993), a training toolkit and research-led resource that promotes practical and creative approaches embedding the UNCRC Article 13. This Article states that children are entitled to show us what they think and feel by any means they choose. After consultation with the child the nappy changing was accommo-dated within his age group's toilet facilities. Reviewing the impact of spaces that children use supports their social inclusion (Moss and Petrie, 2002).

This *pedagogy of listening* (Rinaldi, 2006) is a conscious value that leaders can nurture by the way in which they work. Active listening to young children's views means that leaders of learning can engage in a dialogue of reflection. This pedagogy of listening can then naturally extend to an active means of leader-ship, where the EYP consciously uses her listening skills as a key way to engage with the staff group:

> For a pedagogy of listening means listening to thought – the ideas and theories of chil-dren and adults; it means treating it seriously and with respect; it means struggling to make meaning from what is said, without preconceived ideas about what is correct or appropriate.
> (Rinaldi, 2006: 15)

Standard 18 reflection points

- Do the leadership and staff team have a working knowledge of the policy and legislation?
- Have staff developed skills of active listening?
- Do the views of children and parents inform change?
- Have audits of provision, resources and interaction taken place to review this aspect?
- Are staff skilled in peer observation and how to feed back constructively?

Standard 18 stakeholder comment

Anti-discriminatory practice for EYPs is a complex and significant area of work. One nursery manager of a childcare provision worked alongside her EYP to review this aspect and made a conscious decision to start with a resource audit to review any discriminatory bias. As this work unfolded, the EYP found that the level of resources needed review but actually that this was of secondary concern to the staff's level of awareness of the policies and practice. With the support of the EYP a small working party from the staff team began to research into the rationale of anti-discriminatory practice. What was most significant for them was the notion that: 'The way children feel about themselves is not innate or inherited, it is learned (Siraj-Blatchford and Clarke, 2000: 3). As part of this working party a parent was invited to listen and contribute. As

→

→
> *the parent described his own experiences of childhood and the discrimination he had experienced firsthand, the staff team found themselves wanting to review their whole policy, practice and procedures. Starting with the provision in their 3–4-year-old room they introduced adult peer observation, reviewed resources but most significantly challenged each other in the language and underlying attitudes that underpinned their interactions with children, parents and each other. In terms of leadership, empowering staff groups to reflect on their practice is a powerful tool (Moyles, 2004).*
>
> *This set of standards can also be understood on a more human level of giving children and adults the dignity of reciprocity (Rinaldi, cited in Moss and Petrie, 2002). Simply put, if we listen to children and adults, empathise with their view, tune into their responses and use that knowledge to develop our practice and provision we let their voices be heard. This goes some way to embed values and practices that enable the promotion of children's rights, equality, inclusion and anti-discriminatory practice. We cannot know what it is to be a young child at this place and time, but what we can do is be respectful and responsive in our practice and build provision that provides a haven for children and their families that respects their rights and entitlements. Archard reminds us in his conclusion: 'To that extent the oft repeated claim that its treatment of children says most about a society expresses a deep truth' (Archard, 2004: 219).*

Standard 19 – establish a safe environment and employ practices that promote children's health, safety and physical, mental and emotional well-being

Examples of standard 19 in personal practice

Every setting should be a safe environment and the EYPS candidate will be aware of ways to ensure this. They will be very familiar with the welfare requirements of the EYFS and will be able to see the link with the setting's policies for related areas. When updating or producing a new document they will refer to the statutory framework for the EYFS for guidance on the legislation covering the subject of the policy. They will find that this links with standards 5 and 35.

The candidate will ensure that appropriate measures are taken to ensure the children's safety at all times. Routine risk assessments for both indoors and outdoors are essential, and the candidate will be familiar with the process and, ever vigilant for new risks as equipment and procedures change, they will ensure risk assessments are updated accordingly.

Candidates, whilst being aware of the need for safety, must also understand the need to allow children to take risks. Edgington (2008) comments how disconcerting it is that many children are now over-protected. 'They are therefore denied the opportunity to make their own judgements about risk in the way that children did years ago . . . ' (Edgington, 2008: 95). It is difficult to balance the need to provide a safe environment where parents/carers feel happy to let their children play and one in which children can experiment and take chances and run the risk of being hurt. The candidate needs to be able to express how important this is to parents/carers. They need to highlight that, whilst safety is paramount, it is very important for children to learn to assess risks for themselves and that they need to learn from the consequences of their actions in order for them to make more appropriate decisions next time. The candidate may also involve other professionals to discuss aspects of safety to the children. Many local authorities have a road safety team who are happy to come and give a simple talk to young children about the importance of wearing a seatbelt in the car or holding the parent/carer's hand when walking in the street; police community support officers will visit and discuss 'stranger danger' and the fire service will discuss fire safety, especially in the weeks leading up to bonfire night. These activities address serious issues for the older children, but encouraging children to learn about risk-taking is equally important for younger children and babies. This will be of a different nature depending on the age and stage of development that the child has reached; e.g. the youngest baby may investigate textures, sounds or tastes and in doing so is taking risks and learning. If the practitioner encourages children to investigate musical instruments, one child may find the noise too loud, another may try using a beater to hit him/herself – they will both learn from this experience and change their approach when they next access the instruments. The successful candidate will be able to provide evidence of their support for risk-taking in a safe environment across the three age groups.

The candidate, whilst encouraging children to take risks, will also help children to take responsibility for what they do. They will ensure that children are aware of the consequences of their actions and through this help them to develop a respect for the environment and everything in it.

The candidate will be familiar with the key person approach and will use their skills to develop their effectiveness in this role. They will develop a relationship with both parents/carers and child before the child begins at the setting and have an understanding of the child's likes, dislikes and routine, all of which will help them to deal with upsets in the most appropriate and supportive way. This enables the child to relate to a special adult that they have already met, when they first attend the setting. The parents/carers feel confident leaving their child as they too have begun to develop a relationship with that person and know who they can talk to about their child whenever they are worried or have news to share.

The use of information communication technology (ICT) is becoming increasingly prevalent in early years settings and candidates need to show an understanding of safe procedures necessary for children to use this productively. The candidate may use research of literature or websites such as healthycomputing.com, kidsafe.co.uk or thinkuknow.co.uk. These give sound up-to-date advice on a variety of issues associated with children using ICT. The candidate needs to be aware of the need for furniture to be the correct height for children, that monitors are positioned correctly and that keyboards and mice are at the correct level and, if possible, designed for young children. Safety using the internet as a resource must also be considered; the candidate could discuss and demonstrate the use of parental control software on the setting tour.

This standard also refers to the promotion of healthy eating and exercise. The candidate will have a sound understanding of the legal requirements of the statutory framework for the EYFS and how it promotes the need to provide healthy foods and freely accessible drinking water for children. The candidate will ensure that they have had training in how to prepare and handle food appropriately and show awareness of special dietary needs that any children in their care may have. Policies and procedures regarding this and other health-related practices, such as safe administration of medicines, disposal of waste and infection control procedures, must be demonstrated in the candidate's practice and this could be evidenced in written tasks, witness interviews, documentary evidence and on the tour of the setting.

Examples of standard 19 in leadership

The leadership aspect of this standard requires the candidate to ensure that colleagues are aware of the need for safety within the setting, but also have the self-confidence to encourage children to investigate, experiment and take risks without fear of failure. This can be a difficult responsibility, especially with staff who have been involved with problems over an injury. The candidate needs to show strong support, working with less confident staff, role modelling good practice, discussing how the children themselves assess risks and ensuring that staff feel confident that, if any injury were to occur, they would be fully supported and not blamed, providing they had followed the risk assessment procedures in place. This aspect of practice should be monitored by the candidate during staff appraisal meetings, peer observation or staff meetings, by enquiring if colleagues are having difficulties in this area. Has new equipment been acquired and do they feel confident using it? The candidate should ask questions and feel confident that the children are allowed to take risks in a safe environment with adults who are confident and capable as, if this is not happening and an accident does occur, it is the leader of the setting who is ultimately responsible.

A common misunderstanding is that children can access any resource and that staff must follow their lead, whatever they choose to do. The candidate must ensure that colleagues understand that, while this is true to a certain extent, the children need to learn to respect their environment and all the resources within it. Colleagues need to understand that children need to learn the consequences of their actions and why certain activities and behaviours are inappropriate. The candidate may support this through role modelling, staff training or discussion.

The candidate also needs to ensure that colleagues feel confident using ICT equipment. They need to understand that this does not simply involve the computer, but cameras, CD players, programmable toys and an ever-increasing variety of toys. The candidate may provide training on the use of these either within the setting or through external courses.

As a leader, the candidate will be fully aware of the need for food hygiene training for colleagues and will support them in attending courses and gaining a food hygiene certificate at the necessary level. Colleagues should have training and be aware of the setting's policy on storage and administration of medicines. The candidate will support staff to train in paediatric first aid and, if possible, will access this training themselves.

They will also ensure that colleagues understand the benefits of exercise and how outdoor play can develop this. The candidate will ensure that there are plenty of resources and opportunities for children to exercise in a variety of ways and that colleagues understand how to promote and develop this appropriately. Tovey (2008) discusses the importance of adults listening to children outdoors. What do they like or dislike? Are they frightened of anything? The candidate will support colleagues to ask these questions and act upon the answers they receive to ensure children can access all the resources and activities outdoors.

Also within this standard, the candidate needs to show that they understand how the working environment can impact upon colleagues' ability to function. They will be aware of the health and safety guidance for the workplace and will ensure that this is followed; however, there may be new issues and colleagues need to know how to inform the leader/manager of these. Any issues must be addressed quickly and efficiently to ensure the safety and wellbeing of staff and this in turn will ensure that their work with the children does not suffer.

Standard 19 reflection points

- Examine the risk assessments performed within your setting. Are they appropriate? Do they cover any new equipment?
- Are they performed regularly by colleagues who understand their importance? Is any extra training required in any areas?
- Observe colleagues in practice. Do they understand the importance of allowing children to take risks and learn from their mistakes? Do they feel confident and supported enough to allow this to happen?
- Examine the information that parents are given from the setting. Does it explain the setting's policy on risk-taking?
- Do colleagues support the parent/carer's understanding of this in their role as key person?
- Do colleagues have training using ICT? Do they understand how to support children using equipment and programmes?
- Audit the ICT equipment you have in your setting; is it appropriate for young children?
- What training have you and colleagues undertaken with regard to health and safety? Are there areas to be addressed? If so, how will you go about this?
- Are there any issues within the workplace that colleagues are upset or worried about? How can you address these issues and improve the workplace environment, thus enabling colleagues to maintain a positive attitude to work?

Standard 19 stakeholder comment

Stakeholder 1

Sue Huntbach has run her preschool for 25 years. With the government's aim to have every setting with a graduate leader by 2015 she decided to begin her 4-year study pathway in 2006 by completing a foundation degree, topping up to a BA(Hons) professional development and, finally, completing her EYPS in 2010.

To show evidence towards this standard, she included a letter from a fire fighter in her documentary evidence. He was a past parent who was familiar with the setting and Sue invited him in to carry out a fire inspection and to see where she could improve to ensure her setting minimised fire hazards to maintain the safety of the children.

The inspection showed that they had the wrong type of fire extinguisher in place, and proposed improvements to replace this with the correct extinguisher and site it correctly, and also to give staff training. It highlighted that there were not enough smoke alarms and proposed improvements by putting up extra smoke alarms. The toaster was kept underneath a cupboard and staff were advised to pull out the toaster from underneath the cupboard when in use. No other significant improvements were needed but the inspector suggested that more fire drills using alternative fire exits would improve everyone's safety.

Sue followed this up by having a meeting with the head of the primary school (with whom the setting share grounds). They discussed fire evacuation procedures and how they could work together to improve these. They then agreed a timetable for regular fire drills.

Stakeholder 2

Clare Roberts is one of the owners of a nursery group called Kids Planet. She decided to undertake EYPS to ensure that she was leading the way within her nurseries with this new qualification. She also felt that it supported the company ethos of continual looking to improve practice and raise the standards that all the children were receiving in the group's care. She is a mentor to any students within the nurseries who undertake EYPS and has just become a mentor for Edge Hill University. She is also the chair of the Warrington EYP Network to try to help to share best practice throughout our local authority.

→

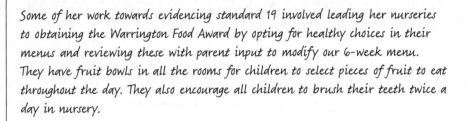

Some of her work towards evidencing standard 19 involved leading her nurseries to obtaining the Warrington Food Award by opting for healthy choices in their menus and reviewing these with parent input to modify our 6-week menu. They have fruit bowls in all the rooms for children to select pieces of fruit to eat throughout the day. They also encourage all children to brush their teeth twice a day in nursery.

Stakeholder 3

Viv has recently achieved EYPS and provided evidence towards this standard by developing safe transitions from nursery to reception. She invites the children to come and visit her for three mornings during the start of July in school – they go and 'explore' ... the classroom, the playground, the school garden, the willow dome, the toilets etc .... so that the children have an understanding of the layout of the school and the type of things they will be able to play with. She encourages them to talk together about being safe and happy while having fun and some of the rules to keep safe. From these first settling in days the children are shown, for example, where we keep the paper and the paint pallets and how to get their own brushes and water. The children are remarkable and very quickly become independent – this often amazes parents and staff new to the foundation stage!

Viv has created a welcome website on the school virtual learning environment 'Moodle' for the transition period. She has taken photographs from all around the school and then recorded the present reception class describing them; for instance, this is where we wash our hands', 'I like stories in the garden'.

Parents are then given a password unique to their child and can visit the site with their child from home time and time again over the 6-week holiday to familiarise the child with the class/school, etc. and hopefully alleviate any worries they may have. At this point she can also address the use of ICT and safeguarding.

The parents/carers are all given a booklet that made by Viv called 'All about me' to fill in about their child ... what they like to be called ... their family ... their likes/dislikes/fears ... what they like to do/where or who they like to visit ... any allergies etc. Viv shares this information with the teaching staff in the class and they use it to plan around each child's interests.

Standard 20 – recognise when a child is in danger or at risk of harm and know how to act to protect them

Example of standard 20 in personal practice

Research by Browne (1989) revealed that child abuse was the fourth commonest cause of death in preschool children – sadly, 20 years later little has changed. It seems that barely a week goes by without some tragedy hitting the news, with distraught parents ending the lives of themselves and their children, social services and other agencies failing to intervene swiftly enough, parents fabricating the symptoms of critical illnesses in relation to their children, child on child abuse, teachers, caretakers, nursery workers, people in a position of trust contributing to this dreadful pattern, paedophile rings, children left to fend for themselves and neglected by parents who have other priorities, and so the list goes on. It soon becomes apparent that we all have a responsibility and a legal duty to protect the children in our care – they are to be our first priority, and this is what standard 20 covers.

The best way that an EYP can safeguard the children in their care whilst promoting the welfare of those children is to ensure that they always adhere to the guidelines contained within *Working Together to Safeguard Children* (DfES, 2006: 18), which states that:

> Safeguarding and promoting the welfare of children is defined for the purpose of statutory guidance under the Children Acts 1989 and 2004 respectively as:
>
> - Protecting children from maltreatment
> - Preventing impairment of children's health or development
> - Ensuring that children are growing up in circumstances consistent with the provision of safe and effective care
> - Undertaking that role so as to enable those children to have optimum life chances and to enter adulthood successfully.

If the EYP strives to follow these guidelines carefully and employs these principles to underpin their practice, then they are part way to achieving this standard. Another specific requirement is that the EYP is fully aware of and contributing to the setting's policies and procedures. The EYP should read and have an understanding of the surrounding key legislation in relation to safeguarding children and promoting their welfare to be able to apply the strategies properly. It is recommended as a minimum that the following are consulted:

- Children Act 1989
- Education Act 2002

- Children Act 2004 – Every Child Matters: Change for Children
- Safeguarding Vulnerable Groups Act 2006
- Childcare Act 2006.

Again, this list is not exhaustive, and a good EYP will keep up to date with ongoing changes in the industry as a result of enquiries into such tragedies as the Soham murders, where the Bichard Report made 31 recommendations, and follow these up to see how they are progressing.

It is crucial that an EYP can recognise the signs and symptoms of actual abuse, danger and harm. If any clarification is needed, then I suggest a visit to the NSPCC website to embed this knowledge before taking this standard any further.

The EYP needs to ensure that the environment in which they are working is one that safeguards children's welfare, that risk assessments are adhered to and constantly reviewed. The EYP needs to explain to the children the importance of being kind to each other, kind hands, kind words, kind feet, kind friends, and get them to discuss what they understand that to mean. Talk about 'stranger danger' and invite your neighbourhood police officer into the setting to expand upon this. Positive behaviour, values and expectations need to be promoted within the workplace, and the EYP should be an exemplary role model to both the children and staff at the setting. The children need to be able to think about their own safety and risk assess themselves. For example, if playing on the large construction bricks they build a model that they want to climb upon and you can see it wobbling, before rushing in to remove the child from the situation, ask the child 'do you think it's safe?' They will know the answer, and from that you can help them to create a more sturdy structure. However, it is important that the EYP recognises the difference between allowing a child to make their own risk assessment as opposed to letting them become involved in a dangerous situation that could cause them harm.

The EYP has a responsibility for children's wellbeing, learning and development and with regard to this standard there are a number of things they can do in their daily practice to promote this. Encourage the children to talk about and understand their feelings and experiences; get the children to do self-portraits with collage materials on paper plates and then explore what emotions they have chosen to portray – happy, mad, sad, glad. Check the books within the setting – do they have any that address the issues of safeguarding in a child-friendly way? The EYP should endeavour to exploit any opportunity they can to enable children to contribute to discussions about staying safe and the rights of the child. Young children need to feel that they are listened to and, above all, the EYP should start making clear to them *that love means telling the truth*. There are a couple of good preschool books that can aid the EYP in this field, predominantly best used with those mature 3-year-olds and those 4 plus:

- *My body is mine, my feelings are mine* by Susan L. Hoke – is a story book about body safety and contains an adult guidebook with it
- *The Right Touch* by Sandy Kleven – is a story to help prevent child sexual abuse
- *Every Child has a Right To ...* by Unicef – is a list of phrases and lovely pictures highlighting the entitlement of a child.

It is imperative that every EYP should be confident with the correct referral procedure if they are to achieve the requirements of this standard.

If for some reason you feel you are unable to approach your manager/safeguarding person because, for example, you feel that they are implicated in the situation and doing so could prove detrimental, you can contact Ofsted's whistleblower hotline, which is designed for an employee who has concerns over practice and procedure in the workplace, with regard to safeguarding children (tel. 08456 404046 or email whistleblowing@ofsted.gov.uk).

Once the EYP has mastered the practical elements of this standard, they are then in a position to move on to demonstrate their leadership skills in this area.

Example of standard 20 in leadership

A good way to evidence strong leadership skills is by the EYP holding a training session or workshops to share good practice. If the EYP has made efforts to conduct activities with the children during personal, social and emotional development (PSED), or read a book to which they have been particularly responsive, this can be shared with other staff, who can make suggestions to work with the EYP developing any next steps for learning, in a relaxed discussion style forum.

Bringing in current newspaper articles re ongoing cases of child welfare and abuse issues and putting them up on the staff noticeboard keeps the issue at the forefront of everybody's mind. Do not assume that all staff are up to date with what is going on in the news. Explore how the situation could have been avoided – what went wrong?

The EYP could be responsible for developing a new policy or providing an appendix to an already established one. Does the setting have a policy on mobile phones? If so, is it separate or mentioned in the safeguarding policy. Recently, staff at a nursery have been found guilty of taking sexually explicit photographs of children. Does the setting you are in do enough to prevent this type of incident occurring in the first place? These are important factors in safeguarding children, and as an EYP, if stringent measures are not already in place, then you can take action and be the catalyst for change. By working with others, lead them to understand why you are doing what you are doing.

Are all team members aware that any little remark made by a child that seems inappropriate, any unexplained bruising, change in behaviour or general deterioration of a child should also be entered into the incident book at the setting? One remark on its own may go unexplored, but if several practitioners have made previous entries concerning a particular child, a pattern may start to emerge which could otherwise have been missed.

Use activities to educate other staff about what exactly is meant by the terms 'abuse' and 'neglect'. Split this into the four categories (physical, emotional, sexual and neglect) and then give the staff some scenarios and see if they can put them into the correct grouping.

Are they aware that a pregnant woman involved in substance abuse constitutes neglect of an unborn child? When a parent fabricates the symptoms of illness in a child, as has recently been in the press, it is a form of physical abuse. Sexual abuse can be committed through a child's involvement in a non-contact activity such as watching an inappropriate DVD. All forms of maltreatment will have some emotional impact upon the child and that too is a form of abuse; however, it should be noted that emotional abuse can exist in its own right.

Remember this is not about making people scared or encouraging them to jump to unsubstantiated conclusions – it is about raising awareness.

Standard 20 reflection points

Take the following scenarios and put them into the category in which they fall.

1. Criminal
2. Harm (or likely to cause harm)
3. Unsuitable (person to work with children)
4. Employer actions.

- A parent collects their child from nursery – you observe that there is no car seat in the vehicle
- A member of staff breaks up a fight between two children, resulting in one of the children having a broken arm

→

→

- The police are called to a domestic at the home address of a young girl who attends your setting; the perpetrator is a paediatrician
- A member of staff brings a pornographic DVD into the setting
- A staff questionnaire highlights that a member of your team drinks two bottles of wine every Friday night
- A member of staff comes into work smelling of alcohol; you know that they have driven themselves to work that day
- An aggressive child is put in an unused room on their own to cool down after a temper tantrum
- You speak to a parent about their son's biting. He is always targeting the same child; however, the parent laughs it off and says he'll grow out of it
- You notice a burn mark on the thigh of one of the children at your setting – the child says his dad did it
- You see a mother smack her child because the child is misbehaving and doesn't want to come to nursery today, consequently making the mother late for work
- You witness a pregnant parent smoking cannabis in the local pub
- An extrovert child suddenly becomes withdrawn for no apparent reason.

Compare your answers and the rationale behind your decision with another person, or do the activity as a group. The situations are designed to be deliberately vague in order to promote discussion and debate. Create more of your own scenarios and extend the activity.

Standard 20 stakeholder comment

All practitioners should have an up-to-date understanding of safeguarding children issues and be able to implement the safeguarding children policy and procedure appropriately ... (all) staff should be able to respond appropriately to any:

- significant changes in children's behaviour;
- deterioration in their general wellbeing;
- unexplained bruising, marks or signs of possible abuse;
- signs of neglect;
- comments children make which give cause for concern.   (DCSF, 2008: 22)

In relation to this standard, assessors will judge whether candidates for EYPS:

1. Can act decisively to protect children who are in danger or at risk of harm.
2. Ensure that colleagues are sufficiently knowledgeable about local policies and procedures for safeguarding children, and know how to apply them at an appropriate level.
3. Lead and provide support to colleagues in specific situations.   (CWDC, 2010)

→

→
There are many opportunities for an EYP to incorporate these requirements into their daily practice. It is not enough to say that as an EYP you conduct risk assessments and adhere to health and safety policy, and that therefore you are protecting children from danger and harm. Of course, that is an important basic statutory requirement, but to satisfy this standard you need to go much further. The flow chart for referral should be known inside out, and an EYP should always know who the designated safeguarding person is at the setting to which they are attached. To be able to implement the actions with regard to the referral procedure, you first need to be familiar with the signs and symptoms that intimate danger or harm. An EYP needs to know in depth about the four main categories of abuse (sexual, physical, emotional and neglect) and be confident about how to determine these. By having this knowledge underpinning your practice, if or when the need arises, the EYP will be fully prepared to offer direction to help other practitioners identify issues of concern, or provide support to colleagues at specific critical times. Perhaps the EYP can impart their knowledge during a staff meeting – consider creating further scenarios and conduct the previous reflective task with colleagues, thus creating an environment for discussion and debate which can be led and evaluated by you, the EYP.

The EYP assessor understands that a student may not have encountered a 'live' experience with regard to this standard but, if the time comes, they need to be certain that an EYP can deal confidently and competently with the situation presented. It is vital that the EYP finds innovative ways to evidence to assessors that they know how to recognise that a child is in danger or at risk of harm, and they know how to act to protect the child.

Standard 21 – assess, record and report on progress in children's development and learning and use this as a basis for differentiating provision

Example of standard 21 in personal practice

This standard links closely with standard 10 and the candidate may well find that certain pieces of evidence can be used for both standards. The candidate needs to understand the necessity for continuous assessment of individual children and how this can be utilised to help each child progress in their own unique way. The EYFS states

'All effective assessment involves analysing and reviewing what you know about each child's development and learning. You can then make informed decisions

about the child's progress and plan next steps to meet their development and learning needs'.   (DCSF, 2008: 12)

Therefore the candidate needs to show a thorough understanding of the
observation, assessment and planning cycle. While this is an ongoing sequence,
it is worth noting that the starting point must always be observation of the child.
Developing an understanding of what the child's interests are and what their
understanding of the world is must be the first step in getting to know that child
as an individual. This knowledge can then be used to develop provision and
resources that will stimulate the child to learn.

The successful candidate will be able to provide evidence of successful practice in this across the three age ranges. What they observe will differ from babies
to toddlers to preschool children, but all of these are equally important. A baby's
gaze on an object or enjoyment in putting a certain rattle into his/her mouth is just
as significant as the 4-year-old writing their name for the first time.

Using these observations and analysing them effectively will enable the candidate to identify any additional needs a child may have, and these regular observations and assessments, together with information obtained from the parent/
carers, will enable the candidate to contribute a clear picture of the whole child if
it becomes necessary to contribute to a common assessment framework (CAF)
for them. The candidate will undertake CAF training to ensure that they feel confident with the purpose and procedures involved. They will show that they understand the importance of information sharing and supporting other professionals
to address difficulties outside the setting that are affecting a child's progress.

Once the candidate has completed these observations the significant evidence for this standard is the next step of assessment. What do the observations
signify? Hutchin (2007: 49) states that every observation should be assessed
and that there are two key questions that should be asked:

- What does this tell us about the child's learning and development?
- What areas or aspects of learning and development are evident?

Answering these questions will enable the practitioner to build up a complete
picture of each child as a unique individual.

Assessment can be divided into two types: formative assessment (which is
the regular observations used to inform planning, as discussed previously) and
summative assessment (which occurs at the end of a stage of learning or at a
certain age). The main summative assessment that the candidate may experience is the EYFS profile.

Completing the profile may initially appear challenging, but if practitioners have kept frequent, quality observations then most of the evidence required will be readily available.

It is important to involve both children and parents in the assessment process. The EYFS requires practitioners to 'involve parents as part of the on-going observation and assessment process' (DCSF, 2008: 3.1) Hutchins (2007: 40) encourages practitioners to use parents as 'the starting point of a child's records, as they contribute key information about their child's learning and development at home.' The parents/carers have a wealth of knowledge about the child and their information about likes and dislikes, routines and preferences is particularly significant for babies and young children during their first transitions to a setting and will enable them to settle, safely and comfortably. This is only the beginning of the involvement with parents. The candidate will use this to develop a strong relationship, where parents/carers know that their contributions are valued and used to inform planning for their child's progression. They will ensure free access to learning journeys and other records and encourage parents/carers to add to them. Siraj-Blatchford *et al.* (2002) observed during the effective provision of pre-school education (EPPE) project that 'the most effective settings shared child related information between parents and staff, and parents were often involved in decision-making about the child's learning programme'. This highlights that this needs to be a continuous process. The candidate will be able to demonstrate to the assessor how important the parent/carer's contributions are throughout the child's time at the setting and how their contributions are included from the initial home visit to transition to the next setting. Hutchins (2007) has produced 10 principles of observation, one of which is to involve children in their assessment. This is possible for children of all ages; the candidate will show how this is done by listening to children, making their observations and photographs available to them to look at and talk about whenever they want – even babies as young as 6 months have shown an interest in these (Hutchins, 2007). Children may have set times to discuss what they have done and how they felt about it; the practitioner may be able to show how they have discussed this with the child and supported them to discover what they are good at and areas for development.

The analysis of the observations must then be used to develop planning for the children; the candidate will be able to show how this is done in their key person group. They will be able to provide evidence of how this enables them to differentiate their provision for the individual children in their group.

Example of standard 21 in leadership

To evidence leadership in this standard, the candidate needs to show how they have supported colleagues in understanding the importance of assessment, recording and reporting. This may involve the production or contribution towards policies and procedures to support the effective cycle of observation, assessment and planning. Regular team meetings to discuss observations are very effective and the candidate may organise and lead these. Meetings will give colleagues the opportunity to share ideas about the meaning of what they have observed and different methods of recording this. Developing this further, the candidate could support colleagues to work together to ensure that assessments are fair and accurate, taking into consideration the fact that there can be personal opinions and preferences between staff and children, and that what is observed is not always interpreted in the same way by two people.

They will support new colleagues in developing their assessment skills, demonstrating what information an effective observation contains and how to use the EYFS Development Matters to identify the child's progress.

Colleagues need to understand how the assessments of individual children can develop planning and how to differentiate provision for individual children's needs. The candidate will work with them to develop understanding of differentiation and review how effective it was after the session. They will encourage colleagues to reflect on their practice and support them in developing a creative approach to differentiation.

The candidate will review methods of recording assessments with colleagues to ensure that they are effective and uncomplicated. They will ensure that colleagues also understand that parent/carer's and the children's views must be included in the assessments and work with them to find the most effective way to put this into practice for the setting.

As an effective leader, the candidate will support colleagues in reporting to parents on a regular basis. This may be informally on a day-to-day basis, through displays and photographs or more formal events such as parents' evenings. The EYFS states that 'parents should review their children's progress regularly and contribute to their child's learning and development record' (DCSF, 2008: 2.2).

The candidate will give colleagues the support they need to develop their own skills by encouraging them to achieve CAF qualifications and contribute to CAF procedures involving their key children. Sharing this responsibility will give colleagues confidence in their own abilities and the experience of working closely with other agencies that will enable them to better understand their roles and responsibilities and how their observations, assessment and record-keeping can help to create a complete picture of the child, thus enabling the team to ensure that all areas of difficulty are addressed. The candidate will show how they have supported their colleagues in written tasks, witness statements, minutes of team meetings and witness interviews.

Standard 21 reflection points

- Review how the observation, assessment and planning cycle works in your setting
- Who has responsibility for this?
- How do colleagues contribute to the planning? Is everyone's voice heard?
- Are you/colleagues confident analysing observations?
- Does the assessment influence planning?
- Does your setting work as a team to review assessments and develop planning?
- How confident are you/colleagues in providing differentiated provision for individual children?
- How often does the team reflect on practice?
- Who deals with common assessment framework procedures? Could this role be shared to support colleagues' professional development?
- Do all colleagues have the opportunity to contribute to CAF meetings?
- How are parents/carers involved in assessment of their children?
- How are the children involved in their assessment?
- Do you have evidence to show that you are confident with this standard for all age groups?

Standard 21 stakeholder comment

Pat is a children's centre teacher and works closely with early years practitioners to raise quality in learning and development for the children that attend early years settings.

When considering standard 21, which recognises the need for ongoing assessment of children's progress as an integral part of their development, Pat offered training for a group of practitioners covering the themes of the EYFS and different types of observations. She gave all the practitioners a copy of the EYFS and provided opportunities for the staff to discuss their previous experiences, discussing good

→

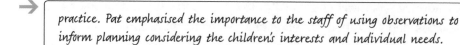

practice. Pat emphasised the importance to the staff of using observations to inform planning considering the children's interests and individual needs.

Pat then worked with the practitioners to devise an 'observation and children's interest proforma' and 'incidental observation form' that would support the planning. The planning included next steps for individual children and individual children profiles were produced based on the planning and observations.

Pat also worked with an individual child where there were some concerns about his development. She evaluated a range of observations, identifying the Development Matters bracket within which the child was working. The observations identified the child's interests, and activities were planned around the individual needs but still involved a group of children. As the activities were planned especially for this child's interests and ability level, this enabled him to progress and develop as he was engaged in the activity. The activity was recorded via picture evidence and annotations. This then formed the basis of the next planned activity, allowing a cycle to take place. Throughout this process his parents and other relevant professionals had been involved, ensuring a consistent approach and effective sharing of information.

On her tour of the setting, Pat was able to show boards she had set up that included planning next steps for children and an overview of the Development Matters statements. She showed the children's profiles stored so that parents could access them and an incidental book she had set up where staff could record children's play. Pat had implemented continuous provision so each child could access the resources independently and be able to engage in child-initiated play. She had linked each area to the EYFS.

In demonstrating this standard Pat has verified her own personal practice and the leadership and support of others.

Standard 22 – give constructive and sensitive feedback to help children understand what they have achieved and think about what they need to do next and, when appropriate, encourage children to think about, evaluate and improve on their own performance

Example of standard 22 in personal practice

The Department for Children, Schools and Families (DCSF) clearly states that children need to feel pride in their own achievements and requires that practitioners provide children with experiences and support to help them to 'know themselves and what they can do' (DCSF, 2008: 24).

Supporting children in the six areas of learning is a fundamental part of child-care. EYPs recognise that every child is a competent learner who can be sup-ported, through feedback, to help develop independence and a positive attitude to learning.

The EYP assessor will judge, for standard 22, whether candidates:

- Give constructive and sensitive feedback to help children to understand what they have achieved and think about what they need to do next; and
- Create an environment that enables children to think about, evaluate and improve on their performance.   (CWDC, 2010)

EYPs need to provide children with activities and experiences that will be both challenging and achievable. This means allowing children opportunities to be responsible and make decisions, whilst offering non-verbal positive reinforce-ment or immediate verbal feedback, so that the children have an understand-ing of what has been accomplished and what they need to do for further achievement.

Observations based on an individual child's interests and current stage of development enable practitioners to plan challenging activities to extend chil-dren's knowledge, and help children to understand what they have achieved and what they need to do next.

Practitioners need to provide an 'enabling environment', and offer feedback/encouragement to children to help them to evaluate and improve on their own performance. Effective practitioners are aware of the additional learning and development available to children who can stay focused on an activity, and they give children encouragement to solve problems, particularly if the activity is challenging.

Example of standard 22 in leadership

EYPs demonstrate excellence in their personal practice, lead the curriculum within a setting and support staff to maintain effective practice. 'EYPS is the gold standard for those working with children under the age of five' (CWDC, 2010: 1). Research from the EPPE project has demonstrated that the most effective way of ensuring that every child receives the best start in life is through settings having a graduate-led workforce who have extensive knowl-edge and experience of how children learn and develop in the early years.

The EPPE report states that children make the most progress in settings where staff engage in open-ended questioning and give formative feedback to them.

The EYP assessor will judge whether candidates lead and support colleagues to develop and extend the ways that they encourage children to celebrate their successes, and to persevere when they are less successful.

Candidates for EYPS frequently report that entering a setting to lead its workforce is a daunting task, although leading in some way or another is something they do every day. They believe that demonstrating leadership may prove difficult when on placement, but their knowledge of children's learning and development, coupled with a thorough understanding of the statutory and non-statutory frameworks, will demonstrate to any setting a strong commitment to early years. These attributes, together with enthusiasm, an ability to share knowledge, role model and advise colleagues on good practice, will demonstrate to the assessor and the setting their ability to lead.

Rodd (2006: 29) says that it is difficult to define leadership broadly and exclusively in the early years sector. She says in her book *Leadership in Early Childhood* that successful leadership is central to 'notions of trust, sharing, collaboration and empowerment'. Teamwork is important in early years and, to lead and support, you must become part of the team. Badaracco (2002) presents a leadership style which fits well with Rodd's collaborative and trusting leadership style – that of the 'quiet leader'. Described as a person who has the best interests of the company and their colleagues at the forefront of any decisions made, 'they do what is right, for their organizations, for the people around them and for themselves' (2002. 1). The quiet leader does not look for recognition but leads by taking small steps. Badaracco says he 'saw lots of careful thinking and weighing of possible outcomes' in this leader (2002: 188). Rodd believes that the effective leader needs 'to be capable of maintaining a balance between getting the job done and meeting people's needs' (2006: 28). When leading colleagues, the EYP should aim to develop a balance between leading and supporting. They should respect and value their colleagues and work together to provide a high quality provision.

By being a good role model and by challenging poor practice, the EYP should be able to lead others in effective practice. A good EYP needs to infuse others with enthusiasm, to guide them to be the best they can be to make a difference to the lives of the children in their care.

Standard 22 reflection points

- What resources do you have which are adaptable?
- How do you show enthusiasm and interest to the children?
- What open-ended questions do you ask?
- How do you know the child's interests?
- What opportunities are available for children to problem-solve and evaluate?
- How do you use your skills to model good practice to your colleagues?

Standard 22 stakeholder comment

EYP Martina Cooper explained how she met standard 22 by setting up an outdoor activity. The aim of her activity was to demonstrate to the staff how to listen and respond to the children by role modelling how to use both verbal and non-verbal feedback to encourage the children to evaluate and improve on their own performance.

Martina ensured that every person taking part in the activity knew exactly what their role was before they went outside. She and the staff helped the children to put on wet weather suits, using positive reinforcement and encouraging them to explore what they can do on their own and to be confident in their own abilities.

Once outside, one child was finding it difficult to walk unaided on the balancing beam. After initially offering some encouragement, Martina offered the child her hand, which was accepted. She praised the child for his efforts and guided him slowly across the beam. The child showed delight and Martina did this again, offering praise and encouragement and some advice on where to put his feet. After a couple of goes on the beam the child went across the beam alone. She clapped and praised him on his achievement and he then went across several times unaided.

Martina felt that she had achieved standard 22 by being a good role model to her staff and ensuring that they understood the reasons for the activity. She also felt that many of the children taking part in the session benefited through being able to explore their strengths and weaknesses in a safe and secure environment through positive and purposeful feedback and that, as they conquered one activity, they felt comfortable in attempting something more challenging.

Martina explained that throughout the task she used lots of positive reinforcement and verbal feedback to encourage independence, allowing the children to explore what they can do on their own whilst developing their understanding of what they have achieved. She encouraged the children's natural enthusiasm and inquisitiveness.

Standard 23 – identify and support children whose progress, development or well-being is affected by changes or difficulties in their personal circumstances and know when to refer them to colleagues for specialist support

Example of standard 23 in personal practice

For this standard the candidate must consider their relationships with children from birth to 5 and their knowledge of each child's level of development and their understanding of child development as a whole.

When the importance of a significant person for each child in the setting first became policy they were named 'key workers'. This terminology has now changed and, as Nutbrown and Page (2008) observe, the role has moved away from simple record-keeping and working with parents and other agencies to the 'key person' who develops a close relationship with the child and their family and carers. Whilst developing a close relationship is important for all children, in respect of this standard it is essential for very young children, particularly those with no spoken language as yet. As a key person, the candidate will have a sound understanding of the child, their stage of development, their routines, their likes and dislikes, and this is vitally important if they are to notice any change in behaviour or progress. In building a supportive relationship, the practitioner will develop an understanding of how best to communicate with the child; they will be able to elicit responses that other practitioners could not. They will also know the most appropriate way to enable the child to express his/her feelings and use this knowledge to help the child to work through their difficulties.

The candidate will be a constant support in what may be a very inconsistent time in a child's life. In cases of relationship breakdown or bereavement, for example, the child's home life may be tumultuous, and the candidate and setting will provide a safe haven for the child where they can be secure enough to express their feelings. The child will need a great deal of support and extra attention to help them deal with these issues and cope with the changes they are going through.

Alongside this, as a key person, the candidate will be building a relationship with the parents/carer. This can be a very difficult process that may take a great deal of time and effort, but is essential in order to deal with difficulties quickly and effectively. If a good relationship has been established, the candidate will feel confident in discussing the change in behaviour and finding the root of the problem quickly, enabling them to work with the parents/carers to find an effective solution together.

Grenier (2007) discusses the need for staff to 'tune in' to children's feelings, whatever the behaviour. He highlights how a child who hurts another may evoke a feeling of dislike or anger in the practitioner. Tuning in to the child's feelings '... might help us understand something about the child who is doing the hurting, who may feel angry about something, or feel rejected and unliked' (Grenier, 2007: 3). This may help the practitioner realise that something is amiss with the child, especially if this behaviour is out of character.

The use of observation is essential to have a record of behavioural changes or change in progress. It may be that only by evaluating these over a period of time are changes noticed and concerns raised. Having clear concise observations which are evaluated and recorded will give substance to the candidate's concerns, both to parents/carers and other agencies if there is a need for referral. This will also provide evidence towards this standard, as well as many others.

As mentioned earlier, good relationships with the family are essential. Whilst some may appear hard to reach or uncooperative, the candidate will show a skill in understanding possible communication difficulties and creating ways of addressing these. Macleod-Brudenell and Kay (2008: 291) discuss the need to 'communicate regularly', 'actively seek out "hard to reach" parents', 'give regular feedback about children', 'recognise parents' reasons for avoidance', 'seek out parents' opinions' and 'plan'. The successful candidate will be able to show evidence of how they have addressed these and how effective they have been in establishing the cause of the problem. Using this positive relationship will enable the candidate to open a dialogue with parents/carers and establish a plan of action.

The candidate must be aware of how much intervention they can provide. A junior member of staff may feel it necessary to refer their concerns to their line manager immediately and follow their directions on how to proceed, whilst a more senior member of staff will be able to discuss the changes with the parent/carer and begin to implement an agreed form of intervention in the setting and at home. They may only need to inform their manager of their concern, but it is imperative that they understand the limits of their role and when it is pertinent to ask for more specialised help.

Everyone working with children needs to be trained to do their own job well. They also need to know how their role fits with that of others.   (DfES, 2004: 86)

Example of standard 23 in leadership

The leadership aspect of this standard involves ensuring that all members of staff understand their role as a key person. The candidate will ensure that all staff, whatever their level of qualification, understand the need to develop a close relationship with the children in their group, whatever their age, and develop a solid understanding of their normal behaviour, needs and preferences. They will work with them to assist them to produce clear relevant observations and enable them to evaluate them accurately.

Establishing clear roles is another important factor for the leader to address, making sure that staff are aware of their own role as soon as they commence employment. The candidate will also ensure that staff are aware of the procedures in the event that they become concerned about a child's wellbeing, so that a senior member of staff will be kept informed of all discussions, interventions and progress and will be able to support the key person in realising when they need to refer the problem to someone who can give specialist support.

In leading practice, the candidate must ensure that whilst enabling a colleague to take on this responsibility, they are regularly updated with the child's progress. The nature of the personal circumstances can be wide ranging, from something that may be a major event for the child, but can be easily addressed, to a massive upheaval for the whole family. Even experienced members of staff may become overly involved in the trauma, initially to help the child, but if they do have good relationships with parent/carers they could become too involved. It is the candidate's responsibility to support that member of staff and advise them of the limitations of their role.

The candidate will ensure that staff feel supported throughout this process, and will give advice on methods of intervention, role modelling good practice, thus ensuring that the child and family feel they are supported and any difficulties are dealt with efficiently.

Standard 23 reflection points

- Consider how you use your observations. Do you evaluate them solely using Development Matters or do you include a child's likes and demeanour and any changes in these?
- Do you know what the setting's policy is if you notice changes in a child's behaviour? Is this a written policy? If not, could you create one?

→

→

- Do you know your responsibilities in a case such as this? How is it addressed in your job description?
- When would you consider referring a child to another professional? What procedures would you follow?
- In a leadership capacity, do you feel confident that your staff would deal with this in an appropriate manner? Do they understand the limitations of their roles?
- Could you invite professionals to staff training events to talk about their roles and do you know how and when to contact them?

Standard 23 stakeholder comment

A candidate studying on the full time pathway had a placement in a 2–3-year-old room. She had used her serial visits to establish relationships with several children and shortly after starting her placement observed that one of them had become quiet and withdrawn and found it hard to settle. She made several observations to support her concerns and shared these with the room leader and they discussed how she could deal with this problem.

During this time she had been making time to talk to the child's mother as often as possible, developing a relationship with her, and it was decided that she should broach the subject of the child's changed behaviour. The child's mother was surprised at this as she had not perceived any differences, but she did mention that the child's father had gone to work away for several weeks and that the child was missing him.

The candidate asked if the child could bring a photograph of her father in to talk about and planned some activities for the child to write and draw pictures that her mother could post and encourage the father to write back. The candidate also suggested the use of a webcam at home so that the child could see her father each day. This was arranged and the child became much happier and returned to her normal demeanour.

The candidate used this example in her written task and also used a witness statement from the mother in her documentary evidence; finally, the setting manager also discussed this in her interview, giving good evidence for this standard.

Standard 24 – be accountable for the delivery of high quality provision

Example of standard 24 in personal practice

The statutory framework for the EYFS (DCSF, 2008) states that the purpose and aims of the EYFS are for every child to have the best possible start in life to fulfil their individual potential. All young children achieving the five *Every Child Matters* outcomes of 'staying safe', 'being healthy', 'enjoying and achieving', 'making a positive contribution' and 'achieving economical well-being' (DfES, 2004) is the overarching aim of the EYFS.

Standard 24 requires EYPs to have a secure knowledge and understanding of the principles and content of the EYFS and how to put them into practice (standard 1) (CWDC, 2010: 14) and to recognise that the quality of care and education that every young child experiences has a significant effect on their individual progress and development. It is the EYP's responsibility, in their setting, to raise the quality of early years provision and to make a positive difference to young children's wellbeing, learning and development.

High-quality provision is never easily defined. Often definitions of 'quality' vary, and perceptions can be influenced by the context, feelings and past experiences (Abbott, 1994).

Early years settings are expected to engage in a process of continuous quality improvement to influence outcomes for young children (DCSF, 2008). Local authority 'Quality Awards', underpinned by the principles of the EYFS, the outcomes from the *Every Child Matters* document and the national quality improvement principles, offer early years practitioners support in establishing the ethos of their individual settings, unpicking and embedding their philosophy and values and thus developing the confidence to broaden their thinking, share consistent approaches and impact upon the quality of the provision with this self-evaluation tool. Self-evaluation is the process of looking at what is happening and then considering and implementing improvements to bring about change – a systematic reflection, introduced alongside the framework for the inspection of schools (Ofsted, 2008). Ofsted's role is to 'inspect and regulate to achieve excellence in the care of children and young people' (Ofsted, 2008) and to ensure that every setting meets the statutory requirements of the EYFS in providing quality care and education.

Experienced practitioners recognise and value that children learn everything through sensory experiences – babies and young children are sociable beings and competent, inquisitive learners from birth. In a high quality, continuously improving setting, children learn by:

- Exploring
- Experimenting
- Creating
- Imagining
- Collaborating
- Organising
- Explaining
- Recalling
- Discovering
- Sharing their thoughts, feelings and ideas
- Labelling
- Negotiating
- Making choices
- Making decisions
- Questioning
- Describing
- Predicting
- Experiencing
- Investigating.

Inevitably, the physical environment directly influences children's learning and development and plays a major role in how children learn. EYPs are required to know all they can about the indoor and outdoor environment – how to design it, manage it, use it and how to ensure that others use the environment to support young children's learning and development at its best. They are accountable for the delivery of high quality provision, accountable to children and their parents (first and foremost), families, managers, proprietors, governors and external agencies such as Ofsted. Improving practice, reflecting upon practice, using commendations, complaints, reviewing policies and procedures, flexible planning and ensuring that early years staff have specific training in child development and early childhood education and continue with their further professional development is key to the accountability of the delivery of high quality provision.

Example of standard 24 in leadership

> All early years practitioners should demonstrate certain core characteristics: a passion for and strong commitment to quality provision for young children; a flexible approach to practice; the capacity to work independently and as part of a team; skills in caring for, nurturing and teaching young children; patience; sensitivity; and a sense of humour.
> (Whalley *et al.*, 2008: 52)

EYPs must have a sound working knowledge and understanding of the current legal requirements, national policies and guidance on health and safety, safeguarding and promoting the wellbeing of children and their implications for early years settings and also lead and support to influence colleagues' practice (CWDC, 2010: 18).

EYPs are expected to support colleagues in their professional development to provide, develop and maintain high quality provision (CWDC, 2010). As a starting point for reflection and as a review of current provision, local authority Quality Award information suggests organising a 'walkthrough' of the 'enabling environment'. A walkthrough would be a very useful way to reflect upon current daily working practice, provide an ongoing rationale for all staff, identify quality indicators and update staff training. Practitioners could:

- Discuss shared aims
- Clarify the ethos and atmosphere of the setting (how are children learning to learn?)
- Review the open-ended opportunities offered within each play area – quality play?
- Discuss sustained shared thinking – do all practitioners know what this means?
- Review children's wellbeing and involvement
- Review the policies and procedures and discuss current practice on safeguarding, inclusive practice, risk assessment, etc. and identify further staff training opportunities as necessary
- Ensure that diversity, gender, ethnicity, culture, religion, customs and traditions, family structures and children's specific needs are accurately reflected and understood
- Establish interactions: how practitioners interact with each other; how practitioners and children interact; how engaged practitioners are with children's activity and learning
- Question whether children are given independent choices – how often? Why not all the time?

- Review whether children's ideas and imagination are valued and demonstrated within practice and provision.

Effective leadership involves improvement, development and enhancement (Aubrey, 2007). Effective leaders and practitioners are enthusiastic, energetic, dedicated and absorbed (Rodd, 2006). EYPs should lead discussions and open dialogues about what quality looks like for children, parents, staff and then review their everyday practice, resources and premises to improve provision.

EYPs can seek out examples of high quality early learning and visit settings that have a reputation for high quality provision, and attend local authority and national networks to support each other. EYPs are expected to use quality as a continuous guide for decision-making and change – ask yourself 'Will this improve the quality of the provision we offer?'

Standard 24 reflection points

In a quality learning environment children will be:

- Learning about rules, grace, courtesy, manners and showing politeness and consideration for their friends, peers and adults
- Making decisions, talking about their personal preferences
- Engaged and interested in finding out things for themselves, supported by caring, sensitive, nurturing adults
- Encouraged to predict possible endings to stories, events and interesting happenings, talking in familiar groups and sharing ideas with others
- Working together to help and support each other
- Showing respect for others, their needs, feelings and wishes, understanding the difference between right and wrong
- Developing a positive image and showing respect for themselves and for people of other cultures and beliefs
- Enjoying sharing books with others, recognising the difference between pictures and print
- Beginning to recognise letters within familiar words and the letters of their own names, and signs and symbols
- Exploring and experimenting with construction; making models, developing skills of cutting, joining, folding
- Exploring and experimenting with information, communication and technology (ICT), using computers, interactive whiteboards, remote control toys, digital cameras

- Enjoying finding out about past and present events in their own lives, talking about 'when I was a baby ...' 'I remember when I ...'
- Enjoying mark-making – 'writing', attempting to write their own name and becoming interested in writing for a purpose (making lists, maps, drawing pictures, circle, lines)
- Showing an interest in numbers and counting, joining in number songs and rhymes, counting, matching numbers, placing numbers in order and recognising numbers all around
- Comparing and ordering shape, size, position, length and volume
- Suggesting explanations to problems, concentrating and persevering on a task
- Using their senses to explore, experiment, comment and describe
- Noticing and talking about patterns and change, everyday materials and natural objects, indoors and outdoors
- Balancing, climbing, moving with control and coordination indoors and outdoors
- Developing an understanding of the importance of exercise, eating, sleeping and hygiene.

Reflection checklist

Do all young children in your setting:

- Have access to resources related to cultural diversity, gender, mother tongue learning, children with disabilities and other special educational needs?
- Have space to work, eat, sit and snuggle in?
- Experience sun, shade, rain and grass, natural materials in an expanding outdoor environment?
- Engage in first hand interactions with adults – receive individual instruction, feed back about their learning experiences and beyond?
- Have warm respectful attentive relationships with adults and peers?
- Have adults that understand, listen, comfort and support children in their social interactions?
- Have sufficient time to become absorbed in their own learning?
- Have continuous learning experiences?
- Have access to adequate, appropriate materials to promote exploration and development of more advanced knowledge and skills – having enough materials is essential to a smooth running classroom. Enough means several of the same items so that more than one child can use them at the same time?
- Have consistency and continuity between home and nursery?
- Have opportunities for families to be involved in their children's education?

→

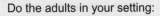

Do the adults in your setting:

- Reflect upon all aspects of their own and others' practice?
- Stimulate children's use of language through conversation, sustained shared thinking, reading and asking open-ended questions?
- Have high expectations for children?
- Know and understand the importance of safeguarding, child protection, health and safety, and risk assessment and provision?
- Know and understand the unique and diverse ways in which young children learn?
- Provide honest, open-minded, real life experiences?
- Provide personal care designed to meet individual needs and encourage the development of self-help skills?
- Understand and address the needs of diverse learners?
- Know how to access a wide range of services to support parents?
- Take responsibility for their own beliefs and consequences and have a high regard for moral, political, social and ethical issues?
- Regularly and continually challenge self and others?
- Listen to views and consider all possibilities?
- Visit a range of early years settings that have a reputation for high quality?

Standard 24 stakeholder comment

The following comment is from an early years professional working as a nursery manager in a private, voluntary and independent (PVI) setting, after delivering a team meeting entitled 'What does quality look like?' (linking to the setting's self-evaluation form (SEF) for Ofsted):

'I was surprised by the team's responses – it created a tremendous opportunity for reflection from a completely different perspective – we had previously explored the question "what is it like for a child here?" and had similar aims and themes, so we were able to complete this section happily.'

'But then, thinking about 'quality' and what it should look like opened up such different viewpoints! Some team members reflected back to when they were a child, while others focused more on resources and areas, rather than learning experiences offered to the children. I decided to take some members of the team to visit other settings known for their quality provision and which have also been recognised as "outstanding" by Ofsted. Then we met

→ 'again as a team and listed all the things that clearly defined "quality" to us: noisy, purposeful, messy, active, imaginative, well organised, clean, calm, tidy, safe, interesting, healthy, happy, comfortable, lots of language, attractive, cosy.'

'We then looked around our nursery rooms and tried to make sure that we offered all this and completed an action plan for our next meeting.'

Comment from a new staff member in a private day nursery setting:

'I had just started my new job. I had lots of previous experience in private day nurseries and I really did think I knew what was expected of me. I had a good job description and I was finding my way around happily. My line manager held a training session for all staff one evening. I was a bit annoyed that I had to stay late! It was called an environmental walkthrough. She took us to each area and explained what the purpose of it was — for the children's learning. It felt like the first time I have ever had everything all explained to me! She talked about the painting easel — making sure that there was always paper on it as it was too tricky for the little ones to put the paper on, but then that she wanted the children always to attempt to write their own name on their paintings and we were supposed to support. She gave us a copy of the way the letters should be formed. She said that she expected the children to take off their own painting and put it to dry on the rack as this was a good hand–eye coordination skill for them to be learning. She also explained that, nearby, the children should always have some rollers, pens, collage materials, sponges and boxes, etc. so that they could mix their media and use their imagination. She reminded us that the aprons should always be the right way round as this might put some children off painting if they couldn't get an apron on in the first place, but that the children should ask their friends to help them fasten each other's aprons so that they were linking up with each other for support, from the EYFS curriculum Development Matters.'

'My line manager explained each activity and area in detail and there was a point to everything in the room and outside. It was great because I was confident to explain all this to any parents that asked me then. It was really useful and actually only took about ¾ of an hour. I looked forward to the outdoors one next term.'

Conclusion

The group of standards 'effective practice' is the largest group of standards. They encourage practitioners to consider how they listen to children and meet their individual needs, giving recognition to children's rights. Practitioners are required to demonstrate how they observe, plan and assess children's development and use this information to differentiate the provision they offer. Practitioners will need to lead colleagues in considering how they extend children's learning and reflect upon how they ensure that all children can reach their full potential.

References

Abbott, J. (1994) *Learning Makes Sense: Recreating Education for a Changing Future.* England: Education 2000.

Alderson, P. (2008) *Young Children's Rights: Exploring Beliefs, Principles and Practice.* London: Save the Children.

Anning, A., Edwards, A. (2006) *Promoting Children's Learning from Birth to Five: Developing the New Early Years Professional.* Maidenhead: Open University Press.

Archard, D. (2004) *Children; Rights and Childhood.* Abingdon: Routledge.

Aries, P. (2002) *Centuries of Childhood. A Social History of Family Life,* 2nd edn. New York: Vintage Books.

Athey, C. (1990) *Extending Thought in Young Children.* London: Paul Chapman.

Aubrey, C. (2007) *Leading and Managing in the Early Years.* London: Sage.

Badaracco, J. (2002) *Leading Quietly: an Unorthodox Guide to doing the Right Thing.* Boston: Harvard Business School.

Baldock, P., Fitzgerald, D. and Kay, J. (2005) *Understanding Early Years Policy.* London: Sage.

Bowen, H. (1907) *Froebel and Education by Self-Activity.* London: Heinemann.

Browne, K.D. (1989) The health visitor's role in screening for child abuse. *Health Visitor,* **62:** 275–7.

Bruce, T. (2004) *Developing Learning in Early Childhood.* London: Sage.

Brunton, P. and Thornton, L. (2005) *Understanding the Reggio Approach.* London: David Fulton Publishers.

Colloby, J. (2008) *The Validation Process for EYPS.* Exeter: Learning Matters.

Crystal, D. (1986) *Listen to your Child.* Harmondsworth: Penguin.

CWDC. (2010) *Guidance to the Standards for the Award of the Early Years Professional Status.* London: CWDC.

DCSF. (2007) *Letters and Sounds.* Nottingham: DCSF.

DCSF. (2008) *Early Years Foundation Stage.* Nottingham: DCSF.

DfES. (2004) *Every Child Matters: Change for Children*. Nottingham: DfES.

DfES. (2006) *Working Together to Safeguard Children*. Nottingham: DfES.

Edgington, M. (2008) *The Foundation Stage Teacher in Action: Teaching 3, 4 and 5 year olds,* 3rd edn. London: Sage.

Farrelly, P. (2010) *Early Years Work-Based Learning (Working with Children, Young People and Families)*. Exeter: Learning Matters.

Featherstone, S., Louis, S., Beswick, C. (2008) *Again, Again!: Understanding Schemas in Young Children*. London: Featherstone Publications Ltd.

Fisher, J. (2008) *Starting from the Child: Teaching and Learning from 3 to 8*. Maidenhead: Open University Press.

Froebel, F. (1901) *Autobiography of Friedrich Froebel*. London: Swan Sonnenschein & Co. Ltd.

Froebel, F. (1907) *The Education of Man*. New York: Appleton & Co.

Goldschmied, E., Hughes, A. (1992*) Heuristic Play with Objects. Young Children In Day Care*. Video London: National Children's Bureau.

Goldschmied, E., Jackson, S. (2004) *People Under Three*: *Young Children In Day Care,* 2nd edn. London: Routledge.

Gopnik, A., Meltzoff, A.N., Kuhl, P.K. (1999) *The Scientist in the Crib: Minds, Brains and how Children Learn*. New York: Harper Collins.

Greenland, P. (2009) *Developmental Movement Play.* Final Report and Recommendations from a 10-year action research project investigating the way the early years sector supports the youngest children to be fully physical. Leeds: JABADAO Publication.

Grenier, J. (2007) *(Extract From) All about . . . Developing Positive Relations With Children*. Nottingham: DCSF.

Hutchin, V. (2007) *Supporting Every Child's Learning Across the Early Years Foundation Stage*. London: Hodder Education.

Kazdin, A. (2009) *The Kazdin Method for Parenting the Defiant Child*. London: Houghton Mifflin Harcourt.

Lancaster, Y.P., Broadbent, V. (1993) *Listening to Young Children*. Maidenhead: Open University Press.

Landsdown, G. (2005) *The Right of Children to Participate in Decisions Affecting them*. Hague: Bernard Van Leer Foundation.

Macleod-Brudenell, I., Kay, J. (2008) *Advanced Early Years,* 2nd edn. Essex: Heinemann.

Mercer, N. (2006) *The Guided Construction of Knowledge*. Bristol: Multi-lingual Matters Ltd.

Montessori, M. (1988) [1912] *The Discovery of the Child* (originally published as *The Montessori Method*). Oxford: ABC–Clio, Vol. 2.

Moss, P., Petrie, P. (2002) *From Children's Services To Children's Spaces: Public Policy, Children and Childhood*. London: Routledge.

Moyles, J. (1999) *The Excellence of Play*. Maidenhead: Open University Press.

Moyles, J. (2004) *Effective Leadership and Management in the Early Years*. Maidenhead: Open University Press.

Nutbrown, C. (2006) *Threads of Thinking*, 3rd edn. London: Sage.

Nutbrown, C., Page, J. (2008) *Working with Children and Babies from Birth to Three*. London: Sage.

Oates, J., Wood, C., Grayson, A. (2005) (eds) *Psychological Development and Early Childhood*. Oxford: Wiley-Blackwell.

O'Connor, A. (2009) A unique child: role play – practice in pictures. *Nursery World*, 3 December 2009.

Ofsted. (2008) *How we Inspect*. http://www.ofsted.gov.uk/Ofsted-home/About-us/How-we-inspect/Learning-and-skills (accessed 29 September 2010).

Post, J., Hohmann, M. (2000) *Tender Care and Early Learning, Supporting Families and Toddlers in Childcare Settings*. Michigan: High/Scope Press.

Rinaldi, C. (2006) *Early Childhood Education in Reggio Emilia*. Oxon: Routledge.

Rodd, J. (2008) *Leadership in Early Childhood, 3rd edn*. Maidenhead: Open University Press.

Sharman, C., Cross, W., Vennis, D. (2007) *Observing Children and Young People*, 4th edn. London: Continuum International Publishing Group.

Siraj-Blatchford, I., Clarke, P. (2000) *Supporting Identity, Diversity and Language in the Early Years*. Maidenhead: Open University Press.

Siraj-Blatchford, I., Manni, L. (2007) *Effective Leadership in the Early Years Sector*. University of London: Institute of Education.

Siraj-Blatchford, I., Sylva, K., Muttock, S., Gilden, R., Bell, D. (2002) *Researching Effective Pedagogy in the Early Years*. London: DfES.

Sylva, K., Siraj-Blatchford, I., Melhuish, E.C., Sammons, P., Taggart, B. (2004) *The Effective Provision of Pre-School Education (EPPE) Project: Final Report*. London: DfES/Institute of Education, University of London.

The National Literacy Trust. (2010) *Transforming Lives*. http://www.literacytrust.org.uk/ (accessed 29 September 2010).

The Warnock Report. (1978) *Special Educational needs*. London: HMSO. (Report by the Committee of Enquiry into the Education of Handicapped Children and Young People.)

Thomas, N. (2005) *Sociology of Childhood*. In T. Maynard and N. Thomas (eds) *An Introduction to Early Childhood Studies*. London: Sage Publications.

Tovey, H. (2008) *Playing Outdoor – Spaces and Places, Risks and Challenge*. Maidenhead: Open University Press.

Vygotsky, L. (1978) *Mind in Society*, M. Cole, V. John-Steiner, S. Scribner, and E. Souberman (eds). Cambridge, MA: Harvard University Press, p. 86.

Webster-Stratton, C. (2005) *How to Promote Children's Social and Emotional Competence*. London: Paul Chapman Publishing Ltd.

Whalley, M., Allen, S., Wilson, D. (2008) *Leading Practice in Early Years Settings*. Exeter: Learning Matters Ltd.

Wood, D., Bruner, J., Ross, G. (1976) The role of tutoring in problem solving. *Journal of Child Psychology and Psychiatry*, **17**: 89–100.

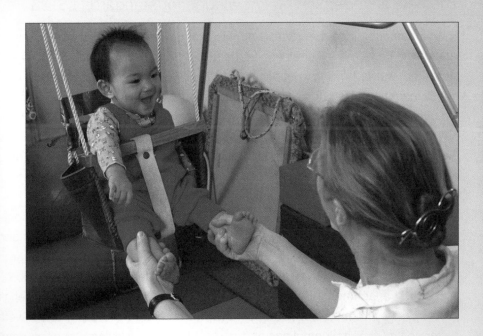

Chapter 5

Relationships with children

Introduction

This chapter details how to communicate effectively with children and build constructive relationships in a fair and respectful way.

Objectives

By the end of this chapter you should have:

- Gained an overview of the key theoretical perspectives on the importance of establishing and maintaining respectful and supportive relationships with children

- Reflected on how you can promote through your practice the requirements identified in standards 25–28

- Reflected on how you can lead and support others in relation to the requirements identified in standards 25–28.

Theoretical underpinning knowledge for standards 25–28

The fundamental idea that underpins this group of standards is clearly articulated in the Early Years Foundation Stage (EYFS) framework (DCSF, 2008), which states that warm, trusting relationships with knowledgeable adults support children's learning more effectively than any amount of resources. Beyond doubt, the quality of young children's lives depends on the quality of their relationships. Key components of child-centred approaches in early years settings include the building of relationships based on respect for children's rights and providing children with the opportunities to develop secure attachments to their carers at home and within the early years setting.

According to Oates and Woodhead (2007: 1), attachments are 'the emotional bonds that infants develop with their parents and other key caregivers, such as their key person in an early childhood setting'. Past and current research (Bowlby, 1979; Doherty and Hughes, 2009) supports the assertion that children with strong attachments in their early years are less prone to attention deficit problems; they normally separate from their main carers more easily and have a better control over their emotions and personal feelings. Having a positive emotional attachment to people helps babies and young children feel self-assured that the carers and practitioners are always available to give the children the love, respect and support that they need. On the other hand, if children feel uncertain about what to expect from the people on whom they depend, they can become anxious, withdrawn and cautious in expressing their true feelings. As the EYFS stresses 'every interaction is based on respectful acknowledgement of the feelings of children and their families' (DCSF, 2008).

EYPs need to acknowledge the significance of listening to children, paying attention to what they say and valuing their views. To develop effective practice and leadership skills in this area, EYPs have to gain sound knowledge and understanding of the key theoretical perspectives on children's rights, along with the practical strategies of how these rights can be protected within the context of early years settings. The contemporary sociology of childhood is characterised by the increasing recognition that children must be seen as 'social actors in their own right' (Thomas, 2005: 80). This change in our understanding of children's role in society led to modification of the child's position from a rights-holder to a citizen, whose opinion has to be considered and whose voice has to be heard.

Nowadays, children's rights are seen as a universal norm that has been established in the majority of countries, including the UK, through a number of both international and national treaties, such as the Declaration of Human Rights, UN Convention on the Rights of the Child (1989), as well as the Children Act 1989, the Education Act 2002, the Every Child Matters (2003) framework and the Childcare Act 2006. Article 12 of the UN Convention on the Rights of the Child (1989) obliges adults as parents and professionals to ensure that children are enabled to and encouraged to contribute their views in all relevant matters and to provide age-appropriate information, which helps them to form their views. It is important to emphasise that the UN Convention on the Rights of the Child formally acknowledged for the first time in international law that children are the subjects of rights, rather than just recipients of adult protection (Lansdown, 2001). The Childcare Act 2006 can be considered a ground-breaking piece of legislation, being the first act to be exclusively devoted to early years and child-care. Measures in the act make official the roles and duties of local authorities, including the improvement of the five Every Child Matters outcomes for all pre-school children and reducing inequalities in these outcomes.

These developments show that children today are no longer seen as incomplete adults not yet able to participate in social life, but as 'co-constructors of childhood and society' (Qvortrup et al., 1994: 14). The government strongly supports participation of children, young people and their parents/carers in the expansion and improvement of children's centres, children's trusts and Sure Start units. These settings and organisations provide a combination of services that contribute to the Every Child Matters outcomes through a number of measures, such as promoting children's participation in community matters, reducing child poverty, improving the health of both children and their families, and removing barriers to help all children and parents in accessing early years services. *Support for All: the Families and Relationships Green Paper* (DCSF, 2010) once again affirms the government's intention to continue to implement the UN Convention on the Rights of the Child by promoting children's wellbeing and developing further positive relationships with children and their families.

Conversely, EYPs need to recognise that, notwithstanding efficiency or inadequacy of any of the strategies, no all-embracing package has been devised that proposes a perfect solution for developing and promoting children's rights and participation. It seems unrealistic to expect a selected model to offer ultimate solutions in the context of a certain educational institution in view of the fact that a wide variety of different theories and approaches continuously develop to meet new sociological, legislative and educational needs. In the face of the changes that time brings into education, we must recognise that the process of developing the ideas of childhood is a continuous non-stop practice, which helps us to comprehend the children and their lives as they really are and in this way give the children's views a central role in our explorations and perceptions. It is only through developing and maintaining personal relationships with children that EYPs will be able to lead effective practice that supports the wellbeing, learning and development of babies, toddlers and young children. As Brown (1994: 180) reminds us, 'Relationships are ultimately what the world is about and ones which are mutually loving and caring, honest and supportive create an atmosphere for healthy human growth.'

Standard 25 – establish fair, respectful, trusting, supportive and constructive relationships with children

Example of standard 25 in personal practice

It is important to begin your deconstruction of this standard by considering the nature of your relationships with young children. Froebel described the importance of the parents as the first educators, suggesting that they were partners in children's learning, not a threat to it: 'First the adults in the family then the teacher help and guide the child into the wider community' (cited in Bruce, 2005: 30).

Acknowledging the contribution that parents make to children's learning is of paramount importance. By valuing their input and working with them, you will develop a sound, trusting relationship which is of vital importance in developing the trust between you and the child. This aspect could also link to standard 30.

Developing positive relationships is fundamental to providing high quality early years provision. One of the EYFS principles attached to the 'Positive Relationships' theme is that 'children learn to be strong and independent from a base of loving and secure relationships with parents and/or a key person' (DCFS, 2008: 5), which also reflects two of Tina Bruce's Bedrock Principles:

- Children are whole people who have feelings, ideas, a sense of embodied self and relationships with others and who need to be physically, mentally, morally and spiritually healthy
- Relationships with other people (both adults and children) are of central importance in a child's life, influencing emotional and social wellbeing.

(Bruce, 2005: 30)

Sylva *et al.* (2004) reported that where staff had formed positive relationships, children made better progress; the candidate needs to begin developing these relationships from the first encounter with the child, usually on the home visit. Both the parents/carers and the child are in the place they feel safest and most comfortable. This enables the practitioner to understand the importance of certain people and items in a child's life. EYPs will be able to learn about family, close friends and treasured possessions, all of which helps them to support the child during the transition to the setting. While EYPs will ensure that the setting is as comfortable and welcoming as possible, they should also be aware that it is not the same as home, but complementary to it. The child needs to feel happy and safe, and the candidate can then support them to access new experiences and activities they may not experience in the home environment.

The candidate needs to show evidence that they understand the different needs of children of varying ages, diversity and ability.

Very young children who are unable to communicate verbally need to develop a relationship in which the adult shows interest, curiosity and affection. They notice the tiny details of how they are held, and spoken to and, even, if an unfamiliar adult treats them in a similar way, they will be aware of the differences 'in detail (smell, facial gestures, physical handling, tone of voice) and can be experienced as completely "wrong", thus replacing delight with anxiety, stiffness and distress' (Elfer *et al.*, 2005: 12).

The candidate's role as key person for the child should provide strong evidence for this standard. They must use their relationship with the child to recognise his/her unique qualities and develop individualised provision to enable that child to develop at their own pace with the support of the key person and the freedom to experiment and investigate without fear of failure. This requires a sound understanding of child development and a working knowledge of the EYFS, linking to standards 1, 2 and 4. Evidence could include how they have used observations to identify the child's interests and how they have used these findings to develop planning to provide for these. This could also relate to standards 10, 11, 12, 13 and 14.

It is important to be able to develop these relationships with children from birth to 5. The candidate must be aware of the differing needs and approaches required with children of different ages. How does a young baby relate to a carer? What are their physical and emotional needs? How does the candidate cater for these to ensure the baby feels safe and happy? How does this differ from the needs of the toddler or preschool child?

The candidate must have the experience to ensure she/he can provide solid evidence that they can meet this standard for all ages.

The candidate needs to show how they initiate these relationships, how they develop them over time, consider the young child's routines, personal care; how do they ensure that each child is treated with dignity and respect? How do they work with the setting's policies and procedures, building on them, finding ways of ensuring that all children are treated equally?

The candidate must develop an understanding of the child's background, embracing their culture, diverse needs, family and society. There may be traditions and behaviours that the candidate does not understand and they must address this through research, courses and speaking to family and friends.

This close bond that forms will enable the candidate to be aware of the child's needs and expectations; they will also be able to recognise changes in behaviour and respond to them appropriately; this could also relate to standard 23.

Example of standard 25 in leadership

As a leader, the candidate should demonstrate how to develop good relationships with children and support staff to do the same. Inexperienced staff will need to understand how to begin a relationship with young children. Initially the candidate will consider role modelling good practice with the staff member playing a supporting role, but as their confidence increases the roles will reverse as the candidate steps back and takes on a supporting role until she/he is no longer needed. The candidate needs to be confident in her/his ability to deal with the wide variety of issues that staff may discover as they learn about the children in their care and be there to guide them through procedures and policies to deal with the problem efficiently and effectively, ensuring the best outcomes for the children. The staff must feel that they can turn to the candidate in confidence when they come across issues they are not experienced in dealing with.

Candidates could look at the self-evaluation form to assess how well the setting is performing in this area; from this they may identify areas for development. They need to consider how well the setting reflects the relationship and respect for the children; are the displays portraying the children's work and the process behind their creativity? Do the children's learning journeys demonstrate how the constructive relationship with the key person has enabled sustained shared thinking and helped the child make progress in their thinking and understanding?

Candidates may wish to develop peer observations to include how staff relate to children and identify areas for development leading to staff training.

Standard 25 reflection points

- Ask staff to think about the following question: What does our setting look like through the eyes of a child? Staff could either take an area of the setting or an area of learning to examine over a period of time. Relationships would be a useful focus for this
- Hold a staff meeting to review findings and formulate an action plan. This would be good evidence of how you lead and support colleagues in developing their practice in this area.

Standard 25 stakeholder comment

Alice Apel is the head/owner of three settings: Atherton House School in Crosby; Homeland Day Nursery, Altrincham and Richmond House Kindergarten, Hale. Alice undertook the validation only pathway in September 2007.

This standard is sometimes considered by candidates to be challenging in terms of finding 'proof'. Firstly Alice reflected on the focus of this standard in terms of how she could evidence a relationship with children and show how she built fair and respectful relationships with the children and also how she promoted that with her staff. As an initial step, Alice discussed this with the manager of one of her settings, Jackie, and asked key questions such as 'how do I do this?' and 'how do you know that I do this?' As a result of this, Alice approached evidencing the standard in several ways through the varied opportunities for presenting evidence that exist in the assessment process.

One of the things that Alice discussed was the way in which she engaged the children in finding out their opinions on things such as the choice of lunch menus, and showed how she respected their opinion, changing content and choices – in one case adding more sweetcorn as a vegetable choice! This also demonstrated how she involves the children in decisions that concern them.

Alice found that finding documentary evidence for this standard was challenging until Jackie suggested annotated photographs which showed Alice engaging with the children in constructive ways and showed a progression of asking opinions and acting on the feedback from the children. She included this in her evidence file and, of course, essential to demonstrating the standard with this evidence was the annotation that went with the photographs themselves.

Key to demonstrating this standard, however, was the witness evidence provided during the assessment visit itself. The witnesses that Alice nominated were briefed

→

by her beforehand on what the standards meant and she had discussed with them how she showed the standards in her practice. The responses that they gave in the interviews told of how she modelled behaviours to form positive, supportive and constructive relationships with children. In each case, the witnesses were able to give examples of the practice that they had seen Alice demonstrate or the way in which she supported them as practitioners to do this in their own practice.

Additionally, the tour evidence also showed how Alice related to the children when they approached her during this part of the visit. Alice asked open-ended questions of the children when talking to them and this was noted by the assessor.

This blended approach enabled Alice to give a strong account of how she met this standard and supported others in their practice.

Standard 26 – communicate sensitively and effectively with children from birth to the end of the foundation stage

Example of standard 26 in personal practice

Communication is not just about the words you use, but also your manner of speaking, body language and, above all, the effectiveness with which you listen. To communicate effectively it is important to take account of culture and context, for example where English is an additional language.

(DfES, 2005: 6)

This standard requires the candidate to consider the development of communi-cation skills from birth to 5 years of age and be confident in their own ability to communicate with all children in this age range.

A baby begins to learn to communicate from the moment of birth; they soon learn that a cry gains attention and that adults will respond to the sounds they make. They are beginning to learn the purpose of communication; that these sounds elicit a response and their needs will be met. The successful candidate will be able to demonstrate their understanding of how communication involves listening, not only with the ears but with the eyes, heart and mind so that we can 'pick up' on the cues other people are giving us (Robinson, 2008).

Robinson continues to discuss how the way we dress the children or dress ourselves, our piercings and tattoos, all communicate a message to others. The candidate must show a clear understanding of these issues when dealing with babies and children who use non-verbal communication.

As a baby learns that making certain sounds ensures their needs are met, they soon discover the pleasure of communicating with others, they realise that when they make sounds, adults join in. Adults usually make high-pitched singing sounds – infant-directed speech (IDS) or 'motherese', when talking to young children. This is a natural response and is effective because a baby's hearing is set at a considerably higher level than our own, so they hear it clearly and enjoy the sound.

The overall pitch of infant-directed utterances is higher, and the pitch range is expanded. Although the extent to which pitch is expanded is culturally determined, expansion itself has been observed in many different languages and cultures, even in languages where pitch can distinguish meaning, i.e. tone languages. IDS also has a slower tempo than adult-directed speech. The syllable nuclei are considerably stretched (de Boer, 2005).

Becoming confident enough to communicate with young babies in this way can be very difficult, but experience will show that babies respond to this type of speech in a positive way even if the speaker is using a different language to the one with which they are familiar. As children grow older, they realise that communication is an excellent way to learn; they are innately curious and using language allows them to ask questions, experiment and consider the mysteries of the world around them.

The practitioner should show how they value these blossoming communication skills and need to demonstrate their understanding that communication is a two-way process and how they use this to develop positive relationships.

Lee (2006) conducted research into the development of relationships in a childcare context and observed that developing a strong relationship was of great importance to both the children and the carer: 'Relationship development also made for easy and smooth communication, sharing of thoughts and emotions and mutual understanding between infant and care giver' (Lee, 2006: 146).

The candidate will show their understanding of how developing this communication and a sound positive relationship will take time and therefore understand that it cannot be rushed. They may contribute to policies and procedures which will highlight this, and in practice will ensure that they give themselves and the child time and space to learn about each other.

In the effective provision of pre-school education (EPPE) report (Sylva *et al.*, 2004), the authors highlighted that the quality of interactions between staff and children were particularly important; where staff showed warmth and were responsive to the individual needs of children, children made more progress. This emphasises the need for the candidate to have a good relationship with each of their key children and use their communication skills to ensure that they meet their individual needs.

Children with learning difficulties, disabilities or English as an additional language may need provision to be adapted for them. The candidate will be aware of this and will be able to differentiate practice without the child feeling different and excluded from the rest of the group. Through effective communication EYPs will understand children's learning styles, their interests, their fears and what stimulates their imagination. Practitioners can change their approach for the more confident child and the reserved child, enabling them both to feel safe and secure in the setting. Through this insightful understanding, the candidate can then ensure appropriate time and opportunities are provided for the child to play, experiment, socialise and through these activities develop their communication skills.

Developing this relationship will allow the candidate to understand the child. They will notice changes in behaviour, however slight, and because of their knowledge of the child will be able to discover sensitively and effectively what it is that is affecting her/him, thus enabling them to deal with the problem quickly and efficiently.

Example of standard 26 in leadership

Grenier (DCSF, 2008) states that practitioners also need to use the skills they have developed from experience and training: communicating in a way that is appropriate to the child's development, remaining calm and ensuring that an orderly environment is maintained for all the children in the group.

The candidate needs to demonstrate this calm control to their staff; they must exemplify good practice and highlight the importance of good communication. In many busy settings, the quiet, reserved child may access activities, appear occupied and never misbehave, and as a result they attract little attention and may not communicate with an adult for more than a few brief minutes upon arrival. The candidate must be aware of this and encourage staff to spend time with all their key children. They may provide training and write policies to support staff development in this area.

They will provide new members of staff with an experienced mentor to help them develop the necessary communication skills. Talking to babies and young children is not always a natural skill, and many inexperienced staff will feel ridiculous trying to use IDS; they also need time and space to develop these skills so that they understand why babies respond to these sounds, and so feel confident doing it. They will also need to gain experience across the age range to develop their understanding of how a child's communication skills develop from non-verbal to verbal and that, even when linguistically confident, non-verbal communication is still very important even in adulthood. The candidate must ensure that all staff have opportunities to develop this level of understanding.

The candidate can become involved in programmes such as I CAN, a children's communication charity which runs accredited training programmes to enable practitioners to develop children's communication skills.

Every Child a Talker (ECaT) is a national project to develop the language and communication of children from birth to 4 years of age. It was produced because of concern for the low standards of language acquisition in the UK and resulting poor progress in school. The candidate may undertake training for ECaT and cascade this to members of staff to ensure that all children in their setting receive the best possible opportunities to develop sound language skills.

They may also consider enabling staff to study alternative methods of communication, such as Makaton, sign language including baby signing, and the picture exchange communication system (PECS). These will all enhance the children's communication skills whatever their age or ability.

Standard 26 reflection points

- Make a list of the different languages spoken in your setting. Do you have similar resources to support each one?
- Consider how effective these resources are. Do they meet all the children's and parents'/carers' needs, or are they token gestures?
- Reflect upon your list of languages. Have you considered spoken language only or have you considered non-verbal communication?
- How can you ensure that your staff understand all of these methods of communication?

Standard 26 stakeholder comment

Jill Elizabeth Anderton BSc (Hons) is an early years professional and daycare provider, implementing 'effective' childcare and development strategies whilst placing importance on a skilled and 'varied' staff team with positive professional relationships.

Jill had a wide variety of evidence for this standard. She had observed children and practitioners communicating in a variety of situations and used these to

→

→

develop her planning, ensuring that she provided space and time for staff to develop their communication skills and role model these to the children. Jill also used her observations to assess children's current level of development and plan for next steps, ensuring that children's interests were used to help them feel safe and confident when engaging in the activities. This individualised planning also supported those children with special educational needs (SEN).

As part of her documentary evidence, she included minutes from a speech and language therapy meeting (depersonalised) discussing a child with specific language difficulties and working with the therapist to deliver an agreed programme to support the child. Another piece of documentary evidence was examples of learning journeys, highlighting children's development in this area and how she had involved parents in this, giving them support and encouragement to help their child's communication skills at home.

Jill showed her leadership in this standard by including minutes from staff training that she had delivered on developing communication skills. This highlighted the variety of ways in which young children communicate and the benefits of effective communication with children, finding the way that is best for them, be it speech, signing, Makaton or some other method. She also encouraged staff to observe how the family communicated with the child as this might provide new methods to ensure effective communication with them.

Standard 27 – listen to children, pay attention to what they say and value and respect their views

Example of standard 27 in personal practice

The United Nations Convention on the Rights of the Child states in Article 12:

> Parties shall assure to the child who is capable of forming his or her own views the right to express those views freely in all matters affecting the child, the views of the child being given due weight in accordance with the age and maturity of the child.

The UN convention was subsequently ratified by the UK government when the committee responsible for this process added a general comment to Article 12:

> Respect for the views and feelings of the young child. The Committee wishes to emphasise that article 12 applies to both younger and to older children. As holders of rights, even the youngest children are entitled to express their views.

This highlights the importance of listening to children and taking their thoughts, feelings and needs into consideration. Gordon-Smith (2008) describes how she observed children in a setting that valued children's choices by encouraging them to move freely around the well resourced environment. She noticed an instant change when children were asked to sit on the carpet for a large group session. The children's behaviour changed, and the practitioners felt the sessions were disrupted:

> Involving the children in shaping these sessions – sharing their news, choosing a story or talking about what they wanted to do tomorrow – would have shown the same respect for their opinions and abilities as existed in all other aspects of the setting. Greater involvement may also have engaged the children's interest more fully, enabling them to be constructive members of the group and helping practitioners to feel under less pressure.
> (Gordon-Smith, 2008: 22)

This standard does not simply refer to listening to children's choices but has wider implications. The amplification for standard 27 says, 'children have a right to be listened to and for their responses and views to be taken seriously about matters that affect them' (standards).

The candidate should be aware of projects such as Young Children's Voices Network (YCVN), which is a national project working with local authorities to develop listening in the early years, enabling policies and practice to reflect young children's views, and the Children's Rights Alliance for England, which works to protect the rights of the child and is part of Participation Works – 'a consortium of six national children and young people's agencies that enables organisations to effectively involve children and young people in the development, delivery and evaluation of services that affect their lives' (CRAE, 2010). These projects emphasise the need to listen to young children's opinions in all areas. Does the candidate consider the children's interests and experiences when acquiring new resources, or are they thinking of how to make the setting look more interesting to adults? When creating new policies and procedures, are the children's thoughts included, and how do they feel about the actions adults decide for them?

Showing the children that they have been listened to is of paramount importance. If the suggestion is unrealistic, the candidate should show that they have considered it and explain to the child why it is not feasible, going on to develop a discussion about how their ideas may be adapted to be workable. The candidate will support children to understand that adults will listen to them and respect what they say; they will know that their ideas and views are valued because the adults will act upon them and involve them in the changes made because of what they have said. This will develop the children's self-confidence and encourage them to share more ideas. Knowing that they have a right to be listened to and heard will help them to listen and hear others and acquire skills of working in pairs and small groups, such as taking turns in a conversation.

Bryson (2007) discusses how she 'listened to' the views of babies accessing a 'baby social'. She and her colleagues observed the children over 6 weeks and recorded the types of activities they engaged with, what they liked and what they didn't; they also consulted with parents and key workers for their views. This way they could ensure that effective provision was made for all of the children. This method of listening to the children was then implemented in toddler groups and became a regular practice.

The candidate must be able to provide evidence of how they listen to the children in their care and how they show the children that their ideas are valued. This may be through similar observations and demonstrating how the findings are put into practice and that the process is ongoing so that changing interests and familiarity with resources are noted and appropriate changes made, enabling the children to gain in confidence and enthusiasm.

In practice the candidate will make a concerted effort to ensure that all children are listened to equally and all ideas and opinions are considered, protecting the children from discrimination. They will investigate ways of ensuring that every child, at whatever age or stage of development, is heard. There are many ways of 'listening' to young children. Observing a baby's reactions to certain situations and resources will inform you of how they feel. This knowledge will influence practitioners to change procedures, activities or resources, and further observations will enable them to understand how the baby feels about this.

Young toddlers may have a limited vocabulary. The candidate may use different methods of 'listening'. This may involve mark-making or taking photographs of what they like or dislike. The close bond that forms between the candidate as a key person and the children in their group enables them to become familiar with the subtle nuances that each child displays, such as the different cries, facial expressions and movements, all of which may be lost to the casual observer, but which the key person will know and understand.

The successful candidate will be able to demonstrate not only how they listen to children, but also how they show that they respect and value their views. A way of evidencing this could be recording their observations and how they are used for assessment and planning; recording findings in learning journeys and how the candidate has implemented changes because of the findings.

Example of standard 27 in leadership

The candidate will be able to demonstrate that listening to children is a key principle in their setting. They will be aware of the variety of experiences that young children have of being listened to. While some may speak one to one with an adult and engage in rich conversations that value their thoughts and ideas on a frequent basis, others may have very few such opportunities and may even find not speaking to be more rewarding. Research has shown that many children feel that parents do not listen to them (O'Hare, 2006) and, while the EYFS specifies speaking and listening as part of the communication, language and literacy area of learning, how much emphasis is put on listening?

The candidate will ensure that colleagues understand the importance of listening, not just to ask for children's opinions on new resources or what they would like in the role-play area, but consistently to find out the child's interests and understanding, their needs and feelings.

The candidate will ensure that the staff understand the role of the key worker in its entirety by ensuring adequate staff training and role modelling high-quality practice. They need to ensure that adults are confident in interpreting body language to assess how both verbal and non-verbal children are feeling as well as using appropriate body language themselves to encourage children to initiate conversations and invite child interactions.

They will use staff observations to consider the ways in which adults talk and engage with the children, and discuss the language used and discuss whether it allows children to express feelings or views or simply answer 'yes' or 'no'? Is their practice equally effective for children with English as an additional language or with limited vocabulary?

Young children may reveal personal information of a sensitive nature and the candidate should have implemented clear policies and procedures for staff to follow so that any concerns can be addressed in the correct manner.

Standard 27 reflection points

- Observe members of staff in their interactions with children. Do all practitioners listen to children's ideas, thoughts and needs?
- Consider how practitioners show this – is it reflected in assessment and planning? Do they change their approach as a result of communication with the children? Do they take what they hear seriously?
- Video your own practice. How well do you listen?

Standard 27 stakeholder comment

Leon Coupe spent 25 years in the family business before deciding to return to education. He started to do some volunteer assistant work with reception classes and completed a returner's course for the primary phase but it wasn't until he went for EYP status on the full time pathway that things really took off. After dropping off his CV with several local nurseries, he was taken on as a practitioner, with funding to support a child with additional needs. When, after a year, that funding ended, he managed to find another position, this time as a senior practitioner, and will soon be moving to a partner setting as the EYP to lead and support changes in the setting. He loves his job, and working with team management and practitioners, and being part of the development and education of children in the early years is the most satisfying thing he has ever done. He is excited by the possibility of the move to another setting and finally stepping into the role of EYP. He believes that this is the start, not the end.

Leon found the remarkable thing about the evidence for standard 27 was that it also supports standards 25, 26, and 28. In other words, the practice of listening, supporting, talking with and modelling all go together and seem to be embedded in his practice.

The evidence covered in the file ranged from the profiles of children, plans and notes for activities, observations which fed into planning, development tasks and write-ups of supporting child-initiated activities. Of 23 evidence documents, 13 supported the standards involving relationships with children.

Leon was able to evidence these standards not just in written accounts but was able to demonstrate good relationships, including listening to and taking on board the contributions of children. He had a practitioner to support his evidence as they worked in the same room and the practitioner observed him. The director of operations at the setting also monitored him and acted as a witness. So his evidence was a mixture of his own accounts and being able to call on witnesses who were in a position to comment and who were willing to discuss their observation of him across his work in all settings. He used experiences of supporting heuristic play outdoors; of exploration of a pomegranate; of a shell-sorting activity; three children's profiles; supporting play with ICT; an account of supporting child-initiated play watering plants; an account of making an interactive jungle display; an account of introducing and reorganising outdoor resources and an account of working to support a child who was not walking or talking in the setting.

He was aware of the wide range of opportunities to listen to children, to pay attention to what they say, and to value and respect their views, and utilised these to produce high quality evidence that he met this standard.

Standard 28 – demonstrate the positive values, attitudes and behaviour they expect from children

Example of standard 28 in personal practice

No printed word, nor spoken plea can teach young minds what they should be. Not all the books on all the shelves – but what the teachers are themselves. (Rudyard Kipling)

The successful candidate will be able to provide evidence that they understand the values and attitudes that children should be encouraged to develop from the earliest age. They will have a full understanding of the Development Matters section of the EYFS for personal, social and emotional development. Candidates will encourage young babies to become familiar with routines and people. They will ensure that the key person approach is functioning well and that staff have time and support to develop a sound relationship with their group. Babies who have developed close attachments tend to be more content and happier, their key person has an in-depth knowledge of their routines and reactions and can identify when there is something amiss. This close relationship ensures that problems are dealt with quickly and in the correct way for the baby, which in turn leads to the baby feeling safe and secure, confident and happy.

This relationship will continue to develop and enable the key person consistently to support and encourage the child to recognise boundaries and consider the consequences of their actions.

The candidate will ensure that the learning environment is stimulating and adequately resourced so that children are able to be occupied and investigate. Resources will be at the children's height and suitably marked to enable children to access them, giving them confidence to make choices. They will develop the child's confidence that they will be able to have a turn using equipment and that they will not have to leave their activity suddenly because of lack of time, all of which can contribute to a child reacting negatively.

The candidate will feel confident demonstrating the values and attitudes that they wish children to develop. They will show that they value the children by their attitude toward them and the emphasis that they put on ensuring that they receive a quality experience whilst in the setting. They will show that they value children's work by displaying it with pride, saving part finished pieces for the child to return to when they are next able.

Fisher (2008) discusses how encouraging children to understand why they need rules and supporting them in creating their own is a successful way of encouraging them to take responsibility for their own behaviour. Good relationships with children enable the candidate to understand how to adapt formal theories of behaviour management to meet the needs of individuals. Moore and Sutcliffe (2009: 68) discuss how 'all learning behaviour is dependent upon relationships'. They go on to examine how these relationships are influenced by a wide variety of factors and that practitioners need to observe for these external influences so that they can be addressed quickly and efficiently.

Successful candidates will be aware of how a young child observes their behaviour and that they need to set an excellent example to help children to develop positive values, skills and behaviour. They will always give priority to the children; they will listen and act on what they hear. They will address unaccept-able behaviour quickly and appropriately and give positive reinforcement to all children, not just those who demand attention.

Example of standard 28 in leadership

As an effective leader, the candidate will be aware of the need to role model positive values, behaviour and attitudes not only to the children but also to col-leagues and students. Some adults in the setting may still regard their role as a supervisor of children's play and not give all their attention to their work. If they do not see a leader taking on this role, they may be inclined to think that this method of working is acceptable; therefore it is essential that the candidate shows strong leadership in this area.

The candidate will ensure that colleagues understand the importance of their behaviour and how children naturally imitate what they see. They will ensure that colleagues develop their own values and attitudes that support the development of the child, so that they are genuine in their approach: '...children can be most perceptive, sometimes far more than adults, and will see through the lack of integrity of any educator' (Rose, 2004: 1).

The candidate will ensure that staff have access to continuous professional development, both internally and, if possible, external courses. Staff need to develop a deep understanding of the ways in which children learn and that their role in this is highly significant. A consideration that the candidate as a leader may want to take into account is how, in a large number of early years settings, colleagues live locally and children may see them outside of the setting. It is important for staff to understand that role modelling does not only happen in the setting but in their behaviour outside too.

A major influence on the children will be the attitude of colleagues and students towards each other. Children learn a lot from this observed behaviour and the successful candidate will be aware of any stresses or difficulties within these relationships and ensure that they are addressed immediately. Staff must treat themselves, others and the children with respect at all times and the candidate is integral in this process. A good leader will listen to staff and involve them in all aspects of provision and ensure that they feel valued and respected; this will influence how they behave as role models for the children.

Standard 28 reflection points

- Consider your own interactions with all stakeholders in this past week. Do you feel you acted appropriately at all times? Did you feel uncomfortable or leave a situation feeling you could have addressed it in a different way? Write down these occasions. What do you think went wrong? How can you develop your practice to ensure you are more effective in the future?
- Observe your staff within the setting. What sort of role models are they? Is there a common area for development? How can you address this?
- Do any of your staff live locally? Are you confident that they understand the need to demonstrate positive values, attitudes and behaviour when they are not at work as well as when they are?

Standard 28 stakeholder comment

Jennifer Lee is an associate tutor at Edge Hill University. She completed her postgraduate certificate in education and then accessed the full time EYPS course.

Jenny organised a visit from a dental health professional for a group of 13 children aged from 2 to 5 years of age during her final placement. The reason for this visit was Jenny's good relationships with the children and her observations of them enthusiastically brushing their teeth after lunch every day and asking questions about teeth. The visit was arranged and the children were prepared through stories and role-play. Jenny discussed their visitor and explained what the lady was going to talk about. When the visitor arrived, Jenny greeted her and introduced her to the children, role modelling how to greet a visitor and demonstrating that this new person was approachable and friendly. She supported the children to join in and say hello. Jenny ensured that more reserved children

→

had a key person to support them so that they felt safe and confident enough to join in.

The visitor had been supported with information on the age, interests and number of children and was able to address them appropriately, using a large toy rabbit to demonstrate tooth brushing. The key person and Jenny were on hand to join in and role model expected behaviour to the children; this gave them confidence to join in and enjoy the activities.

When the visitor had finished talking to the children Jenny thanked her for coming to see them and asked the children to say thank you too. The visitor said how much she had enjoyed her visit and how well behaved the children were. She gave stickers to the children and some colouring sheets to reinforce what they had learnt and to support discussion later with their parents.

Jenny learnt that role modelling activities is a very effective way of helping children to learn. The children not only learnt about brushing their teeth but they also learnt about how to behave with visitors, therefore focusing on their personal, social and emotional development in a different way. Also, very importantly, Jenny learnt that there are plenty of adults in varying roles who may be able to come in to the nursery to talk and role model values, attitudes and behaviour; it is not just the regular staff who will take on this role.

Conclusion

The group of standards 'relationships with children' encourages the EYP to recognise the importance of good relationships and understand how this is the basis for any learning to take place. There is a particular emphasis in standard 26 on effective communication with children from birth to 5, and the full age range must be covered to achieve this standard. EYPs are required to help colleagues understand how listening to children can help the adults to understand the child's thinking and identify their interests.

References

Bowlby, J. (1979) *The Making and Breaking of Affectional Bonds*. London: Tavistock.

Brown, B. (1994) *Unlearning Discrimination in the Early Years*. London: The Cromwell Press.

Bruce, T. (2005) *Early Childhood Education*. London: Hodder Arnold.

Bryson, S. (2007) Listening to the views of very young children. Available from http://www.teachingexpertise.com/articles/listening-to-the-views-of-very-young-children-2500 (accessed 28 September 2010).

CRAE (2010) *Participation Rights*. Available from http://www.crae.org.uk/networks/participation.html (accessed 27 September 2010).

DCSF. (2008) *The Early Years Foundation Stage*. Nottigham: DCSF.

DCSF. (2010) *Support for All: the Families and Relationships Green Paper*. London: TSO.

de Boer, B. (2005) Infant directed speech and the evolution of language. In: M. Tallerman (ed.) *Evolutionary Prerequisites for Language*. Oxford: Oxford University Press, pp. 100–21.

DfES. (2005) *The Common Core of Skills and Knowledge*. Nottingham: DfES.

Doherty, J., Hughes, M. (2009) *Child Development: Right from the Start*. London: Pearson.

Elfer, P., Goldschmeid, E., Selleck, D. (2005) *Key Persons in the Nursery*. London: Routledge.

Fisher, J. (2008) *Starting from the Child*. Maidenhead: McGraw Hill.

Gordon-Smith, P. (2008) All about . . . children's rights. *Nursery World,* July 2008: 19–22.

Lansdown, G. (2001) Progress in implementing the rights in the convention. In: S. Hart, C.P. Cohen, M.F. Erickson and M. Flekkoy (eds) *Children's Rights in Education*. London: Jessica Kingsley Publishers.

Lee, S.Y. (2006) A journey to a close, secure and synchronous relationship: infant–caregiver relationship development in a childcare context. *Journal of Early Childhood Research,* **4**(2): 133–51.

Moore, A., Sutcliffe, J. (2009) Behaviour for learning. In: A., Walton, G. Goddard (eds) *Supporting Every Child*. Exeter: Learning Matters.

Oates, J., Woodhead, M. (2007) In: J. Oates (ed.) *Early Childhood in Focus 1: Attachment Relationships*. Milton Keynes: The Open University.

O'Hare, N. (2006) *Listener – the Things that Matter*. Available from http://www.literacytrust.org.uk/talktoyourbaby/Listening.html (Accessed 17 September 2006).

Qvortrup, J., Bardy, M., Sgritta, G., Wintersberger, H. (1994) *Childhood Matters: Social Theory, Practice and Politics*. Aldershot: Avebury.

Robinson, M. (2008) Child development. Your guide to the first five years, part 8. *Nursery World,* June 2008.

Rose, D. (2004) *The Potential of Role-model Education, the Encyclopaedia of Informal Education*. Available from www.infed.org/biblio/role_model_education.htm (accessed 29 September 2010).

Sylva, K., Melhuish, E., Sammons, P., Siraj-Blatchford, I., Taggart, B. (2004) *Effective Provision of Pre-School Education*. Nottingham: DfES.

Thomas, N. (2005) Sociology of childhood. In: T. Maynard, N. Thomas. *An Introduction to Early Childhood Studies*. London: Sage.

Chapter 6

Communicating and working in partnership with families and carers

Introduction

This chapter deals with how to build constructive relationships with families and with recognising the contribution they have to make and how information can be shared between the setting and the family.

Objectives

By the end of this chapter you should have:

- Gained an overview of the key theoretical perspectives on the importance of establishing and maintaining effective partnership with families and carers
- Reflected on how you can promote through your practice the requirements identified in standards 29–32
- Reflected on how you can lead and support others in relation to the requirements identified in standards 29–32.

Theoretical underpinning knowledge for standards 29–32

'Never fear spoiling children by making them too happy. Happiness is the atmosphere in which all good affections grow.' These words belong to Dr Thomas Bray, a famous English clergyman of the seventeenth century. Today, in the twenty-first century, this idea still remains relevant: we still believe that happy children achieve more, and that every child deserves the best possible start in life to fulfil their potential. A happy and secure childhood is important in its own right, and it provides the base from which children grow and develop to make the most of their abilities and talents. Much developmental research has focused on the fact that a child's experiences in the early years have a major impact on their future life chances. We all recognise that one of the key factors contributing to children's wellbeing and happiness depends on the quality of their relationships with the people they love and to whom they are attached. As the Early Years Foundation Stage (EYFS) document (DCSF, 2008) states, children learn to be strong and independent from a base of loving and secure relationships with parents and/ or a key person. Without any doubt, parents, carers and families in general have the most powerful influences on children's lives, especially during the early years of their lives. This group of standards (29–32) lays emphasis on the importance for EYPs to appreciate these influences, to establish and maintain respectful and constructive relationships with children's families and to involve parents and carers as much as possible in a mutual information sharing process in relation to their child's learning and development.

The impact of parent–child relationships on a child's overall development has been most explicitly acknowledged in the work of a number of theorists and researchers. In his attachment theory, Bowlby (1979) argued that children have a tendency to make strong affective bonds to their parents and carers throughout life. The bonds, or attachment relationships, that are formed in the first 3 years of children's lives are especially important for children's social and emotional development in the future. According to Bowlby, children can form two types of attachment with their primary carers – secure and insecure. Children who form secure attachments are more likely to see the world around them as a much safer and happier place, whereas children with insecure attachment relationships often develop different forms of personality disorders, emotional distress, anxiety, depression and emotional detachment. Key aspects of Bowlby's theory of attachment can provide EYPs with additional criteria for understanding various patterns of child–parent relationships and the ways in which children and parents/carers relate to each other in times of stress.

In his theory, Vygotsky (1978), a follower of social constructivism, also referred extensively to the importance of positive child–parent relationships. He argued that children's cognitive development is a result of a dialectical process, where the children co-create meaning out of their early interactions with parents and other adults around them as well as with their siblings and peers. Vygotsky's theory considers language to be an essential part of this process, as it is the developmental advancement of the language skills supported and encouraged mainly by the parents that will help children to shape their understanding of the world around them. The more positive parent–child interactions that children have, the more enhanced their development becomes.

Vygotsky argued that parent–child verbal communication provides the child with certain clues to understanding, reflecting upon and expressing themselves in a variety of social situations. During the early years of children's development, parents take more responsibility in the process of creating and co-creating these clues together with the child. Later on, these messages are internalised by the child as the child develops their own skill of problem-solving in a variety of social contexts. As a result, social interaction and communication with parents and carers contribute significantly to a child's cognitive development.

Along with the belief that parents and carers co-construct meaning together with a child and that this meaning is ultimately internalised by the child, Vygotsky also argued that the process of acquiring this new meaning results in the 'zone of proximal development' (ZPD), which Vygotsky described as '. . . the distance between the actual development level as determined by independent problem solving and the level of potential development as determined through problem solving under adult guidance . . .' (Vygotsky, 1978: 86). Undoubtedly, for a child to achieve their full developmental potential, parents and carers need not only to expose the child to as many social situations as possible, but also to introduce children to the ideas and concepts that are above their existing level of understanding.

Vygotsky' s ideas are also reflected in more recent research into the impact of positive support provided to young children by adults and the importance of developing effective partnerships with parents. The key messages from the research findings suggest that children thrive when surrounded by loving and sensitive adults who are knowledgeable, sensitive and responsive to the children's needs, genuinely interested in their progress and who can provide a safe, secure and stimulating environment (Researching Effective Pedagogy in the Early Years – REPEY, 2002; Effective Provision of Pre-School Education – EPPE, 2003; Parents as Partners in Early Learning – PPEL, 2007).

Understanding theories that call attention to the importance of parent–child relationships can guide EYPs toward better understanding of the value of working in partnership with families and carers, and consequently toward better social and intellectual outcomes for children. The EYFS (DCSF, 2008) places a legal obligation on all early years practitioners to work in partnerships with parents: 'Parents are children's first and most enduring educators. When parents and practitioners work together in early years settings, the results have a positive impact on children's learning and development.' Evidence from recent research studies shows that most successful early years settings put every effort into developing good communication with parents and encouraging high levels of their involvement.

Standard 29 – recognise and respect the influential and enduring contribution that families and parents/carers can make to children's development, well-being and learning

Example of standard 29 in personal practice

Parents' influence is important throughout childhood and adolescence. At different times parents guide, encourage and teach. Children learn from the example set by their parents. The support that parents give for their children's cognitive development is important, as is instilling of values, aspirations and support for the development of wider interpersonal and social skills (DfES, 2007: 5).

Although there are distinct links between each of the standards in this group, standard 29 has a distinct focus on parents and carers being the foremost and most enduring influence on children's early development. The key focus of this standard is to establish a partnership with parents and carers to improve outcomes for children on the basis of respect and shared responsibility.

The phrase 'parents are their children's first educators' is used frequently, but perhaps a more appropriate expression is '. . . parents are their child's first and continuing educators . . .' (Lindon, 2006: 72). This acknowledges the ongoing contribution that parents make to their children's learning and highlights the need for EYPs to recognise this and use the parents'/carers' understanding of their child to ensure that children's individual needs are met.

EYPs will need to demonstrate that they know how and why parents and carers play a crucial role in children's wellbeing, learning and development. The Children's Plan (2007) clearly outlines the importance of the family and their influence on children's development, wellbeing and learning. It states that 'families are the bedrock of society and the place for nurturing happy capable and resilient children' (DfES, 2007: 5).

In today's diverse society, the EYPS candidate needs to be aware of a child's culture, ethnicity and history. An early step towards this would be to go on home visits before the child starts at the setting. This enables the practitioner to begin the relationship with the parent/carers at a very early stage, and time is available to discuss these issues and the practitioner can prepare any special requirements for the child or family before they attend regularly. The practitioner also has the opportunity to discuss the parent's views on early childhood education, assess how they contribute to their child's learning and development and share the principles of the EYFS with them so that they can begin to understand the practice within the setting.

The *Guidance to the Standards* (CWDC, 2008) clarifies what assessors are looking for when it says:

Assessors will judge whether candidates for EYPS:

- recognise and value the influential and enduring contribution that parents can make to children's well-being, learning and development by working positively in partnership with them;
- work to create and sustain opportunities to involve parents as active partners in their children's well-being, learning and development;
- lead and support colleagues in recognising and making the most of parents' contribution to children's well-being, learning and development.

Although this outlines what is being sought, what does this look like in practice?

EYPs' recognition of the important role of parents may be reflected in several ways. How to do this in practice will vary according to the role in the setting and the overarching philosophy that the setting has. For many the challenge may be making contact with some hard-to-reach parents and carers. Not all families are the same and for some parents the setting may be seen as a forbidding place because of their own experiences as a child. This can be a barrier to contact and something of which the EYP needs to be aware. As EYPs we need to approach the family situation with professionalism, empathy and care.

In practice some of the ways in which a candidate can show their recognition of the vital contribution that parents make can be through ensuring that they listen to parents with due respect when they do have contact with them.

This means making time to talk to them, maintaining eye contact and ensuring that your body language tells them that you are listening to them. This needs to happen from the earliest stages in the candidate's relationship with the parent/carers. As the key person, the candidate needs to value the family's beliefs and principles, recording significant information that will enable them to understand the child's previous experiences and their interests and abilities. The candidate also needs to give time on a regular basis to enable parents to share their child's experiences outside of the setting to enable the candidate to adapt planning appropriately, ensuring that new experiences and interests are included. Parents/carers may also wish to join in with activities, or develop their understanding of the EYFS. Candidates should encourage this and give them opportunities to do so. This may involve the parents working with the children and the candidate supporting them, or informative open events in which the candidate may take part to enable parents to understand the EYFS principles and how the setting puts them into practice.

Showing that the EYP values their contributions and actively acts upon the information shared is a valuable way of showing that respect and building an effective partnership. Involving parents in the experiences of the setting is one such vehicle to enable this.

Example of standard 29 in leadership

The leadership aspect of this standard involves the candidate supporting colleagues to develop a secure understanding of the contribution that parents make to their child's development, wellbeing and learning. This will involve staff training, role modelling and innovative practices which help to develop the contribution from parents/carers and families.

Candidates may review current practices, examining when and how the parents/carers are consulted, and how this information is used. They may utilise the skills, talents and experience of parents to develop learning within the setting and to create exciting new experiences for the children. There may be opportunities for training to hold courses for parents, to enable them to understand how their children learn and the best ways to support this. A successful EYP candidate will have investigated a wide variety of methods of involving parents in their child's learning and, in consultation with colleagues, will have implemented the most beneficial for the child, the parents and families, and the setting.

Standard 29 reflection points

- Review the home visiting policy/procedure in your setting. Is it a time for staff to give information about the setting or is it time for staff, parents and child to share information about each other?
- Observe the staff in the setting when children arrive and depart. How much time is given to each parent? Do staff support each other when it is busy? How could you develop this opportunity to share information?
- How are parents' contributions used? Is this visible to all – observation sheets, planning sheets? How can this be developed so that parents can see that their contributions are valued and utilised?
- Evaluate the ways your setting promotes parent involvement. Are there areas for improvement?
- Research ways of developing parents' understanding of the EYFS principles and what they look like in practice. How can you encourage parents to use these principles to develop the child's learning at home?

Standard 29 stakeholder comment

Julie Thornton is the registered person and owner of Eagley School House Nursery in Bolton. Julie spends her time supporting the whole staff team and manager as well as working with all the different age ranges of children as a key person.

As evidence for standard 29 Julie showed how she had set up a reception area in the building where parents and children could take books and games home together to share. The reception area also had lots of information for parents, including the EYFS document which parents could take home. Julie had also created books of events such as trips out to show the parents some of the experiences that the children encounter at the setting. Julie shared this with the staff and encouraged the practitioners to contribute to this development.

In every room and the reception area, Julie had supported the staff to display notice boards on the EYFS. One example was that sticky notes were left on the bottom of every board on which parents could write comments about their children's experiences. This encouraged a three-way relationship between the parent, child and practitioners, enabling parents to recognise that their contribution was important.

Since gaining EYPS, Julie has now progressed onto mentoring other EYPS students, offering advice, support and practical tips throughout the process.

Standard 30 – establish fair, respectful, trusting and constructive relationships with families and parents/carers and communicate sensitively and effectively with them

Example of standard 30 in personal practice

The fact that parents are a child's first educators is well documented. Froebel believed that it was necessary to work closely with the family, as the child will imitate what he/she knows through a direct and real relationship, things learned through familiarity in everyday family life (Dewey, 1990). This highlights the importance of developing sound relationships with parents and carers to enable candidates to be aware of the family's individual circumstances and to better understand the child's previous experiences to build upon them to enable the child to progress.

The EYFS theme 'Positive Relationships' has four commitments to achieving excellent relationships with parents:

2.1 Respecting each other: every interaction is based on caring professional relationships and respectful acknowledgement of the feelings of children and their families.

2.2 Parents as partners: parents are children's first and enduring educators. When parents and practitioners work together in early years settings, the results have a positive impact on children's development and learning.

2.3 Supporting learning: warm, trusting relationships with knowledgeable adults support children's learning more effectively than any amount of resources.

2.4 Key person: a key person has special responsibilities for working with a small number of children, giving them the reassurance to feel safe and cared for and building relationships with their parents.

Candidates may show their understanding of this in the way in which they respond to the parent's/carer's initial enquiries. When parents choose the first setting for their child, they may have very individual perceptions of what is ideal, but one of the deciding factors will definitely be whether the setting has a welcoming atmosphere, friendly, caring staff and happy children. First impressions are of vital importance and will form the basis of any future relationships.

In practice the candidate will look for ways of ensuring that parents/carers and families feel welcome in the setting. This begins from the first contact with the parents. The candidate will ensure that he or she is friendly and approachable; s/he will be knowledgeable and honest, answering initial queries and inviting the parents/carers to visit the setting and discuss their child's needs and require-ments. The candidate will treat these with sensitivity and understanding, ensur-ing that any special measures are put into place, thus reassuring parents that their child's needs are respected and dealt with efficiently. These are the first steps to developing a three-way relationship between child, parents/carer and setting staff. Elinor Goldschmeid described this triangular relationship to empha-sise that each part of the triangle is equally important and, if any members of this three-way relationship have difficulties or anxieties, the others will be affected by it (Lindon, 2001).

It is vital that staff understand parents' own theories about the development of their child and their children's learning at home. It is also essential that nurs-ery staff share with parents their theoretical and practice-based understand-ing of children drawn from their observations of the child in the nursery setting (Whalley, 2007: 201).

The candidate will have an excellent understanding of their role as the child's key person and will ensure that parents/carers also understand this role. Having one person as the main carer, who will develop a strong relationship with the child and make time to talk to the parents daily, will develop a solid support for both the child and the parent/carers. In this way the parent/carer will feel sup-ported and that their child is being cared for by someone who respects them and their choices. These relationships need to be developed and nurtured at the earliest possible stage.

In demonstrating this standard, candidates will understand the benefits of establishing positive relationships with parents and carers and what these ben-efits can bring to the child and learning environment. They will have discussed and put into practice a variety of methods of instigating and developing these relationships to ensure they can be a support to the family in times of need and thereby improve and enhance individual holistic learning and development opportunities for the child.

Example of standard 30 in leadership

The importance of good relationships with parents is also recognised in inter-national philosophies. In Reggio Emilia home–school relationships are of para-mount importance. Children, parents and teachers work together, programmes are family-centred, and parents and family are involved in activities and projects, consulted about their child's progress within the school and encouraged to share information about their child's home experience.

The Te Whāriki curriculum acknowledges the diverse backgrounds children come from and regards them as opportunities for new learning, for children to reflect on alternative approaches, examine alternative points of view and to develop the ability to meet new challenges.

The Swedish approach to families is one of support and involvement. From the birth of the child, parents are encouraged to link with family resource centres and here the parents are supported in developing their new role. Once the child attends preschool, there is a well structured transition period, not only to help children settle in, but also to foster good relationships between the staff and the parents. Families and carers are encouraged to develop an involvement in the setting, including helping to make decisions about finances and policies as well as joining in with centre activities.

As a leader the candidate will be aware of how important relationships with parents are considered internationally and will endeavour to highlight these examples of excellent practice to their colleagues.

Every family is unique and therefore has differing needs. The key to positive partnerships with parents lies in having a network of strategies that can be employed so that different flexible approaches are used with different families, approaches that support and build on the families rather than undermining what the parents/carers already do (Bruce, 2005: 176).

The candidate will demonstrate their understanding of how relationships are developed and maintained by acting as a role model to colleagues. They will always be welcoming and supportive of parents/carers, making time to speak to them and, using their knowledge of multi-agency working, will offer appropriate support when required. In their leadership role, they will try to ensure that there is a quiet place to speak to parents to ensure privacy and demonstrate the importance of confidentiality, while showing an understanding of the limits of this and when further action must be taken.

> conversations need to acknowledge the expertise that parents have about their own children and the understanding that parents have about their children's current needs and interests. They [staff] should be respectful of the parent's own perspectives and not seek to mould the parent's views to coincide with those of the setting.   (Fisher, 2008: 23)

The candidate needs to support colleagues by allowing them time to meet with parents, reinforcing the role of the key person. Another key skill is the ability to remain neutral, not discriminating, assuming or stereotyping and always providing an inclusive practice. Many children come from diverse backgrounds – they may have more than one family and/or home, transferring from one to another during the week, there may be religious or cultural differences that the candidate needs to address, personal opinions must not be shared with the parents and the candidate should support colleagues in ensuring that they understand why this should not happen.

As a leader the candidate will work with colleagues to help them develop their relationships with parents by sharing responsibilities with junior staff initially and discussing issues and advising them on the best course of action, then showing support for their decisions and any action they take. By the candidate providing support, encouragement and showing confidence in the member of staff, the candidate will empower the staff member's self-confidence to improve and as a result the parents/carers will feel more secure building a positive relationship with them.

Standard 30 stakeholder comment

Karen Howard is a teacher and assistant manager of a 52-place nursery catering for children from 2 to 5. She says 'Gaining EYP status has enabled me to promote a culture of reflection and adaptability to change'. She has recently reduced her working week at the nursery to 3 days to take on the role of associate tutor and mentor at Edge Hill University. 'I like a challenge and am finding that my nursery work and university work complement each other.' Karen is also a member of Warrington Borough Council's EYP network group.

Karen's professional experience was with children aged 3–5, so she took the short pathway to enable her to gain experience of children from birth to 3 years. This gave her an opportunity to work in a setting with this younger age group. While on this placement, one child developed a high temperature and a parent was called to come and take him home. The parent arrived and was clearly unhappy about being called out of work and more so when the member of staff explained that the child could not return for 24 hours. Karen observed that the situation was getting out of hand and sensitively stepped in. She took the parent to a private area and calmed him down. She explained the nursery's health and safety 'common ailments and exclusion' policy and explained how poorly the child seemed. Once the parent was given time to think about the situation and see how ill his child was, he soon agreed that the child would be better at home with 1:1 care and a visit to the doctor. Karen observed the challenging behaviour and dealt with it by giving the parent time and space to calm down, giving him an opportunity to discuss

→

the problem in a constructive way, communicating the setting's policy regarding sickness and explaining why it was important to give the child a day off to recover.

Karen used this piece of evidence as part of her written Task 1.

To help reduce parents' anxiety when their child starts at nursery, Karen devised a booklet called 'All About Me' which she gave to new parents and children before they started at the setting. It enabled parents and their child to discuss nursery and the types of activities they could look forward to when they started there. It also helped to develop the key person's knowledge of that child and his/her parents which eases transition by sharing information about the child and their likes and dislikes, family, favourite activities and gives the key person a strong foundation to develop a positive relationship with the whole family. This resource also enables the key person to be aware of any diversity and gives them an opportunity to ensure that resources and procedures are in place to ensure that the child and their family feel comfortable and welcome within the setting.

Karen used an example of an 'All About Me' booklet as part of her documentary evidence.

As part of written Task 5a, Karen discussed an incident with a child who was on the child protection register. Karen led her staff in dealing with the situation, ensuring that two staff members were present to ensure they were not compromised. Karen explained how she had worked with the child's mother over a period of time, ensuring privacy and confidentiality at all times, enabling the mother to feel safe and supported throughout. They had an arrangement that the mother could always be contacted by telephone and so Karen was able to relay the problem to the mother and she was able to say how she would like the staff to deal with it. This supportive relationship ensured that an incident that could have been very embarrassing for both the child and parent was managed in a sensitive and constructive manner.

Karen arranged an interview with the parent of a child whose development across most areas of the curriculum would define him as gifted and talented; however, he had some social and emotional difficulties especially when relating to his peers. She began by giving his mother lots of advice about what she might be able to do with him regarding his areas of strength, e.g. starting a reading scheme and developing reading strategies at home as well as explaining how libraries might also help. Karen felt that it was more constructive to begin on a positive note and developed a supportive relationship with the parent and grandparents, who played a major role in the child's life, before addressing his social issues. Once the parent felt confident and empowered to support her child's learning, areas of difficulty could be discussed. Karen worked with the family to see how best to enhance his *personal, social and emotional development and, as he was an only child who had little contact with other children outside nursery, arranged some play dates with other children by working with parents to get them to swap phone numbers. This gave the child much more opportunity to learn to share and turn-take, which enabled him to take part in the activities in the nursery in a much more positive and constructive way.*

Lindsay McGregor is a play development worker for Sure Start, practising at both Warrington Road and Kingsway Children's Centres, Widnes, and was part of the first cohort of short pathway candidates for EYPS in 2007.

Lindsay's first feelings when looking to evidence this standard were that she did this on a daily basis and would find no difficulty gathering evidence. However, initially she broke the standard down into smaller sections and thought about how she could evidence the elements of the standard; this made her reflect on her practice. On a daily basis, she met with a diverse range of families with individual needs which were often complex, and she worked in partnership with other agencies (for instance, family support, social services, education and health) to try to support and manage those needs on a daily basis. In her role, she provided opportunities to develop positive relationships through a variety of play services, crèche provision, respite, home visits and one-to-one support to encourage learning and development through play.

Lindsay considered how she communicated with families. What did she do? Who did she work with? What worked and what didn't? The standard opened up a lot of thought-provoking personal questions. Lindsay is an EYP with a vast experience of working with families and young children, incorporating effective communication strategies, adopting sensitive approaches, and she felt that she had a natural empathy with both parents and their children; this in turn promoted security, trust and mutual respect. She enabled colleagues to develop their skills in this area by role modelling good practice, offering support and encouragement, and was confident in her ability to do this because feedback from managers, colleagues and parents about the way that she interacted, communicated and shared information with families was extremely positive. Within her role she developed various forms of communication to deliver information about the importance of learning through play in early years settings to try and meet even the hardest-to-reach families. Considering standard 30 made her more reflective as a practitioner, it encouraged her to re-examine her practice and observe others to increase her knowledge and skills when working with families. Just reflecting on the standard was a positive experience.

Standard 31 – work in partnership with families and parents/ carers, at home and in the setting, to nurture children, help them develop and to improve outcomes for them

Example of standard 31 in personal practice

Common definitions describe partnership as a relationship between organisations and individuals based on mutual cooperation and responsibility for the achievement of specified compatible goals. Although today the idea of working in partnership with parents is a widespread notion in the context of early years, the true value of partnership with families has been acknowledged relatively recently. According to Sallis (1988), the initial establishment of formal schooling was based on an understanding that the functions of an educational setting and a family were incongruent, the first one being concerned purely with education and the other with care. Today all early years settings aim for a strong two-way relationship with children's families that take full advantage of the expertise of both the practitioners and the parents/carers to create meaningful, enjoyable and pedagogically sound experiences for young children.

Elements of good practice that EYPs have to consider in the process of building such relationships are as follows:

- Recognising that the partnership has to embrace not only mothers and fathers, step-parents and carers, but also siblings, grandparents and members of the wider family
- Understanding that there is a variety of different family structures and avoiding making judgements about the nature of families when setting up partnerships with parents
- Taking account of parents' points of view and considering their perspectives when planning activities for their children
- Allowing and encouraging parents to take the lead in some of the aspects of their children's learning and development
- Sharing with parents information about their child's progress and using parents' expertise to ensure continuity between setting and home
- Involving parents as much as possible in their children's learning and development.

The most effective strategies that EYPs employ to lead some of these elements of practice include arranging home visits, providing joint courses and workshops for parents and practitioners, recommendation of specific activities for parents to carry out with their children at home ('story sacks', home-setting journals, lending digital cameras for children to take home and take pictures of family outings and other activities), providing 'morning coffee' discussions during drop-off time and organising joint activities for children and their families.

EYPs also have to accept that there are certain challenges in the process of establishing effective partnerships with families. One of the challenges for EYPs will be to reconsider the balance of power within these partnerships and to avoid the urge to dictate to parents the terms of the partnership and deciding on the extent of parents' participation. It is not uncommon for some EYPs to assume that they have better knowledge of parents' and their children's needs (Edwards, 2002), thus causing the partnership to be inequitable and one-sided. EYPs need to acknowledge that all forms of parental partnerships are potentially valuable and that most parents do want to play an active role in their child's learning and development. As a recent study, 'The impact of parental involvement on children's education' (DfES, 2003) found, 72 per cent of parents said that they wanted more involvement. Developing genuine partnerships with parents is a vitally important aspect of the EYP's role. Effective collaboration between early years practitioners and parents creates a fundamental base that empowers every child to thrive and develop to the best of their abilities.

Example of standard 31 in leadership

The EYFS (DCSF, 2008) theme, 'Positive Relationships', section 2:2, 'Parents as Partners' states:

- Parents and practitioners have a lot to learn from each other. This can help them to support and extend children's learning and development.
- Parents should review their children's progress regularly and contribute to their child's learning and development record.
- Parents can be helped to understand more about learning and teaching through workshops on important areas such as play, outdoor learning or early reading. Some parents may go on to access further education at their own level.
- In true partnership, parents understand and contribute to the policies in the setting.

The word partnership suggests equality within a relationship. However, the expectation for an EYP to promote the development of this relationship, within their role, can be a challenging one. Successful relationships become partnerships when there is two-way communication, where parents and practitioners really listen to each other and value each other's views and support in achieving the best outcomes for each child (DCSF, 2008).

The relationships should not appear enforced; they need to be inclusive and often personalised depending on the diversity of the setting, children, parents/carers, families and community. Partnership development takes determination, perseverance and a willingness to be open to scrutiny. This openness can make people fearful and wary of developing relationships, both as a provider and as a parent.

The importance of a two-way flow of information between parents and early years childcare provision is vital, and EYPs can often be the catalyst for developing, monitoring and evaluating this communication. The importance and value in encouraging all staff to meet and greet parents and facilitating key workers to have time to prepare and share information with parents should be stressed. This could be considered through encouraging families to participate in activities at home or in the early years setting, such as sports day, festival celebrations and music or dance sessions, enabling and encouraging children's learning and development.

Some parents are unable to attend sessions in the day but other more creative access to partnerships may be useful, such as websites, portals, key worker or child (age-dependent) emails, weekend community activities or evening classes. Home links and visits can be vital in ensuring and supporting links with parents, for example, if parents have mobility issues or require support to care for siblings or the child him or herself. A proactive EYP can look for ways to enable and support the team to encourage sometimes reluctant families to attend the early years setting and consider wider options for parents to make a contribution to their child's wider wellbeing.

For parents to take advantage of the services designed to help them, they need to know what is available. If they are not aware of what is out there they could be missing out (DfES, 2007).

Standard 31 reflection points

- What is the process of initial engagement and ongoing involvement of parents in your setting?
- According to research, what are features of effective communication with parents to enhance relationships?
- Critically assess the opportunities for parental involvement and partnership in your setting.

Standard 31 stakeholder comment

Paddy Burgess is an associate tutor at Edge Hill University. She is sharing her views of how a candidate has demonstrated standard 31 on a setting visit.

It is crucial that early years practitioners work in partnership with families and parents/carers, paying due regard to children's home circumstances and the impact of this on a child's learning and development. This is an integral part of EYFS and the key messages from EYFS in terms of effective practice for partnership with parents support current research in this area:

> Successful relationships become partnerships when there is two-way communication and parents and practitioners really listen to each other and value each other's views and support in achieving the best outcomes for each child.   (DfES, 2007)

Furthermore, when working in partnership with families, practitioners bring their own values and experiences to their role and therefore may find some parents and parenting styles easier to value than others and this can impact on the quality of the partnership. Time is needed within settings to explore these issues and clarify the shared values of the setting, so that practitioners and parents can build relationships which value everyone:

> Part of the professional duty of educators is to see the world through the eyes of others, both parents and children, in order to understand, support and extend their learning.   (DCSF, 2008)

To meet standard 31, practitioners must have a clear understanding of the term 'partnership'. The amplification of the standard sets out how it differs from standards 29 and 30:

> Standard 29 describes the crucial role of parents and Standard 30 sets out how to establish positive relationships with them. This Standard (Standard 31) translates these two aspects into establishing a partnership with parents in order to improve outcomes for children.   (CWDC, 2008)

A good example of this standard in terms of practice and leadership was seen as part of an EYP setting visit at a private daycare setting. The candidate had recently implemented a system of home visits for children who were due to start at the nursery. The candidate had initially involved staff to gather their views about the idea. In response to this initial meeting she had prioritised the issues of staff safety and the type of information they would gather and how this would inform practice. She then led a staff meeting explaining the rationale behind the implementation. The candidate developed a policy for

→

home visits and has been fully involved in the visits. The visits have allowed the setting to:

- Take account of the child's home circumstances, which enables them to identify any factors which may affect the children's learning and development
- Initiate a two-way flow of information between staff and parents in a friendly, informal way
- Identify if the parent needs any support or advice nurturing or caring for their children and offer appropriate support.

One of the parents from the setting acted as a witness for the candidate and corroborated the evidence for standard 31 that was in the written task and the policy acted as documentary evidence.

All aspects of the standards were covered in terms of practice and the leadership evidence for this standard was also very strong.

Standard 32 – provide formal and informal opportunities through which information about children's well-being, development and learning can be shared between the setting and families and parents/carers

Example of standard 32 in personal practice

Communicating effectively and sharing information with parents is a vitally important aspect of the EYP's role. According to the EYFS (DCSF, 2008), relationships between settings and parents/carers become partnerships when there is two-way communication between practitioners and children's families that involves listening to each other, respecting each other's opinions and sharing information about children's progress. Research evidence of the impact of parental involvement on children's learning and development (DfES, 2003) makes the process of establishing successful communication between early years settings and home a high priority for EYPs.

In simple terms, communication can be defined as a process of conveying information that generally anticipates a response from a recipient of the information. Means of communication employed by practitioners for sharing information vary depending on the circumstances; however, there are certain common aspects that EYPs need to consider to ensure the effectiveness of this process. Firstly, it is important to create a welcoming and relaxed atmosphere that will foster successful communication with parents. Some settings choose to have an 'open door' policy that allows parents to come to the setting and speak to practitioners at any suitable time. Using this strategy gives parents/carers a natural opportunity to have an informal discussion with a member of staff, thus promoting two-way communication, allowing practitioners not only to share information with the parents but also to listen to their opinions and plan future steps together. Another aspect that EYPs need to consider involves the frequency of communication and the amount of information that they wish to share with parents/carers. It is important to keep regular contact with children's families, and practitioners need to think carefully about the effective use of time and different methods of communication appropriate to specific situations. For example, on some busy days it is more manageable to offer parents an opportunity for a longer discussion during 'morning coffee' time than during spontaneous visits throughout the day.

The amount of information also needs to be taken into account: issues such as lack of information or its overload can create a barrier in the communication process. This especially applies to sharing information by sending home leaflets, newsletters, reports, etc., which can be referred to as an 'outward' process that does not always require a response from parents/carers. How can practitioners be sure that all parents have received the information, understood it and acted upon relevant issues appropriately? The key point is that dialogue should not end with sending the information to the parents/carers; this should encourage some action and feedback from the parents. Some settings try to achieve this goal by asking parents to sign and return reply slips; however, examples of effective practice entail instigating further discussion with the parents, whose views benefit children and settings much more than just their signatures (DCSF, 2007).

EYPs also need to make every effort to gain better knowledge about each family's preferences in terms of the forms and the language of communication: awareness of the parents' literacy level and the languages spoken at home will help EYPs to obtain more response from parents/carers in the process of sharing information and create more sincere dialogue with families. Evidence from successful early years settings shows that practitioners in these settings use a wide range of opportunities to build meaningful two-way communication links for sharing information about children's learning and development. Some of these opportunities include an 'open door' policy, home visits, social events, involving parents in outings, joint workshops and play sessions. Figure 6.1

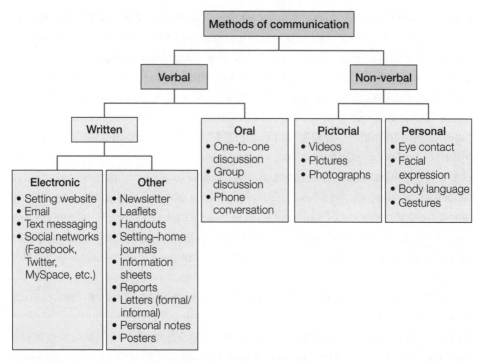

Figure 6.1 **Specific ways of sharing information that EYPs might consider employing within different aspects of the communication process**

shows specific ways of sharing information that EYPs might consider employing within different aspects of the communication process.

Example of standard 32 in leadership

The CWDC has a vision that EYPs will become the catalyst for change and innovation within the many varieties of early years provision in England. To be able to carry out that role effectively they have to develop as perceptive skilled professionals and to be able to encourage, model and analyse the development of outstanding provision for very young children.

'Leadership is understood as shared process where effective leaders draw on a range of strategies to achieve positive and ethical outcomes for members of the group or organisation' (Rodd, 2009: 12). In the developing complex working environment of services for children and families the position you hold is not as important as the quality of practice you provide and the reflection in which you engage. Thus you provide opportunities to inspire, encourage and stimulate your own learning as well as that of colleagues, children and families.

The initial visit to a setting for a parent can be one of mixed emotions: fear of leaving a child for possibly the first time, stress in regard to finding a place that the parent feels will welcome them as a family and provide the personalised care they seek, or anxiety about placement availability and choice. How a setting plans for and provides a welcoming approachable environment is crucial in the development of trust and mutual collaboration that underpins standard 32.

EYPs leading the initiative to develop formal and informal opportunities to share information with families need to demonstrate and discuss with their team how to develop positive relationships with parents and carers. The more approachable a team appear, the more involved families will feel and the more likely they are to build strong relationships which allow the sharing of what might be sensitive information.

Developing the use of learning stories to be able to capture and illustrate the learning taking place within certain structured and unstructured activities can be a way of allowing access for parents who would not normally see those interactions to share them. Enabling colleagues to have access to cameras and computers and supporting any training that they may need to use this technology can provide excellent channels of communication with parents.

Providing a regular system of reporting to parents formally in regard to children's achievements and progress will provide support with the next steps of learning and development. It should be accessible to all, not too complex to manage or complete. It should encourage a two-way input of information, maybe in the form of a journal, a video diary or a photographic record. It could be drawn, written or voice recorded but should give all stakeholders a chance to contribute if they so wish.

EYPs should make arrangements to facilitate the effective exchange of information when families find communication difficult or are not fluent in English. This could be through supporting key workers during initial discussions with the family to ascertain specific requirements that the child and family may have to ensure a smooth transition into the setting. It may involve supporting or finding specific training for staff in regard to personalising provision for this family or looking into community links which may be able to provide cultural or language support.

> Much of the knowledge about the child which professionals require is held by the parents; hence you have to develop strong trusting relationships with them to be able to access it.
>
> (Ward, 2009: 2)

Standard 32 reflection points

The children's centre manager has identified that a group of staff new to the setting are not seeking opportunities to talk to parents in the morning when they welcome children into the room or as the children are collected at the end of their session. She asks you as the EYP to find out why they are avoiding interactions?

● How would you approach this task?

One of the members of staff says that they are not sure of the policy for interacting with parents and if it should only be the key person that greets the children?

● How would you answer this question?
● What would you need to know first?

One of the members of staff says that they are unsure on what is the best way to approach the parents.

● How would you tackle this concern?
● What support could you provide?

In terms of long-term planning what systems could you put in place to ensure that the support and induction for new staff deals with these kinds of problems as they commence their post?

Standard 32 stakeholder comment

Laura Grindley is a deputy manager at Thatto Heath Children's Centre. Here she describes how, in her role as an EYPS mentor, she helps her mentees to deconstruct standard 32.

'When looking at standard 32 I feel it is important to break the standard down and look at each component individually to ensure that the standard is met. This is something that I did when working towards my Early Years Professional Status and I encourage my mentees to adopt the same approach.'

'Firstly, when looking at providing both formal and informal opportunities to share information I looked at what was already in practice at our setting. At the children's centre we ensure that at the beginning and end of our respite sessions we make time for key workers and any other members of staff to informally share information with both families and parents/carers. When looking at more formal opportunities we ensure that every child who attends the respite group has an

→

→

introductory visit in the home so that information can be shared between the setting and the family to ensure that the best possible care is given to each child and all welfare requirements are met.'

'To ensure that records are kept about children's wellbeing, development and learning we ensure that information is shared in different ways. At the end of every session parent/carers are asked to sign a record about their child's wellbeing throughout the session, e.g. toileting. Records of development and learning are also kept for each child who attends the group and these records are shared regularly with parent/carers, and their views and opinions are listened to and influence the records throughout. As EYP at the setting I have ensured that each member of staff has been given appropriate support and guidance before completing any of these documents and that each has sufficient knowledge of the EYFS to relate this document to children's progress.

'Another informal opportunity to share information that I have introduced is a photographic display, which is shown as a slide show on a television in reception. This display is renewed monthly and includes photographs of children during sessions of the respite group and comments from staff and children. The display ensures that information regarding children's interests and opportunities for learning is shared between the setting and parent/ carers, as well as other members of the family who attend the centre at different times (for example, our grandparents' group). As a reflective practitioner this standard really made me evaluate the holistic way in which information must be shared between settings and families and parent/carers. It also reminded me that this must be a two-way process and information given to settings from families must be taken into account at all times during observation, assessment and planning.'

Conclusion

The group of standards 'Communicating and working in partnership with families and carers' identifies that parents are the child's first educator and recognises that an effective relationship with the family is a three-way process between the child, family and setting. EYPs are required to show how they build relationships with families to enhance the child's learning. EYPs will support colleagues in reflecting on their current relationship with parents and identifying the strengths that can be shared with others as well as the weaknesses which can be developed.

References

Bowlby, J. (1979) *The Making and Breaking of Affectional Bonds*. London: Tavistock.

Bruce, T. (2005*) Early Childhood*, 3rd edn. London: Hodder Education.

CWDC. (2008) *Guidance to the Standards for the Award of the Early Years Professional Status*. London: CWDC.

DCSF. (2007) *Engaging Parents in Raising Achievement. Do Parents Know They Matter?* A research project commissioned by the Specialist Schools and Academies Trust, Professor Alma Harris and Dr Janet Goodall. University of Warwick: DCSF.

DCSF. (2008) *The Early Years Foundation Stage*. Nottingham: DCSF.

Dewey, J. (1990) *The School and Society and the Child and the Curriculum*, expanded edn. Chicago: The University of Chicago Press.

DfES. (2003) *The Impact of Parental Involvement on Children's Education*. Nottingham: DfES Publications.

DfES. (2007) *Every Parent Matters*. Nottingham: DfES.

Edwards, R. (ed.) (2002) *Children, Home and School: Regulation, Autonomy or Connection?* London: Routledge Falmer.

Fisher, J. (2008) *Starting from the Child*. London: Open University Press.

Lindon, J. (2006) *Understanding Children's Play*. Gloucestershire: Nelson Thornes.

Rodd, J. (2009) *Leadership in Early Childhood: The Pathway to Professionalism*. Maiden head: Open University Press.

Sallis, J. (1988) *Schools, Parents and Governors. A New Approach to Accountability*. London: Routledge.

Vygotsky, L.S. (1978) *Mind and Society: The Development of Higher Mental Processes*. Cambridge, MA: Harvard University Press.

Ward, U. (2009) *Working with Parents in Early Years Settings*. Exeter: Learning Matters.

Whalley, M. (2007) *Involving Parents in their Children's Learning*. London: Sage.

Chapter 7

Teamworking

Introduction

This chapter details how to work with others to develop policies and procedures in the setting. It identifies how to create a culture of cooperative and collaborative working between colleagues.

Objectives

By the end of this chapter you should have:

- Gained an overview of the key theoretical perspectives on the importance of effective teamworking within the early years context
- Reflected on how you can promote through your practice the requirements identified in standards 33–36
- Reflected on how you can lead and support others in relation to the requirements identified in standards 33–36.

Theoretical underpinning knowledge for standards 33–36

This set of standards, as described in the *Guidance to the Standards* (CWDC, 2010), deals explicitly with the principal aspects of professional leadership and support: teamwork and collaboration.

It is recognised that teamworking skills are of crucial importance in the context of early years, and within the leadership role in particular. EYPs must be effective teamworkers to be able to achieve their goals and provide the best possible early learning experiences for the children in their setting. The skills of teamwork and collaboration should be practised and reflected upon and improved on a constant basis to ensure that EYPs lead and maintain efficient early years teams.

It is useful to define at this point what a team is. According to Adair (2004: 1), a team is 'a group, in which the individuals have a common aim, and in which the jobs and skills of each member fit in with those of others'. In addition to these aspects of a team, Rodd (2005) suggests a wider definition of a team as a group of people cooperating with each other to work towards achieving an agreed set of aims, objectives or goals while simultaneously considering the personal needs and interests of individuals . . . the pursuit of a common philosophy, ideals and values; commitment to working through the issues; shared responsibility; open and honest communication and access to a support system.

Looking at theoretical perspectives on teamworking, almost certainly the most renowned theory of teamwork was suggested by Tuckman in 1965. His model of staged teambuilding is widely accepted as a useful tool for analysing and informing effective teamwork strategies in early years settings, helping practitioners to realise that forming a team is not an instant event; teams evolve as they go through clearly defined stages of forming, storming, norming and performing (Tuckman, 1965). In 1977 Tuckman revised this scheme together with Mary Ann Jensen and added a fifth stage of 'adjourning', which involves breaking up the team because of completion of the tasks (Tuckman and Jensen, 1977). Although Tuckman's scheme can be used to enhance our understanding of the team formation process, we also need to remember that teamwork and team formations do not always take place in such a straightforward way. With this in mind, EYPs need to consider that every team will have their own unique pattern of development, where these stages overlap, fail to emerge or develop in a non-linear way.

This group of standards also requires EYPs to ensure that their colleagues understand their role and are involved appropriately in helping children to meet planned objectives. In view of this goal, EYPs might consider enhancing their knowledge of theoretical models related to team roles. Dr Meredith Belbin developed a theory of team roles. According to Belbin (2010), people within teams exhibit certain types of behaviour, which can determine their roles within those teams and, also, affect the team's performance. These roles are:

- Completer/finisher
- Coordinator
- Implementer
- Monitor/evaluator
- Plant
- Resource investigator
- Shaper
- Specialist
- Teamworker.

In basic terms, Belbin's theory is based on the assumption that, when team members understand how their skills, abilities and potential can affect functioning of the team, they begin to manage the demands of the collaborative environment in a more effective way (Belbin, 2010).

The concept of team roles links closely to the principle that, to be able to meet children's diverse needs, early years practitioners require skills of multi-professional multi-agency collaboration to ensure effective early years provision. Research indicates that multi-agency working is not a new idea:

> It might be described as a 'Holy Grail' in public policy, which, if achieved, will improve public services. The concept of professionals from different disciplines coming together, sharing their knowledge and skills in a combined effort to support better outcomes for a family or a community is an attractive one, especially for those working in or with public agencies. Indeed, asking 'why people don't work together' is a common question.   (CWDC, 2009: 5)

Over the past few years, the concept of multi-agency working defined within the Green Paper *Every Child Matters* (DfES, 2003) has provided another dimension to professional development for EYPs. As it is stated in the Common Core of Skills and Knowledge (CWDC, 2010: 18), 'to work successfully with children and young people it is important to be clear about your role and to be aware of, and respectful of, the roles of other workers and agencies'. The Government made its goals clear, with the Children Act 2004 defining explicit duties for local authorities to develop multi-agency working environments and to enhance the skills of the workforce for children's services. The strategic directions of the Government in relation to multi-agency collaboration were detailed further in *The Children's Plan: Building Brighter Futures* (DCSF, 2007).

Within this group of standards, EYPs will also need to demonstrate their ability to influence and shape the policies and practices of the setting on the basis of an analysis of current effectiveness and knowledge of best practice, as well as to lead colleagues in a collective process of continuous review of existing policies along with the formulation and implementation of new policies. According to the *Statutory Framework for the Early Years Foundation Stage* (DCSF, 2008a: 20), 'group providers will be expected to have written copies of any policies and procedures which are required, for example, to safeguard children or promote equality of opportunity. Providers should ensure that all members of staff have been given copies of these policies and procedures as part of their induction, and that they are explained to, and accessible to, all parents.'

It appears that the most effective policies are based on the evidence from high quality studies on the effectiveness of different forms of early years provision. One of the most significant examples of the impact of research on government policy is the Effective Provision of Preschool Education (EPPE) study, which has proven that high quality preschool experiences have lasting effects on children's learning and development throughout their early years. According to Sylva, director of the EPPE Project, 'it is possible to influence government policy at national and local level through a combination of rigorous research methods, user friendly dissemination, the combining of quantitative and qualitative approaches, and adequately funded research activity' (Sylva, cited in Whitty, 2006: 170).

It is important that EYPs use their knowledge of current research and effective practices to inform the process of reviewing already existing policies in their setting or developing and implementing new ones. Developing a new policy is a creative process that often goes beyond ready-made samples and formats. As Dickins (2002) rightly points out, while prescriptive or ready-made policies are convenient, they are unlikely to be readily meaningful to individuals who had no hand in putting them together. EYPs need to take ownership of policy statements and requirements in order to implement them effectively.

In conclusion, the ability of EYPs to work collaboratively with other practitioners is imperative to high quality provision in early years settings, where all adults work together to support children's learning and development in the best possible way. An efficient and well organised early years team can only develop if its team members have clear ideas of their roles and responsibilities, possess a range of relevant skills, show positive attitude within the team and are committed to the achievement of common goals. Although we have to admit that it is impossible to suggest one recipe for successful teamwork that would work for all early years setting, we need to remember that the end product of teamwork is an improvement in the quality of care and education for children (Rodd, 2005).

Standard 33 – establish and sustain a culture of collaborative and cooperative working between colleagues

Example of standard 33 in personal practice

The EYFS (DCSF, 2008a) is an integrated framework. In the past there has been a distinction between education and care – now, all settings are concerned with both pastoral care and education. It is recognised that a holistic approach is the best way to provide for children's needs – an approach that puts learning and development within the wider context of children's welfare and wellbeing.

To enable practitioners to work together effectively, leaders need to establish and sustain a culture of collaborative and cooperative working between colleagues. Having a shared sense of purpose and ethos within the setting is important when working together to plan, deliver, evaluate and improve practice and provision.

EYPs will need to demonstrate that they can sustain a culture of collaborative working and recognise the importance of teamworking. Identifying the knowledge and skills of colleagues within the setting is essential in enabling the team to work effectively together. In practice, colleagues should be encouraged to share expertise through mentoring, shadowing or coaching. Rodd (2006) argues that there are two main dimensions involved in teambuilding: staff morale and task demands. It is important that all staff feel valued and are included in the development of policies and procedures. This will give staff a sense of ownership and shared meaning when implementing policies in practice.

Gillian (cited in Smith and Langston, 1999: 44) discusses the following principles of teambuilding:

- **Pull, don't push** – allow the team, not the leader, to set the pace
- **Involve people as much as possible** – encourage the team to take ownership of the ideas
- **Think behaviour rather than personality** – observe individual behaviour
- **Persuade, don't manipulate** – respect the other person and try to see their point of view.

Teambuilding is an essential part of quality improvement in an early years setting. Understanding how teams function effectively in practice is an important aspect of the leader's role.

Tuckman and Jensen (1977) identify five stages of team development: forming, storming, norming, performing and adjourning. The leader's role is to understand the dynamics within the team and identify the 'stage' within which the team is operating. In practice this may mean that some settings will still be in the first stages of teambuilding where the team is still *forming*, and team members may behave independently of one another. The skill of the leader is to harness the ideas, views, issues and possible concerns of the practitioners to gain a shared understanding of learning and development and work towards a 'collective vision' of pedagogy.

Some teams will have reached the *performing* stage. They perform effectively as a unit and team members have become interdependent, competent and autonomous. It could be viewed at this point that they have established and sustained a culture of collaborative and cooperative working between colleagues.

Example of standard 33 in leadership

The leadership aspect of this standard involves the candidate supporting colleagues to work collaboratively and effectively together to enhance children's welfare, development and learning. Whalley *et al.* (2008: 91) state that 'the successful functioning of any team is dependent on each individual member functioning well, where each person acts as a kind of catalyst to the other', and goes on to suggest that 'there are two elements to Standard 33: the establishment of *building* a team and then its *maintenance*'.

This will involve staff training, team development and role modelling. Clear practices and processes need to be effectively communicated to create a shared understanding and good team spirit. The wellbeing of the team will reflect on the wellbeing of the children in the setting. The dedication and passion of the leader to inspire others through articulating a collective vision and encouraging reflective practice is identified in the most effective settings (Siraj-Blatchford and Manni, 2007).

Effective Leadership in the Early Years Sector: the ELEYS Study (Siraj-Blatchford and Manni, 2007: 12) identified a range of 'categories of effective leadership practice'. It is important to reflect and consider how you meet each aspect in your role as leader in:

- Identifying and articulating a collective vision
- Ensuring shared understandings, meanings and goals

- Effective communication
- Encouraging reflection
- Monitoring and assessing practice
- Commitment to ongoing professional development
- Building a learning community and team culture
- Encouraging and facilitating parent and community partnerships
- Leading and managing: striking the balance.

Standard 33 reflection points

- Consider the importance of the leader's role in ensuring a 'collective vision' of pedagogy
- Identify possible issues and concerns in terms of a shared understanding of learning and development
- What does it mean to work collaboratively? How can you demonstrate this in practice?
- What kind of skills do you think you should have as a leader in relation to meeting each member of the team's individual needs?

Standard 33 stakeholder comment

Liz Ludden is an associate tutor and EYP assessor at Edge Hill University. An EYP and a teacher, Liz owns and runs two nurseries in Liverpool and mentors EYP candidates within settings.

'Lisa Fryer was on the full time pathway at Edge Hill and demonstrated leadership and personal practice to support standard 33: establish and sustain a culture of collaborative and cooperative working between colleagues.'

'For this standard assessors were looking for evidence that the candidate was able to work collaboratively and cooperatively with colleagues to enhance children's wellbeing, learning and development, and for the ability to draw on colleagues' knowledge and to encourage them to share their expertise.'

'On placement at Dukes and Duchesses Day Nursery in Liverpool, Lisa quickly established a rapport with the 25 staff. She supported staff in a range of situations, making links to her academic modules and experience gained on previous placements.'

> 'Lisa wanted to build on communication training which had been accessed by two staff and so facilitated a visit to the Early Years Professional Development Centre at Wilton House, Chorley. This is set up to incorporate the six areas of learning. Colleagues observed the areas and thought of what adjustments could be made to their own learning environment to enhance language and communication. Lisa prepared a questionnaire which encouraged them to work towards a shared sense of purpose and establish shared values within the team.'
>
> 'Lisa used this opportunity to engage staff who had attended training on communication-friendly spaces and encouraged them to share their knowledge and understanding. She also encouraged colleagues to utilise other skills such as sewing and painting to transform the learning environment, and to create a space that encouraged communication.'
>
> 'To ensure that the project was developed after her placement, Lisa helped to produce an interactive display for staff to share evaluations and make links to EYFS areas. Lisa was able to draw on this activity and evaluate it as part of her Gateway Review.'

Standard 34 – ensure that colleagues working with them understand their role and are involved appropriately in helping children to meet planned objectives

Example of standard 34 in personal practice

This standard requires EYPs to ensure that their colleagues understand their role in the implementation of the EYFS and their contribution to improved outcomes for children.

EYPs will need to make a positive contribution to the quality and effectiveness of colleagues' practice by seeking their colleagues' views and opinions about the effectiveness of the setting's provision, and supporting colleagues with the decision-making process and the consequent implementation of improvements. Initially, EYPs will need to demonstrate that their colleagues have a clear understanding of their overall role in the setting, ensuring that colleagues understand the planned objectives for each activity and their individual role in achieving these planned objectives. The EYP must then lead and support colleagues in the review and evaluation of the setting's overall practice (CWDC, 2010: 65). The EYP is intended to be a 'change agent', resulting in raised standards in early years settings (Miller, 2010: 23).

This standard does not relate to personal practice with young children nor to any managerial responsibilities. Standard 34 relates to an EYP's personal practice with their colleagues, through which they provide leadership and support (CWDC, 2010: 61). Professional relationships focus on respecting and valuing the strengths, skills and knowledge of the people you work with and recognising the contribution made by everyone in your setting.

There should be open communication to ensure that everyone's views are listened to and considered fairly, always keeping the needs of the children firmly in mind. EYFS Principles into Practice Card 2.1 Respecting Each Other (DCSF, 2008: 2.1) Edgington (2004) suggests that within an early years setting there are three main types of 'team':

- The *cosy* team – well established, unwelcoming to new members, resistant to change
- The *turbulent* team – no clear dialogue for shared decision-making, unrest within the team, disquiet expressed away from the team meeting agenda
- The *rigorous* and *challenging* team – professional, strong commitment to continued professional development, challenge each other thoughtfully.

Effective teamwork does not happen by chance, but has to be given sufficient time and attention to enable all members of the team to play their part to the best of their ability.

A team that functions well:

- Recognises that they are dependent on one another
- Takes joint responsibility for achieving aims and objectives
- The vision and objectives are clear and understood by all
- Each individual is clear about their own role and responsibilities
- Trusts each other
- Communicates openly and honestly – constructive criticism is given and taken maturely and differences of opinion, although inevitable, are seen as a starting point for new ideas or new ways of working together
- Uses good communication strategies – both verbal and written are used to ensure information is shared and distributed
- Ground rules regarding behaviour and confidentiality are established and adhered to
- Aspirations are high and everyone understands that they are expected to fulfil their role in the setting and wider context.

Brunton and Thornton (2006) suggest that a simple way to assess how well a team is functioning is whether the members of the team:

- Enjoy their job
- Cooperate well
- Are keen to accept responsibility
- Work hard and to a high standard
- Complete tasks on time and
- Are rarely absent from work.

There are also strong links to standard 33, requiring EYPs to establish and sustain a culture of collaborative and cooperative working between colleagues (CWDC, 2010: 64). Thus, there is an element of building your team, establishing roles and responsibilities within the team and then managing and maintaining the team. Indeed, as an EYP it is imperative to establish and understand the roles and responsibilities of all practitioners working in an early years setting, however varied these may be. Embedded within these roles, discussions evolve relating to staff training and teambuilding leading on to (hopefully) personal and professional components of confidence, respect, interpersonal skills, consistency, confidentiality and professionalism. Professionalism in the early years is a complex component (Friedman, 2007). Defining professionalism is as wide a discussion as defining quality, yet as beneficial to the learning outcomes of the children.

Example of standard 34 in leadership

Leadership involves communication, direction, inspiring thoughts and ideas that motivate others, building and encouraging teamwork and collaborative working. Successful leadership in early years settings is essentially about clear communication and interpersonal skills (Rodd, 2006).

In summary, the expectation is that leaders are people who have a clear idea of what they want to achieve and why – motivating, setting objectives, initiating change, taking decisions, setting the pace, being self-sufficient and inspiring loyalty (Smith and Langston, 1999). Discussions on how an EYP ensures that adults are involved appropriately in their setting clearly link back to the setting of objectives, the focus on development and innovation rather than the smooth running and management of the setting (Solley, 2003), being accountable for quality, being knowledgeable and an informational resource for the staff team (Moyles, 2006) and being overtly aware of the importance of shared values. Leading practice is about reflecting on roles, policies, procedures, practice, perceptions and constructive discussion (Anning and Edwards, 2006). Reflective practice is about challenging ourselves, 'open-mindedness, responsibility, wholeheartedness' (Pollard, 2002: 17).

Standard 34 reflection points

- Is it sufficient to presume that colleagues will have a clear understanding of their overall role in the setting if they have a clear and concise job description and access to EYFS training and documentation?
- What policies and procedures do you have in place to support colleagues in their understanding of their role?
- What perception do the parents have on your team?
- Is good teamwork visible?

Standard 34 stakeholder comment

Cathy is a nursery owner and manager of an 'outstanding' private day nursery. She has recently completed her EYPS.

'I always spend at least 10 minutes of every day with key members of staff. I find that those 10 minutes equate to the quality and professionalism of my nursery and have a great impact on the children's learning and development. If you spend 10 minutes explaining something initially, spend time working alongside a practitioner, supporting, guiding, prompting, praising, encouraging and building on their existing skills and confidence base – how can that not impact? What's 10 minutes out of your busy working day? I invest as much time in the staff in my setting as I do with the children and parents. I have a clear induction procedure and induction training – as well as the local authority EYFS courses I deliver my own training – often prompted by questions from my staff. I think – well, if one staff member is concerned about that – others will be. I build relationships with all my staff – not just key members. That doesn't mean going out after working hours and socialising with them, although it can be a part of it – but caring about who they are, if they are happy, if they understand what they need to do, how it should be done and why – how it fits into the ethos of our nursery.'

→

'I have set up learning 'journals' for my staff so they can research and develop at their own pace. They manage their own journals – often it is linked to what the children are choosing to be engaged in and moving the children on to the next stage – for example, one member of staff is researching schemas, another is finding out about Islam to support a small group of children and another is looking into research on brain development for babies. I do tell the team that it is an expectation that they do this – I set high expectations but that is how I get my quality – for the children, parents and staff – we all work together.'

Julia is a nursery manager of a private day nursery who is interested in becoming an EYP:

'Supporting colleagues in their role is an issue that I admit I do struggle with. I employ L2 and L3 practitioners in my setting and we also have students. I think I manage the nursery really well – I have a great relationship with children and parents and often a great relationship with staff – but that is not all the time. Occasionally I have unhappy staff – staff that just really want an easy life and are not that interested in knowing and understanding why everything has to be spot on! As with everything it takes time to build up a body of good, dedicated, professional staff – and often when they are dedicated, professional and knowledgeable they go to work somewhere else!'

'For me, it is important to work alongside all the team at different points – I support new members of staff by organising their shifts so that they spend time with me a lot in the beginning. I explain everything, I make prompt cards and leaflets and I involve them as much as possible in planning. Also I find that, if I invest in that time with them in the beginning, it helps with their confidence and knowledge. But then I try to make sure that I keep spending that time with them a bit later on too. I like to work alongside all my team, explaining things, setting the standards – we learn from each other. It does take such a lot of time! If I see something I don't like I deal with it then and there – I don't let if fester and develop into a bad habit or lack of knowledge. I encourage the team to share their staff training events with each other – we hold inset days for this so we all get the same information – again it's about learning from each other. This is why I am interested in gaining my EYPS. I wouldn't want to ask anyone else to do it until I have done it.'

Katie is a nursery teacher in a children's centre, who has achieved her EYPS in April 2010:

> 'I really enjoy my job and ensure that all my colleagues support each other in understanding all our job roles in order to achieve the aims and ethos of the setting. I remind everyone – there's no 'I' in team! One of the strengths identified in both our Ofsted inspection and Quality Award documentation is our teamwork – we don't always agree with each other but we are professional and mindful that each and every one of us works really hard for the children and parents and for each other – we help each other out and parents often comment upon how well we all work together in the nursery. The skill is understanding and appreciating each other. We weren't always such a great team – it has probably taken us about 3 years!'

Standard 35 – influence and shape the policies and practices of the setting and share in collective responsibility for their implementation

Example of standard 35 in personal practice

To show evidence for standard 35, the candidate needs to be involved in the creation and updating of policies and procedures within the setting that 'concern the well-being, learning and development of children' (CWDC, 2008).

Baldock et al. (2008: 3) define a policy as 'an attempt by those working inside an organization to think in a coherent way about what it is trying to achieve (either in general or in relation to a specific issue) and what needs to be done to achieve it.

The candidate will understand that policies and procedures are essential in the setting to promote excellent practice, support colleagues by providing a uniform approach to achieve the best possible outcomes for all children and ensure that all practices are safe, legal and in the best interests of the child.

A sound understanding of the Every Child Matters (ECM) outcomes is essential. The candidate will be able to write and review policies and procedures with each of the five outcomes in mind. They will consider how each one addresses the children's physical and mental health and how it can be improved to develop their understanding of healthy practices; how does it address children's safety and support each child's ability to recognise danger and keep themselves safe? Can any changes be made to ensure the children are getting the most out of their time in the setting, enjoying learning, developing skills and having fun? Do they enable the children to be part of the community, contributing to it, and develop their understanding of how working together can help others? Are there improvements that could develop positive behaviour? Does the candidate ensure that all children have equal access to quality resources to ensure they all have a secure foundation of learning that they can build upon in the future? These questions need to be considered, guaranteeing that the ECM outcomes underpin all practices within the setting. The EYFS document provides essential guidance on early years statutory requirements and the candidate will use this to inform policies and make references to it within the document to support the approaches to be followed.

Policies need to be based on research and legislation; therefore the candidate will use their considerable knowledge of current local and national early years policy and international research to underpin their setting's policies and procedures. The candidate will consider how the policy will move practice forward; they will be creative in adapting requirements to address the particular needs of their setting. They will also ensure inclusivity, that the policy/procedure addresses children of all ages and abilities. Policies need to show 'joined up' thinking; the candidate therefore needs to show a knowledge and understanding of all the policies in the setting and ensure that they all deliver a uniform approach. All policies and procedures must be reviewed and evaluated on a regular basis and, if the candidate can show involvement in this process, it will be an informative piece of evidence.

By contributing to the creation of policies and procedures that address these issues, the candidate will ensure that there is a sound framework supporting a uniform approach to colleagues' approaches to children's learning experiences. They will demonstrate a sound understanding of policies and procedures and ensure that they use them to support all of their practice and implement new changes as necessary. They will monitor and evaluate the effect these have on the children's wellbeing, development and learning, and report their findings to colleagues for further discussion. This may be demonstrated by minutes of staff meetings in documentary evidence, written tasks or witness statements or interviews.

Example of standard 35 in leadership

Whalley (2008: 35) states 'the most effective policies are the ones where there is shared ownership and understanding of the contents. Only then can they be applied effectively'.

The candidate in a leadership role will be aware of this and will ensure that policies adhere to the needs and requirements of all stakeholders as well as relevant legislation. There will be a shared vision for the setting and this will be at the heart of all policies and procedures. The candidate will consult with children, staff, parents and any other parties to gather information as to what they believe to be good practice. They will consider all suggestions as to how to achieve this and, as a leader, create a policy that all will understand and follow.

Within this they must consider the roles and responsibilities of others, and whether colleagues are adequately trained to perform these efficiently. The candidate may arrange professional development to ensure that colleagues are confident and knowledgeable in their area of responsibility. This may require anything from a simple role modelling exercise to a long-term course, but the candidate will be aware of the benefits of supporting colleagues with appropriate training as this makes them feel valued, competent and dedicated to performing to their best ability.

An area that is frequently neglected is that of publication and dissemination. Often policies and procedures are written and one or two copies are made, which are then put with all the other policies and rarely, if ever, consulted. The successful candidate will ensure that there are adequate copies available for all to see. It may be that there are stakeholders with English as an additional language, so the candidate will ensure there are translated copies available for them, or those who have a visual or hearing impairment – copies in Braille or recorded copies should be made available. Any new or revised policies or procedures must be approved by the setting's managers and then delivered to staff for discussion. Staff need to understand changes made and the reasons behind them. They need to know how this will affect their role and have an opportunity to ask questions. If the procedure has involved them throughout, this will be kept to a minimum. In their capacity as a leader, the candidate should feel confident to delegate the writing of policies to colleagues and support them in understanding the whole process.

Once the policy/procedure is in place, the candidate will have a timetable for evaluation and review. They will ensure that stakeholders are involved in this, to ensure that they have a full overview of the effects the policy is having on the provision. Stakeholders need to have the opportunity to make comments and for these to be recorded, so that all contributions are considered in the evaluation process. The candidate can then review areas of strength and areas for improvement and ensure that changes made will make further improvements to the children's wellbeing, learning and development.

Standard 35 reflection points

- Review the policies and procedures within your setting. Are:

  - they consistent, supporting the vision of the setting?
  - they available for all stakeholders to read?
  - they delivered to all stakeholders, with guidance as to how they will benefit children's wellbeing, learning and development?
  - they able to cover all relevant areas? Are there any gaps that need to be addressed?
  - staff aware of their roles within the policies? Are they given adequate training to fulfil these?
  - they such that one person writes all policies? Are stakeholders involved in policy writing anyway?

- Consider how you can become involved in this process, developing practice and provision for all children within the setting.

Standard 35 stakeholder comment

Marion Connett has worked at Little Acorns Pre-school for around 11 years, first as an assistant whilst completing her degree and subsequently as manager. It is a small village preschool run by a voluntary management committee as a registered charity and her experience is very comprehensive – working as a hands-on manager and taking care of all other related duties outside of session times. She tries to keep up with current issues and had heard a lot about EYPS, so she contacted Edge Hill and began the interview process. In the end she undertook the short pathway rather than validation, as she needed to gain further working knowledge of the 0–3 age range. So alongside her Edge Hill sessions she also completed a short placement at a local nursery. She is lucky to work with a small team of very supportive and dedicated staff and was able to organise day release for EYPS sessions but she admits that her 6-month EYPS pathway was a demanding and very busy time – she needed support from friends and family as well as work colleagues.

So it felt like a real achievement when the certificate popped through the letter box! Since gaining the status she has had opportunities to work as both a visiting tutor and student mentor, which have been very interesting and enjoyable next steps.

→

→

Marion considered that she had achieved standard 35 as she had revised all preschool policies in the previous academic year in light of the introduction of the EYFS welfare requirements and practice guidance, and had produced a collated set to be adopted by the committee. She had also produced a new policy about photographic and video footage of children – detailing how the setting stores and uses digital images. She had also worked with the staff team reviewing the observation, assessment and planning process to try and improve assessment of children's progress.

She showed evidence of her work by providing the assessor with documentary evidence of minutes from a committee meeting, with the relevant passage highlighted as well as an annotated copy of the new 'digital image' policy.

In the written tasks, Marion described different elements of the observation, assessment and planning process, including how it included parents as partners in their child's educational experiences for Task 3. For Task 5a she gave a detailed description of the policy review process.

On the tour Marion made the policy file available to the assessor and discussed how she had researched the necessary information and worked with stakeholders to ensure that they could contribute their ideas and opinions in the writing of the document. She showed the assessor how all stakeholders had access to the policies and how she ensured that staff were aware of the policy and how it affected their roles and responsibilities.

This all provided strong evidence of both Marion's personal practice and leadership skills for this standard.

Standard 36 – contribute to the work of a multi-professional team and, where appropriate, coordinate and implement agreed programmes and interventions on a day to day basis

Example of standard 36 in personal practice

Candidates will see a great many links to standard 6 when deconstructing this standard. Standard 6 requires evidence of a deep understanding of the roles and responsibilities of various professionals and when and how to seek their advice. This standard underpins standard 36, which requires the candidate to provide evidence of how they put this knowledge and understanding into practice.

The candidate will need to show that they are proactive in working with all early years providers and professionals. This includes other settings, childminders and family to ensure a consistent approach for the child. Lumsden (2005) discusses how early years practitioners need to be aware of the importance of government initiatives that encourage them to work together and collaborate to ensure improved outcomes for all children. The candidate needs to illustrate how they promote this collaboration, demonstrating an understanding for the need for good communication with all parties. They also need to show an awareness of their own and others' skills, taking responsibility for seeking further advice from professionals experienced in dealing with a particular difficulty when they see that they have reached the limits of their own remit. A candidate with limited experience in this area can extend their knowledge by working with a member of another discipline, attending sessions with children, if permission is granted, and doing their own research into conditions. This could be extended by creating an information leaflet for staff and/ or parents and delivering it to them; this would then show evidence of leadership.

Evidence that the candidate actively promotes an integrated approach must also be seen by assessors. Candidates need to show that they fully understand the Every Child Matters outcomes and how working towards them develops a shared vision between agencies. An understanding of the Common Core of Skills and Knowledge and how it is used to promote collaboration and effective integrated practice is also essential. This can be shown in written tasks to show your underpinning knowledge of why you worked in a particular way. The candidate also needs to illustrate the correct use of information sharing procedures as well as a willingness to 'work across traditional boundaries and learn to communicate effectively with each other in the best interests of service users' (Anning et al., 2007: 123).

Candidates will also show a sound understanding of the common assessment framework (CAF); they may have received training in this and use this as a piece of documentary evidence, while contributing towards the completion of a CAF will provide further evidence towards achieving this standard.

At the heart of all this integrated practice must be the child and family, and the successful candidate will have a variety of evidence showing how they have worked with the child and family to find the best approach to addressing their particular problems. They will ensure that parents/carers are continually updated on their child's progress and that any contributions made by parents/carers are considered and put into practice. They will discuss progress with parents and help them understand that practitioners have done everything their role allows them to and that it would be in the child's best interest to involve other practitioners with more expertise. They will ensure that the parents/carers are fully involved in any planning/review meetings and that their voices are heard.

Candidates will have a variety of experiences of working with other agencies; some may have roles in which they do this on a daily basis whilst others have few opportunities. The practitioner should take every opportunity to work with other agencies whenever possible to enable them to develop a sound understanding of the various roles and responsibilities, as well as developing good relationships and lines of communication with these professionals. Working collaboratively with other agencies will enable the candidate to implement agreed programmes with a full understanding of their purpose and aims. This will enable them to carry out the work with the child with enthusiasm and ensure that they know what they are to do and for what they are observing. The candidate will then feel confident when contributing to planning or review meetings, knowing they are giving pertinent feedback which will enable colleagues to understand the child's responses, and thus plan further effective interventions which will help the child to progress further.

Example of standard 36 in leadership

To show leadership in this standard the practitioner must be able to show evidence of how they develop integrated practice in the setting. This may include writing policies, delivering training to colleagues to develop their understanding and supporting staff to become involved in the process to gain experience and understanding to improve their own practice. This could involve inviting professionals from other agencies to discuss their role and improve colleagues' understanding of how they can involve and support them to enhance the children's development.

The candidate will demonstrate how they have communicated and collaborated with other early years providers and professionals as well as how they involve their colleagues in this. They will be able to show an understanding of how this supports both the child and family.

The candidate will role model good practice when working in a multiprofessional team, they will be aware of common issues both positive and negative arising within multidisciplinary teams:

- Sharing while acknowledging the importance of specialist expertise
- Using common protocols and documentation
- Excluding team members from discussions by the use of jargon
- Brokering links with external agencies
- Resolving differences in the values of team members and tensions arising from devolving activities to generalist workers   (Anning *et al.*, 2007: 89).

They will feel confident working to develop and improve the work of the team, enabling it to function efficiently and all members to feel valued.

Role modelling good practice is an essential leadership skill and the successful candidate will ensure that less experienced colleagues have the opportunity to work with teams in whatever way is appropriate for their level of experience. A junior member of staff may begin by implementing agreed programmes and interventions; the candidate will support them in this and give them opportunity to feed back to the professional involved. A more senior member of staff may be invited to planning or review meetings to contribute their observations to the multiprofessional team. As a leader the candidate will role model these activities first and then support the member of staff until they feel confident to do this independently. In this way, colleagues gain an insight and understanding of the benefits and processes of working in this way, which leads them to take on a more constructive and proactive role.

Standard 36 reflection points

- Consider which agencies are involved in your setting
- How can you liaise with these professionals to gain an understanding of their roles?
- Can you arrange with them and parents/carers of the children concerned to attend sessions?
- If you can arrange this, consider, what do you want to learn from this?
- Make a list of questions you want to ask the therapist and take it with you
- What responsibilities do you have towards the child receiving interventions?
- Consider how you can liaise with specialists to implement planned interventions to give them feedback
- Ask permission to attend planning or review meetings, and to observe or participate if you can
- Attend a course on information sharing
- Research any conditions that children in your setting have; consider what the symptoms and treatment are; how does this relate to the child in your care?
- In a leadership role, consider your setting's policy on multiprofessional working; is it clear and concise?
- Consider a colleague's understanding of information sharing procedures. Can you develop this in any way?
- Do you enable other members of the team to collaborate with professionals involved in supporting children or do you take on this role yourself? Could you share this work with others to enable them to progress professionally?

Standard 36 stakeholder comment

Sandra Harwood has completed the training aspect of the EYPS full training pathway at Edge Hill University.

For standard 36 the candidate needs to show that they are proactive in working with others such as other professionals within or outside their settings to ensure the best learning and development opportunities for children. Sandra had the opportunity to work with the setting manager on new initiatives at this early stage in the life of the children's centre, including FACE (Fathers and Children Engage) – an initiative aimed at encouraging and facilitating fathers' involvement in the lives of young children. She attended meetings with the group of involved settings and was instrumental in establishing the initiative. Sandra included minutes from the meetings to help to evidence the standards, particularly where they showed her contribution to the discussion and her ability to provide support for children and families.

Similarly, Sandra has represented the children's centre at meetings and on home visits as part of their work with other agencies, e.g. Home-Start, aimed at reaching out to families needing support. All of this shows evidence for standard 36 by showing how Sandra is proactive in working with other professionals within and outside her setting.

The manager was one of Sandra's witnesses during her setting visit and talked about Sandra's work to her assessor.

Conclusion

The group of standards 'Teamwork and collaboration' looks specifically at the candidate's leadership of others. Candidates will identify how they create an ethos of support, helping colleagues to feel valued and listened to. They will reflect upon projects they have led and consider how they involved others in creating a culture of collaboration. Practitioners need to have a good understanding of the policies and procedures of the setting and they will have taken a role in influencing and shaping the policies. The candidate will need to understand and recognise the work that multiprofessionals carry out and the impact of this upon their setting.

References

Adair (2004) *The Concise Adair on Teambuilding and Motivation*. London: Thorogood.

Anning, A., Edwards, A. (2006) *Promoting Children's Learning from Birth to Five: Developing the New Early Years Professional*. Maidenhead: Open University Press.

Anning, A., Cottrell, D., Frost, N., Green, J., Robinson, M. (2007) *Developing Multiprofessional Teamwork for Integrated Children's Services*. Berkshire: McGraw Hill.

Baldock, P., Fitzgerald, D., Kay, J. (2008) *Understanding Early Years Policy*. London: Sage.

Belbin, M. (2010) *Management Teams: Why they Succeed or Fail*, 3rd edn. Oxford: Heinemann.

Brunton, P., Thornton, L. (2006) *Creating an Effective Team. 'The Early Years Handbook'*. London: Sage.

CWDC. (2010) *Guidance to the Standards for the Award of the Early Years Professional Status*. London: CWDC.

DCSF. (2007) *The Children's Plan: Building Brighter Futures*. London: HMSO.

DCSF. (2008a) *Statutory Framework for the Early Years Foundation Stage*. Nottingham: DCSF.

DCSF. (2008b) *Practice Guidance for the Early Years Foundation Stage*. Nottingham: DCSF.

DfES. (2003) *Every Child Matters: Next Steps*. London: DfES Publications.

DfES. (2004) *Every Child Matters: Change for Children*. Nottingham: DfES.

Dickins, M. (2002) All about… Anti-discriminatory Practice. *Nursery World*, January 3, pp. 15–22.

Edgington, M. (2004) *The Foundation Stage Teacher in Action,* 3rd edn. London: Paul Chapman.

Friedman, R. (2007) Professionalism in the early years. In: M. Wild and H. Mitchell (eds) *Early Childhood Studies*. Exeter: Learning Matters.

Lumsden, E. (2005) Joined up thinking in practice: an exploration of professional collaboration. Cited in Waller, T. (2005) *An Introduction to Early Childhood. A Multi-Disciplinary Approach*. London: Paul Chapman Publishing.

Miller, L. (2008) Developing new professional roles in the early years. In: L. Miller and C. Cable (eds) *Professionalism in the Early Years*. London: Hodder & Stoughton.

Moyles, J. (2006) *Effective Leadership and Management in the Early Years*. Maidenhead: Open University Press.

Pollard, A. (2002) *Reflective Teaching: Effective and Evidence-informed Professional Practice*. London: Continuum.

Rodd, J. (2005) *Leadership in Early Childhood: The Pathway to Professionalism,* 3rd edn. Buckingham: Open University Press.

Rodd, J. (2006) *Leadership in Early Childhood,* 3rd edn. Maidenhead: Open University Press.

Siraj-Blatchford, I., Manni, L. (2007) *Effective Leadership in the Early Years Sector: The ELEYS Study*. London: Institute of Education, University of London.

Smith, A., Langston, A. (1999) *Managing Staff in Early Years Settings*. London: Routledge.

Solley, K. (2003) *What do Early Childhood Leaders do to Maintain and Enhance the Significance of the Early Years?* Institute of Education, University of London: Early Education.

Tuckman, B. (1965) Developmental sequence in small groups. *Psychological Bulletin*, **63**(6): 384–99.

Tuckman, B.W., Jensen, M.A. (1977*)* Stages of small group development revisited. *Group and Organisational Studies*, **2**: 419–27.

Whalley, M., Allen, S., Wilson, D. (2008) *Leading Practice in Early Years Settings*. Exeter: Learning Matters Ltd.

Whitty, G. (2006) Education(al) research and education policy making: is conflict inevitable. *British Educational Research Journal*, **32**(2): 159–76.

Chapter 8

Professional development

Introduction

This chapter details how EYPS students use their literacy, numeracy and ICT skills. It identifies ways in which practitioners can reflect upon practice and identify improvements.

Objectives

By the end of this chapter you should have:

● Gained an overview of the key theoretical perspectives on the importance of continuous professional development (CPD) for EYPs

● Reflected on how you can promote through your practice the requirements identified in standards 37–39

● Reflected on how you can lead and support others in relation to the requirements identified in standards 37–39.

Theoretical underpinning knowledge for standards 37–39

This group of standards emphasises the importance of personal professional development for EYPs as well as the extent of EYPs' ability to reflect on their learning and to make informed decisions that challenge existing practice.

Providing effective support for children's learning and development across all areas of learning is not feasible unless early years practitioners are clear about their own insights into the learning process along with their competence in literacy, numeracy and information and communication technology (ICT). The importance of looking at the professional development of practitioners in the early years context is particularly pertinent, since the EYFS highlights the need to encourage positive dispositions to learning (DCSF, 2008). Current research (Pound, 2006; Aubrey and Dahl, 2008) suggests that there is an obvious link between the children's negative learning experiences and adults' ongoing difficulties in relevant areas of subject knowledge.

Practice guidance for the EYFS on communication, language and literacy begins by stating that children's learning and competence in communicating, speaking and listening, being read to and beginning to read and write must be supported and extended. Research (Kontos, 1999; Potter and Hodgson, 2007) shows that the course of supporting and extending children's learning in this area of learning and development has proved to be challenging for some early years practitioners. One of the reasons for this situation includes practitioners' insufficient subject knowledge in the area of language and communication development. As studies (Bryant *et al.*, 1993; Potter and Hodgson, 2007) concluded, the settings where more in-depth subject knowledge was required from staff often scored poorly on language and literacy scales. This allows us to suggest that to improve the outcomes for babies and young children, and particularly those from a disadvantaged background, EYPs need to place emphasis on continuous broadening of their subject knowledge in this area, along with further developing their range of strategies for promoting children's language and communication skills.

It is obvious from previous discussion that the learning processes of very young children require tailored pedagogies and highly skilled practitioners. This statement is particularly true when it comes to developing children's mathematical skills; these are incorporated into the EYFS as problem-solving, reasoning and numeracy. The EYFS (DCSF, 2008) communicates clearly to practitioners the importance of nurturing children's early interest in numeracy through a range of experiences and contexts, both indoors and outdoors, that will allow children to develop their confidence in solving problems, asking meaningful questions and reasoning. *The Independent Review of Mathematics Teaching in Early Years Settings and Primary Schools* (Williams, 2008) emphasises the critical role of appropriately qualified staff in early years and acknowledges the increasingly important role of the graduate EYP in the process of extending children's understanding of this area of learning and development. The review also highlights the importance for EYPs to acquire specialist skills and confidence in certain mathematical elements of pedagogy:

Distinctive features that support high quality mathematical learning include:

- Practitioners' enthusiasm for, understanding of, and confidence in, mathematics
- Direct teaching of mathematical skills and knowledge in meaningful contexts
- Opportunities for open-ended discussions of solutions, exploration of reasoning and mathematical logic
- Exploitation of mathematics in everyday activities and in play where children use and apply their knowledge, skills and understanding
- A breadth of mathematical experiences
- Understanding of the links in mathematics
- Understanding of mathematical concepts.   (Williams, 2008: 38)

As the guidelines for practitioners recommend, appropriate mathematical development in young children is context-dependent and should be embedded into daily activities that make sense to young children. Good practice, therefore, suggests that practitioners need an awareness of the cultural and social environments outside the setting in which children's early mathematical experiences and dispositions are being formed, as well as the knowledge and skills they are bringing with them into the setting (Aubrey *et al.*, 2003: 102).

A set of resource materials, *Numbers and Patterns: Laying Foundations in Mathematics* (DCSF, 2009), stresses the importance of laying secure foundations in early mathematics that will equip children with the key mathematical tools and ideas that they will use throughout the rest of their lives. To achieve this goal, EYPs need to ensure that they have secure knowledge and understanding of all relevant areas of mathematics along with the understanding of the processes through which children develop mathematical understanding. As Gifford (2004) points out, there is a need to ensure that pedagogy for mathematics considers and enables the practitioner to develop effective 'sustained shared thinking' and discussion with individual children, not only during planned activities but in everyday opportunities for mathematical development that occur in a range of settings.

This set of standards also refers to the need for EYPs to recognise the importance of enhancing their subject knowledge of information and communication technology (ICT) and developing technological awareness education through using ICT in early years settings. *A Review of the Evidence on the Use of ICT in the Early Years Foundation Stage* (Aubrey and Dahl, 2008) has identified three main areas of early years learning that can be supported by ICT, including developing positive dispositions to learning, extending children's knowledge and understanding of the world and helping children to acquire operational skills. However, the review also highlighted that, although the majority of early years practitioners are generally positive about the role of electronic media and ICT, not all practitioners are fully confident in using ICT; nor are they always able to use ICT to contribute to children's learning or see how this can be integrated into the EYFS curriculum. To be able to lead and support elements of practice and other practitioners in this area, EYPs need to extend their competence in:

- Using ICT, and specifically developing their skills further
- Using interactive whiteboards and software for spreadsheets
- Editing and downloading digital images
- The provision of routine guidance and technical assistance.

EYPs also need to have a greater awareness of different types of adult interaction that dynamically mediate, expand and encourage children's learning across all areas of learning and development.

Recognising the fact that young children's use of technology is guided and focused by an appropriately trained adult, the Department for Children, Schools and Families launched the 'Using ICT in EYs Project' (DCSF, 2006). The main driving force of the project was to support the raising of children's achievements in ICT capability within the early years. One of the key messages to EYPs from the case studies of the project include a strong emphasis upon the importance of embedding the observational assessment practices across the early years and finding new ways to involve children and their parents/carers in that process.

Along with the issues relevant to personal professional development, this group of standards also highlights the expectations of EYPs in reflecting on their own and colleagues' practice, and in acknowledging the importance of positive change and innovation. Hatton (2007) calls attention to the importance of being creative in the process of improving practice and generating new forms of practice, emphasising that the key element of such creativity involves modification of 'existing ways of doing things to make them more relevant to people providing and experiencing services' (Hatton, 2007: 3). These goals require EYPs' involvement in a process of review, evaluation and development followed by initiating changes where improvements are needed. Using a creative approach to innovations based on sound professional judgement will help EYPs to build on the best examples of current practice as well as on the best traditions of pedagogy, both national and international.

Standard 37 – develop and use skills in literacy, numeracy and information and communication technology to support their work with children and wider professional activities

Example of standard 37 in personal practice

Standard 37 'defines the ways in which EYPs maintain and extend their competence in literacy, numeracy and communication technology in order to support children's learning and development across all areas of learning and to facilitate wider professional activities' (CWDC, 2010: 70).

In any early years role there are formal and informal opportunities involving literacy, numeracy and ICT. The National Literacy Strategy Framework (DfES, 1998: 3) states that 'literacy unites the important skills of reading and writing. It also involves speaking and listening skills'. Numeracy is more than just numbers and calculations, it is about understanding mathematical frameworks. Considering the national strategies along with a definition of standard 37 may be a starting point from which to consider the activities with which you are currently involved.

The use of Information Communication Technology (ICT) has been gaining pace in settings, and is used to support children's learning through the use of a PC and interactive educational games, through to staff use for their wider professional activities, keeping registers, accounts and managing occupancy. With high speed broadband, the purpose and use of ICT is recognised in supporting our wider professional activities. Children can develop their learning both about ICT and through ICT. The variety of software and hardware suitable for young children and babies now available is immense, and the candidate should ensure provision is age-appropriate and of excellent quality. Clearly, the way in which literacy, numeracy and ICT are identified in practice will depend on the setting and the role of the EYP.

Each element of the standard can be considered in turn, using a structured approach to identify current effective personal practice. Practitioners who do not view themselves in a leadership position will no doubt seek the opportunity to evidence their leadership through their day-to-day practices. What if you do not hold a senior position? How can you find the evidence?

If you work in a room with other staff you are part of a team, you are in a strong position to demonstrate your leadership by sharing your expertise as a practitioner with other staff.

How may this be done? One way would be to take on a role in a setting-wide project such as Every Child a Talker (ECAT) or Early Years Quality Improvement Support Programme (EYQISP), focusing on an area of practice. In doing so you would be engaging in teamwork and collaboration, maybe having formal or informal opportunities to communicate with parents as well as engaging in activities to promote literacy, numeracy and ICT.

This activity may require further research, browsing the internet to look for resources, completing order forms, collating information and presenting a report of findings.

You may be able to revisit policies to review and update them, continuing then to present them for approval to senior managers, before sharing them with colleagues and parents.

The setting's link diaries, play or individual education plans may be drawn up by you for key children. This information is likely to be shared verbally or in print with practitioners in your team or with parents. Such information may also be shared with other agencies.

The daily observations which lead to planning will be testimony to your skills in literacy. The children's planning may be word processed or hand written; equally, it is documented as are all the other records you keep. Are you responsible for ensuring that risk assessments are completed each day? Do you file them, forwarding necessary information to your seniors?

The Independent Review of Mathematics Teaching in Early Years Settings and Primary Schools, known as the Williams Review (DCSF, 2008), recommended that the DCSF should produce a set of materials on mathematical mark-making and mathematical development. These would be used to support early years practitioners' professional development.

Mark Making Matters (DCSF, 2008) was the first part of the set of materials recommended by Williams. This is a tool for strengthening the quality of provision for mark-making in the EYFS areas of learning and development. This is referred to in the National Strategies publication, 'Children Thinking Mathematically: Knowledge for Early Years Practitioners'. The prime focus of this review was the teacher, and the 'increasingly important role' of the graduate EYP was also acknowledged.

The review also laid great store by play-based learning and the aforementioned mark-making.

Together these publications will support practitioners not only to develop their own practice but the practice within a team. Illustrated by case study and practical suggestions, these pedagogical strategies will extend the children's learning by using existing resources in a new and innovative way.

As a practitioner working within a small team it is these ideas for auditing practice that allow the whole team to be led. The EYP will be responsible for researching the publication to decide on a plan of action. This would be followed by collating findings, maybe noting them or by verbal discussion. Resources may need identifying, reorganising or labelling. These jobs can be delegated to other staff and the outcomes monitored by the EYP. Sharing best practice with the rest of the staff team may be an option and would give the opportunity to support a larger team of practitioners.

Within the EYQISP materials there is an audit tool for problem-solving, reasoning and numeracy (PSRN). This aims to develop a high quality learning environment indoors and out to support PSRN. The EYFS profile scores reveal that boys do less well than girls, especially in the area of calculation, and a focus on provision aimed at boys may be an aspect of practice that could be developed further.

Throughout these activities the use of ICT is obvious, in researching, printing materials, collating and planning. What if you want to consider the use of ICT in a wider context? ICT is inextricably woven into day-to-day activity and play in settings, recognising that this may be sufficient to evidence standard 37. However, again, auditing practice may be a supportive tool and can be shared with others in the team.

Following this through, drawing up an action plan will identify the change process, a timescale and the involvement of others, identifying expected outcomes.

The Naace website, www.naace.co.uk, is dedicated to 'advancing education through the use of ICT'. Within the early years section of the website there are various topics. The primary early years section has links to the early learning goals with the focus on the role of ICT. It identifies further links to websites for additional support and these are wideranging to include talking books, maths games, Tweenies and Bob the Builder.

Example of standard 37 in leadership

The EYP leading practice has many opportunities to consider their competence in literacy. While leading other practitioners, they may be involved in staff training, briefings, coaching or mentoring.

The roll-out of the Every Child A Talker (ECAT) Programme followed an independent review by John Bercow MP. Commissioned by the Government, this review identified communication as a key life skill for every child. Investing in this early intervention programme to identify and tackle communication problems has given settings an opportunity to evaluate their practice before engaging on a programme to improve outcomes for children at school and in later life.

Undertaking a quality assurance programme such as EYQISP also means looking at current practice, evaluating and planning for change.

These programmes require written evaluations initially, undertaken after discussion with other team members. The information is collated and disseminated, delegating roles to staff.

These processes provide a wealth of opportunity for the EYP to provide evidence to meet multiple standards, demonstrating leadership.

Forms will be distributed, completed electronically and printed off for sharing. Resources may be sourced, ordered, taken delivery of and distributed to staff. Staff may need tutoring on their usage or storage identifying and labelling. Written instructions may be needed or a policy for usage.

Everyday activities such as organising staff cover, managing occupancy and communicating with parents will also provide evidence. You may keep this information on a spreadsheet, a paper table, a diary or reflective log – all require skills in evidence of standard 37.

Wider professional activities may include tasks such as organising or attending meetings, taking the minutes and writing them up. Attending training for outdoor play could result in qualifying the needs of the setting's outdoor provision in an action plan. To complete the action plan may require you to canvas parents for their opinion. Once resources arrive, they need to be checked against expected delivery, unpacked and put into use. If the resource is new then it may require a written policy to cover usage or a risk assessment. Staff may need training or written instruction. Undertaking such activity requires written and verbal skills, the ability to engage with staff, to research and formulate policy and clearly you will be aspiring to a vision of which staff will be aware because this too has been articulated and documented.

The authors have used examples of current early years initiatives that are popular amongst our students. For staff leading practice, choosing the best evidence may be their challenge as opposed to finding it.

Standard 37 reflection points

- Conduct an audit of the resources you have to support ICT for all age ranges and how well they are used by the staff
- How can you develop this area if there is a lack of provision for an age group? Do you have ICT equipment other than a PC for the children to experience?
- How do you use ICT to develop communication with parents, book-keeping and other professional activities?
- Conduct an audit of the resources you have to support PSRN for all age ranges and how well they are used by the staff
- How do you use numeracy in your day-to-day work?
- Consider ways to develop staff in their support of children's PSRN experiences
- Conduct an audit of the resources you have to support communication, literacy and language for all age ranges and how well they are used by the staff
- Compare this to the PSRN and ICT audit – are they given equal status in the setting?
- Does each age group have equal access to age-appropriate resources?

Standard 37 stakeholder comment

To gather evidence for standard 37, Nikki spent time working alongside the staff team observing and evaluating the provision in the setting.

Nikki was aware that the setting had invested in a range of resources to promote ICT that were currently not being incorporated into the daily provision for the children. Nikki chose to focus on this area as part of her development plan. Initial discussions with staff revealed that they were lacking in confidence in this ICT, as they had not received training. Nikki realised that her first objective was to develop staff confidence through practical training and support in the use of ICT equipment.

→

She organised a session wherein the staff could explore and experiment with the equipment in a supportive context. The staff enjoyed the session and their confidence grew as Nikki led the gradual introduction of a range of computer programmes, developed the use of the interactive whiteboard, the use of digital cameras with the children and the implementation of a listening centre in the learning environment. Nikki's early observations and discussions with staff also revealed that provision for literacy and numeracy was not based on practical experiences planned as a result of staff observations of children. Nikki identified a training need and offered to provide some input on the EYFS. The staff welcomed the opportunity to engage in professional development as a team.

By focusing on the principles and commitments of the EYFS, Nikki was able to encourage the staff to reflect on their practice and provision and begin to evaluate the children's learning. In this way staff began to discuss and understand the need to use their observations of children to inform them about individual interests and learning needs and to provide meaningful experiences based on those interests.

Nikki supported this process with ideas on how to put EYFS principles into practice and, most importantly, worked alongside the staff with the children to model how to implement those ideas. The staff worked collaboratively to develop their provision. Nikki received positive feedback from the staff highlighting the benefits they had experienced as a result of focusing on children's interests and encouraging literacy and numeracy development through play-based experiences.

Jane came to the full training pathway with a degree in communication and new media. Whilst this shows her ability to think and reflect on her own learning in these areas at degree level, it takes a little time and creative thinking to see how this could translate into a highly committed and effective practitioner able to carry out the leadership element of the EYP. With such a body of knowledge, Jane also needed to develop the personal, human interface of communication in a way that would support highly experienced practitioners, who may have not had the leisure or opportunity to extend their technical knowledge and confidence in using the newer forms of technology.

It was the placements carried out as part of the training pathway that enabled Jane to explore these crucial issues and to gain essential experience in working personally with babies, toddlers and young children in a range of settings. This supported the theoretical background she gained as part of the intensive full training pathway. It also gave her the opportunity to share her knowledge and understanding of ICT to promote her colleagues' own professional development, a crucial element of standard 37. She was able to show how to develop and use skills in ICT with children and wider professional activities, which would support the work of not only herself personally but also that of all the practitioners in the placement setting in a wider context. It can be difficult to appreciate fully the range of techniques available to early years practitioners to engage with children and their parents/carers that have become available through the innovation of new media, but having an 'expert', who was nevertheless also a recognised 'learner', seems to have been key to this success. A model of sharing expertise or co-coaching perhaps?

Jane's first placement enabled her to work on the aspect of supporting her work with children, using 'digiblue' cameras with the children, enabling them to record their own ideas, opinions and concerns. Here she also developed an information booklet for staff, recognising the need to produce a readily accessible format for staff to motivate them, foster and extend their own interest in the use of technology and new media with children. Jane used her skills to develop a promotional leaflet to encourage parents/carers to use the children's centre. An interesting, accessible leaflet acted to encourage parents/carers to use the centre but also acted to illuminate the key points of the high quality education and care that was available.

One of the key attractions of the leaflet shows the level of thinking behind it: it was not too wordy, it recognised and responded to key parent/carer concerns and it illustrated how children might enjoy and learn from attending, thus alleviating parental concerns. A more exciting opportunity perhaps presented itself in the production of a DVD to record the children's participation and engagement with a dance activity led by an external practitioner.

Standard 38 – reflect on and evaluate the impact of practice, modifying approaches where necessary, and take responsibility for identifying and meeting their professional development needs

Example of standard 38 in personal practice

Reflecting on and evaluating the impact of practice is a crucially important aspect of the EYP's role as a 'change agent'. Self-evaluation and the training and development needs of those working in the early years sector have become a key issue in recent policy. The EYFS (DCSF, 2008: 8) states that 'all providers should continuously think about how to improve what they are offering to children and families'. More specifically, the welfare requirements of the statutory framework

of EYFS also state that 'providers must support their staff in improving their qualification levels' and that 'regular staff appraisals should be carried out to identify
the training needs of staff. A programme of continuing professional development
should be applied so that these needs are met' (DCSF, 2008: 31).

Since 2004, the findings of the Effective Provision of Pre-School Education (EPPE)
report have been influential in shaping policy, with a focus on quality and quality
improvement linked to the qualifications of staff and emphasising the role of continuous
self-evaluation. The Ten Year Childcare Strategy of the same year even quoted EPPE to
rationalise the increased spending on early education and care for the improvement of
quality. Throughout this change in practice, the emphasis on the concept of reflective
practice has become synonymous with 'quality'. The Study of Pedagogical Effectiveness in Early Learning (SPEEL) research (Moyles *et al.*, 2006), which aimed to identify
the embedded characteristics of effective pedagogy in the early years, reported that
the personal qualities of an effective early years practitioner include the ability to:

- Be reflective
- Be questioning
- Be analytical
- Be committed to learning and professional development
- Welcome and initiate constructive, critical engagement with peers and others.

(SPEEL, 2006: 58)

The report makes it clear that effective practitioners are reflective and thoughtful people who 'examine, question and evaluate all aspects of effective early
years pedagogy and child development' (SPEEL, 2006: 57).

Similarly, the Effective Leadership in the Early Years Sector Study carried out
by Siraj-Blatchford and Manni (2007) identified that encouraging reflection with
staff acts as an impetus for change and the motivation for ongoing learning and
development. This was one of a range of characteristics they saw when considering effective leadership practice in the settings they used for their research. This
concept is reiterated more currently in the EYQISP (2008), a recent tool designed
to be used by local authorities to determine the quality of its settings and to support continuous quality improvement. It provides a set of audits for settings to be
used for self-evaluation and to form the basis of discussions with early years consultants. One of the non-negotiable audits it provides is entitled 'Strengthening
Leadership for Learning' and asks providers the following questions:

- Is the current improvement plan for the setting based on an audit of current
  practice and needs?

- Does the current improvement plan set out clearly the next steps and identify timescales and evaluation procedures?
- Are all relevant people involved in creating and monitoring the improvement plan?

Clearly, there is currently an important focus on self-evaluation within early years settings and a strong link is being made between leadership, reflection and self-evaluation. This is reflected in the EYPS standards by standard 38 which highlights this as a responsibility of EYPs within their setting. It emphasises a commitment to review and reflect continually on provision but also a commitment to lead others to do the same, making the process of reflection explicit. According to Reed and Canning (2009), in his attempt to define the notion of reflection, reflective learning implies a sense of open exploration to find out how something is or to find out more about it. He feels that this can lead to reflective action – that is, action taken following reflection.

Inspection frameworks have been influential in promoting self-evaluation, with settings now required to complete a self-evaluation form (SEF). In its report in 2008, Leading to Excellence, Ofsted detailed key findings from early years inspections in a review of inspections from 2005 to 2008, with a focus on organisation, leadership and management. They asked the question, what does best practice in organisation, leadership and management look like? One of the findings was that providers further improve on already outstanding practice. Within this report their findings show that in the most effective settings, adults are highly motivated and committed to improvement and that improvement is based on self-evaluation, where all adults share the responsibility for continually improving outcomes for children. Improvements following self-evaluation include recognising and responding better to the child's point of view, better resources, training focused on areas identified, updating of policies and procedures, and better involvement of staff, parents and children, leading to improved outcomes for children. Although it is important to be reflective to develop, the practitioner needs to take care that self-evaluation does not simply mean to deliver and comply with the EYFS. This idea was also expounded by Moss in Reed and Canning (2009: 9), warning practitioners against a narrow interpretation of reflective practice that reduces it to the role of a tool for 'governing early childhood educators' or for 'assessing one's own conformity to externally imposed norms'.

The work of Donald Schon has been influential in defining reflective practice and the concept of a reflective practitioner. Schon (1991) describes two processes of reflection: reflection-in-practice and reflection-on-practice. A practitioner who reflects on the tasks they are carrying out is 'reflecting-in-practice'. Someone who takes this further and links these thoughts with theory and new ways of working would be reflecting-on-practice. An EYP should be engaged in both processes. Reflective practice is about considering the impact of what we do as practitioners on the learning and development of children. It is a way of thinking and translating those thoughts into behaviour, something that becomes a habit. As an EYP, it is important that we create the right culture for this, and train and support staff to become reflective by developing a reflective learning environment. This is strongly linked to practitioners taking part in professional development and becoming part of a community of learning practitioners. A reflective learning journal is a useful tool for an EYP. This may include writing about professional practice, work issues, research, ideas, feelings, readings or websites. This can be personal or shared (Macleod-Brudenell and Kay, 2008: 49).

Example of standard 38 in leadership

'This Standard relates to EYPs' commitment to reflecting on, and evaluating the impact of, their own practice on children's learning and development, and encouraging colleagues likewise to reflect and evaluate their practice' (DCSF, 2008: 73). An example of leadership of this standard is someone who is not only engaged in 'reflecting-on-practice' (that is, linking thoughts, observations and theory with new ways of working), but someone who also supports other staff to do this by creating a culture of reflection for all staff and opportunities for staff to develop their full potential by actively engaging in continuous professional development. Indeed, in the introduction and rationale for the EYQISP it states that the tools are built on four key principles. One of those principles is, 'a continuous cycle of self-evaluation, improvement and reflection, thus empowering practitioners to see themselves as learners seeking improvements in their practice, reducing inequality and narrowing the achievement gap.' The document also focuses on 'the key role of leaders in building capacity and ensuring high quality learning development and provision' (DCSF, 2008a: 6).

The notion of 'quality' and the concept of self-evaluation have become key areas in early years provision recently and this is identified in the EYFS as the responsibility of all staff. Leaders need to ensure that not only do they participate in a variety of professional development events to extend their own knowledge and skills continually but that they also encourage others in this pursuit of knowledge. This professional development could include facilitating opportunities for members of staff to observe other colleagues within their own setting or within other settings to gain new ideas or different insights or perspectives on ways of working with young children. Other ideas include arranging shadowing or mentoring opportunities for staff, based on a good working knowledge of the skills and areas for development of each colleague. This could also include personal study of current research or encouraging colleagues to become involved in action research in an area that has been identified as needing some development.

Many EYPs are members of networks and lead team or network meetings. These are useful opportunities to disseminate information about successful innovations within their own settings that have had positive outcomes. This could include information about the rationale behind the change and preparing briefing papers on the impact this has had on the children. Savage and Leeson (2007: 151) expound the idea that leadership in the early years is 'about empowering people to learn and seek change and improvement, not about controlling them'. This concept of shared leadership is about the leader working cooperatively with a team, seeking to support and empower members of the team to work with children effectively in the pursuit of quality provision. This can only be successful where there is a culture of reflection and self-evaluation and where all staff are fully involved in this and, in a wider sense, in all settings. It is important for an EYP to understand the wider context within which they work and for them to ensure other practitioners are also aware of this.

All settings should now have an appraisal system in place to assess the performance of their staff, and providing this opportunity is important. This too is about the process of reflection, with time, the most precious of resources, set aside for reflecting on individual performance. As an EYP it is important to lead this process of reflection by making use of open-ended questions and guiding reflection through skilled questioning. Leading reflection means encouraging others to continually review and develop their own practice based on self-knowledge. This can be done by regularly making links between theory and practice; identifying a particular member of staff's knowledge, understanding and skills and making effective use of these; making recommendations for adaptations to practice as part of a formal appraisal process but also as part of everyday practice; looking for patterns and making connections with practitioners. It is useful in settings to build up a 'library' of current books about early years theory and practice available for staff use, which could be added to following recommendations from staff. Time within staff meetings could be used to consider some of the theory, with practitioners being involved in the dissemination of some of the relevant information followed by reflection on practice. The internet is a useful tool in this respect as well.

> ### Standard 38 reflection points
>
> - Is there a system of peer observation in your setting?
> - How supportive is this?
> - Do all staff participate fully?
> - Is there a staff appraisal system?
> - How effective is this? Are staff able to contribute to their own targets and how supportive are the management in supporting staff in their professional development?
> - What procedures are in place to allow staff time to reflect on their practice and provision for the children – is time allocated for them to consider this as a team?
> - How open are the leaders of the setting to ideas for change?
> - Do staff have opportunities to contribute to or make changes to policies, practices and procedures?

Standard 38 stakeholder comment

The stakeholder comment in this chapter is from a manager of a preschool who is currently preparing for her EYPS assessment. It is a new setting, with all staff finding their place within the team.

She feels that it is important to really understand the standard you are evidencing and that the best way to do that is to be clear about the amplification within the guidance to the standards. One way to do this is to familiarise yourself with the standards by reflecting on what you do on a day-to-day basis and relating it to the standards. She did this by keeping a rough diary and making links at the end of the week, trying to recognise where she was meeting the standards with an emphasis on the leadership aspect.

> 'Obviously reflection is an ongoing part of what we do at the setting and this is linked with the self-evaluation form and EYQISP, which we are using at the moment to evaluate our provision. One area that we needed to develop, as we are a relatively new setting, is relationships with parents. To do this I wanted to get involved with a local authority project called INSPIRE, which is designed to develop parent's knowledge of the setting and EYFS and how children learn through play, but also to make them feel more comfortable and familiar with the setting through attending a series of informal sessions with staff. As this had been identified as an area for development by all staff, I wanted to ensure that all staff were involved. One member of staff

→ had built a particularly good rapport with parents and I identified her as the most appropriate person to lead the initiative. This involved attending a series of training sessions and disseminating the information to other staff and then implementing the scheme, overcoming all the practical and logistical challenges like safeguarding. We had frequent meetings about the project, giving her opportunities to reflect on what she had learned and how this impacted on all our opportunities and procedures for relating with parents generally. This also prompted her to offer suggestions about procedures and this led to changes being made to provide opportunities for more effective relationships with parents. At one point I felt that this had been too much of a challenge and we discussed what support she needed from me. However, the INSPIRE sessions took place and were extremely successful and well attended, with positive feedback from parents and grandparents. This is now something which will take place annually. By giving my colleague the opportunity to do this, I feel that I led her to reflect on the processes already in place to build relationships with parents and how the INSPIRE project fitted into the context of that. Her knowledge and understanding of what effective relationships look like has been deepened and extended, and her professional development needs have been met, based on an existing strength. As a result we have adapted our approach to developing relationships with parents, which has had a very positive impact. This was also linked to our appraisal system, which has given us further opportunities for reflection.'

'As an EYP it is important that you offer opportunities to others to reflect on practice and to make this part of the wider culture within the setting. There are formal opportunities for this, such as appraisal procedures and staff meetings, but informal opportunities are just as valuable. This leads to a situation where practitioners are constantly evaluating the quality of their provision from a range of perspectives, those of 'experts', parents and children. It is only through these professional discussions, combined with an atmosphere of trust and a growing knowledge and understanding that comes from continuous professional development, that we can provide the best for the children and families at our setting.'

Standard 39 – take a creative and constructively critical approach towards innovation and adapt practice if benefits and improvements are identified

Example of standard 39 in personal practice

Reflective practice is a key constituent of being an effective EYP. Beyond reflection, however, are the insights and skills associated with exploring, developing, delivering and evaluating new and innovative ways of doing things. Whilst an EYP will often be the catalyst for such activity, their role is also to harness the collective energy of colleagues, children and parents in continuously improving practice, provoking thought, stimulating ideas and motivating the team – change should be about refreshing, transforming and reinvigorating. In this respect, an EYP's role is about inspiring, challenging and delivering. It is about optimising potential within a setting. 'It is vitally important that early years provision is of a consistently high standard, and that providers continually look for ways to improve the quality of the learning, development and care they offer' (DCSF, 2008: 8).

In striving for improved standards and high quality provision, an EYP should be guided by evaluations of existing practice and an understanding of 'best practice', including that of other settings. Local authority quality assessors and early years advisors are a particularly useful source of information and ideas based on their knowledge of EYFS requirements and high quality practice observed across a variety of settings. EYPs must heighten and attune their awareness of innovative practice. This can be done in many ways – from attending formal courses to networking with colleagues from other settings. Reading is important – journal and periodical articles, newspapers, textbooks, research and evaluation reports, and generally being aware of media accounts and stories exploring new ways of working and celebrating success. Projects and initiatives undertaken at local and national levels provide a rich source of inspiration and the possible involvement in the development of good practice in a wider context (The Family Nurse Partnership, Every Child a Talker, Quality Counts and EPPE are some examples of this). EYPs should be receptive to new ideas, engage in discussion and debate, welcome constructive criticism and invite thoughtful comment. Such engagement and collaborative practice have many benefits that go beyond those of direct relevance to any one setting – opening the sector to scrutiny, establishing formal and informal support networks which in turn can lead to a sharing of knowledge, expertise and resources.

Any change, however, does present challenges, sometimes large and sometimes small. Some colleagues will embrace change, others will question it, some will resist. In his chapter on Eight 'Forces' for Leaders of Change, Michael Fullan (2009: 10) identifies effective 'drivers' that help to support and sustain change. The first of these is the need to engage people's 'moral purpose' – the importance of establishing the reason(s) why change is necessary. This, Fullan (2009) believes, is fundamental in gaining other people's support. Without a reason, change will seem like a burden rather than an opportunity and colleagues who cannot be convinced of the moral purpose are likely at best to lack motivation, and at worst actively to seek to undermine new initiatives. Practitioners are much more likely to support something that can be justified in terms of improved outcomes. They will also be more accepting of the additional work usually associated with change (even if this is only short term) if they can be convinced of contingent benefits.

Fullan's (2009) second force is 'building capacity' or establishing the infrastructure in which change is more likely to occur. This includes shaping policies, procedures, strategies, resources and actions in ways that support people to, and harbour the expectation that people will, work together in a mutually supportive way – a combination of vision, positive intent, action and teamwork. Building capacity requires investment in your team – both emotionally and through taking practical steps to equip them for change (e.g. providing training, sharing knowledge and good practice, consulting, allowing time to adjust, providing resources). It is about recognising and attending to the individual and collective needs of team members and equipping them with the knowledge, skill and confidence to embrace and deliver new ways of working. Fullan (2009) describes this striving to establish a culture of continuous improvement as 'developing cultures for learning' (another of his 'forces') through which people are encouraged to share good practice and learn from each other as well as becoming collectively responsible for, and committed to, improvement. A culture of shared responsibility and involvement in the development of quality services fosters a sense of 'ownership' which has the potential to achieve much more than the isolated efforts of individual team members alone.

Aldo Fortunati (cited in Moss, 2009: xii) describes his image of the kind of worker he sees as essential to meet the needs of emerging early years practice:

> [The early childhood worker needs to be] more attentive to creating possibilities than pursuing predefined goals . . . [to be] removed from the fallacy of certainties, [assuming instead] responsibility to choose, experiment, discuss, reflect and change, focusing on the organisation of opportunities rather than the anxiety of pursuing outcomes, and maintaining in her (sic) work the pleasure of amazement and wonder.

For Fortunati, an early years worker is not an 'automaton' – there to implement early years policy and practice passively – rather s/he should engage with and co-construct new models of practice based on informed judgement and measured 'risk', something that Rinaldi – also cited by Moss (2009: xiii) – refers to as 'a capacity for transformation . . . where you lose absolutely the possibility of controlling the final result'. None of this is to suggest an abdication of responsibility towards colleagues or children, but rather it is about having the courage and the capacity to lead and develop in truly innovative ways, taking 'calculated' risks to stimulate new ideas and strategies. It is about informed experimentation – trying new systems, methods and techniques, but ones that are based on tested and evaluated models and informed judgements. An EYP will need a combination of skills, including modelling practice, coaching, mentoring, guiding, explaining and questioning, demonstrating and celebrating to engage colleagues in the process of continuous quality improvement.

Examples of standard 39 in leadership

The EYFS (DCSF, 2008) signals the expectation that settings will engage in a process of continuous quality improvement. The guidance expands on the role of the leader in supporting this.

The EYFS practice guidance clearly sees the role of an early years leader as transformational, shaping and developing a culture in which change is not only possible, but welcomed – a culture of transparency and mutual support in which high standards are expected, striven for, objectively evaluated and ultimately achieved.

Sergiovanni (cited in Rodd, 2008: 26) suggests a number of facilitative skills that may be helpful for early childhood leaders to use to get the best out of their team. The first of these is *empowerment* – where the leader shares some of their authority and responsibility with other members of the team, thus increasing accountability and commitment throughout the group. Sergiovanni also emphasises the importance of a leader's support for their team (*enablement*), eliminating obstacles where these might impede progress, and *enhancement*, where 'leader and follower roles are interwoven to produce increased commitment and extraordinary performance' – an approach sometimes referred to as 'distributed leadership'.

Rodd (2008: 25) outlines four basic steps that she believes leaders should follow to move from 'theoretical' notions of change to 'actual' quality improvements:

- Clarify the definition of organisational and individual goal(s) and/or objectives
- Set individual standards and expectations
- Provide support and feedback
- Monitor and evaluate outcomes.

Within a 'quality' early years context, Rodd adds the important requirement that a leader should also 'attend to child well-being, adult morale and goal attainment' (Rodd, 2008: 26).

Developing innovative practice is not for the faint hearted – it is for rising aspirant leaders, leaders who are committed to achieving the best standards for children, the best possible provision and who have both the insight and foresight to create the conditions within a staff team to support and encourage participation in the search for excellence.

Standard 39 reflection points

- What opportunities are there in your setting to discover new practice and initiatives?
- How would you introduce innovative ideas to the setting?
- How would you support colleagues to develop innovative practice?

Standard 39 stakeholder comment

Linda was an EYP long pathway candidate on placement in a children's centre in Lancashire. After her own observations and discussions with staff led her to identify that the sensory room was under-utilised, she approached the centre manager for a meeting to discuss the possibility of basing a project around this. Through a series of informal interviews and a short questionnaire, she discovered that the main reasons for restricting parent access to the room included staff availability for supervision and health and safety considerations. Linda conducted a further survey of parents to establish the level of potential demand for this resource. With the data collected and summarised she once again arranged a meeting with the manager at which she proposed devising a parent induction programme to the sensory room.

The manager invited her to share her ideas at a staff meeting, at which she enlisted the support of a number of other colleagues. This also led to a further suggestion – the development of a resource handbook (containing key operating instructions for the equipment, code of conduct, health and safety information and descriptions of a variety of parent–child activities that could be undertaken in the sensory room with and without the use of specialist equipment).

Linda met with the centre SENCo and other key staff members to move the project forward and was invited to lead the initiative. Through careful liaison with colleagues and further consultations with parents, a standardised induction programme was developed and the handbook produced. This was a lavish affair, containing pictures of children (with appropriate permissions, of course) and parents engaged in play and learning activities. The illustrations showed both basic and

→

innovative use of equipment and resources accompanied by written explanations of learning benefits and extension activities.

The induction programme and handbook were a great success, and their introduction opened access to the room for parents and children to use without direct supervision. The induction sessions were scheduled around the availability of staff, but, significantly, this reduced the overall requirement for staff supervision at every session.

An evaluation of the project showed that the use of the room increased significantly over the next 6 weeks. The initiative helped the centre to develop relationships with parents and new activity groups formed naturally, with groups of parents coming together to use the sensory room in mutually supportive ways. The local childminder network started to access the room and interest in both the sensory room itself and the resource handbook began to extend beyond the registered parents. The children's centre started to receive requests for copies from local childminders, neighbouring schools and children's centres.

Conclusion

The group of standards 'Professional development' encourages practitioners to be reflective in their work. They should reflect upon their own practice and the practice of others, and identify and implement improvements. Candidates will identify their own strengths and understand what they need to do to develop their skills. Standard 37 has a emphasis on how the candidates use literacy, numeracy and ICT within their own work and within their work with children. They must demonstrate all three areas to achieve this standard.

References

Aubrey, C., Dahl, S. (2008) *A review of the evidence on the use of ICT in the Early Years Foundation Stage.* Available from http://partners.becta.org.uk/index.php?section=rh&catcode=_re_rp_02&rid=14901 (accessed on 24 March 2010).

Aubrey, C., Bottle, G., Godfrey, R. (2003) Early mathematics in the home and out-of-home contexts. *International Journal of Early Years Education,* **11**(2): 91–103.

Bryant, D.M., Peisner-Feinberg, E., Clifford, R. (1993) *Evaluation of Public Preschool Programs in North Carolina.* University of North Carolina: Frank Porter Graham Center.

CWDC. (2010) *Guidance to the Standards for the Award of the Early Years Professional Status.* London: CWDC.

DCSF. (2006) *Using ICT in EYs Project.* Available from http://nationalstrategies.standards.dcsf.gov.uk/node/84802?uc=force_uj (accessed 24 March 2010).

DCSF. (2008) *Practice Guidance for the Early Years Foundation Stage Guidance. Setting the Standards for Learning, Development and Care for Children from Birth to Five.* Nottingham: DCSF Publications.

DCSF. (2008a) *Early Years Quality Improvement Support Programme (EYQISP).* Nottingham: DCSF Publications.

DCSF. (2009) *Numbers and Patterns: Laying Foundations in Mathematics.* Nottingham: DCSF Publications.

DfES. (1998) *The National Literacy Strategy Framework.* Nottingham: DfES.

Fullan, M. (ed.) (2009) *The Challenge of Change, Start School Improvement Now,* 2nd edn. Canada: Corwin.

Gifford, S. (2004) A new mathematics pedagogy for the early years: in search of principles for practice. *International Journal of Early Years Education,* **12**(2): 99–115.

Hatton, K. (2007) *New Directions in Social Work.* Exeter: Learning Matters.

Kontos, S. (1999) Preschool teachers' talk, roles and activity settings during free play. *Early Childhood Research Quarterly,* **14**(3): 363–82.

Macleod-Brudenell, I., Kay, J. (2008) *Advanced Early Years: for Foundation Degrees and Levels 4/5,* 2nd edn. Harlow: Pearson.

Moss, P. (2009) Foreword. In: A. Paige-Smith, A. Craft (eds) (2009) *Developing Reflective Practice in the Early Years.* McGraw Hill, Open University Press, pp. xii–xvi.

Moyles, J., Adams, S., Musgrove, A. (2006) *Study of Pedagogical Effectiveness in Early Learning.* Nottingham: DfES.

Potter, C.A., Hodgson, S. (2007) Language enriched preschool settings: a Sure Start training approach. In: *The Sure Start Experience: Lessons from Local Evaluations.* London: Jessica Kingsley.

Pound, L. (2006) *Supporting Mathematical Development in the Early Years,* 2nd edn. Maidenhead: Open University Press.

Reed, M., Canning, N. (2009) *Reflective Practice in the Early Years.* London: Sage.

Rodd, J. (2008) *Leadership in Early Childhood,* 3rd edn. Maidenhead: Open University Press.

Savage, J., Leeson, C. (2007) Leadership in early childhood settings. In: J. Willan, R. Parker-Rees, J. Savage (2007) *Early Childhood Studies.* Exeter: Learning Matters.

Schon, D.A. (1991) *The Reflective Turn: Case Studies in and on Educational Practice.* New York: Teachers Press.

Siraj-Blatchford, I., Manni, L. (2007) *Effective Leadership in the Early Years Sector: The ELEYS Study: Issues in Practice Series.* Institute of Education, University of London.

Williams, P. (2008) *Independent Review of Mathematics Teaching in Early Years Settings.* Available from http://www.education.gov.uk/publications/.../Williams%20Mathematics.pdf (accessed 31 March 2011).

Chapter 9

Beyond EYPS

Introduction

This chapter details the roles of practitioners when they have gained EYPS and gives some case studies. It identifies further continuous professional development (CPD) for EYPS practitioners and gives some examples of how EYPS has changed practice. The chapter gives examples of EYPS practitioners who are working in the field through a variety of perspectives, including managers, owners, local authority workers, practitioners themselves, etc.

Objectives

By the end of this chapter you should have:

- Gained an understanding of some of the roles EYPS that practitioners undertake
- Gained an understanding of the next stages of professional development after gaining EYP status
- Gained an understanding of the difference EYPS has made to other practitioners.

Gaining EYP status gives practitioners recognition of the hard and dedicated work they carry out. EYPs aim to raise the quality of the provision and experiences offered for children and families across a range of backgrounds. They carry out a number of diverse roles and this chapter aims to explore some of the different roles and responsibilities.

EYPs may work as:

- Nursery practitioners
- Deputy nursery managers
- Nursery managers
- Nursery room leaders
- Childminders
- Children's centre workers
- Curriculum advisors
- Creche workers
- Playgroup leaders
- Family support workers
- Local authority support workers.

After gaining EYPS many practitioners question how they will now continue professionally, and how the status may impact upon their role. As EYPs' roles and responsibilities are so varied, the answer to this will depend on the stage of the practitioner's journey and the setting in which the practitioner works. The Children's Workforce Development Council (CWDC) highlights some of the questions frequently asked by employers of EYPs. Please see the website for the most up-to-date and current information (www.cwdcouncil.org.uk). Some of the questions include:

- What exactly should a job description for an EYP look like?
- How much is it going to cost me?
- How much should I pay my EYP?
- If Ofsted doesn't say I have to do it, why should I?
- How do I choose or identify who to put forward?
- How do I keep them? Do I have to release them to other settings?
- Do I have to release them for training?

Practitioners who have undertaken EYPS have described the process as thought-provoking and have explained the difference it has made to them personally and as part of their professional development.

Case study 1 – a nursery manager describes how EYPS impacted upon her role

Catherine Curl – Little Cherubs Day Nursery and Preschool:

'Above all, becoming an EYP has been a personal journey. The EYPS course is designed to appeal to the individual qualities and strengths of a person, and be accessible in a way that many higher education courses are not. It values the students' personal story and works to support achievement through their strengths. Through study on the EYPS course, I realised it was about what I could bring to the table and how I could use my knowledge and skills to become a leader. I believe this was the key to finally achieving my role as an agent of change.'

'I decided to become an EYP because, for me, like many, it was the next professional step to take. I had completed my degree in early childhood studies 3 years earlier, and I went on to work as a supervisor. Some time later I was looking for a new job and a new challenge. I wanted to work to raise standards of children's learning and care, and was desperate to feel fulfilled in my job. I had all these ideas but lacked the facilities and means to put them into action. Becoming an EYP gave me the opportunity I was looking for to achieve this.'

'When it came to getting a new job as a preschool coordinator, I was glad to hear my new employer ask if I was interested in becoming an EYP. I had heard of the EYPS qualification and I knew it was what I wanted to achieve. There was just one problem – my specific learning difficulty in maths. I had only achieved a D at GCSE in school, so I wasn't eligible for achieving EYPS at that point. I took a GCSE maths equivalency course, a number of psychological tests and a numeracy course to finally get me on to the EYPS course. When I was told I had dyscalculia, a difficulty in learning and comprehending mathematics, everything fell into place. Edge Hill University, where I had applied to study, were incredibly understanding about this, and I was offered a place providing that I achieved the required mathematics requirement. Those dark days studying maths and finding my feet in a new job felt like the ultimate test at the time. However, I was determined to get there, and when I passed it was as if I was giving a big hug to my 9-year-old self. I had proved myself, and I felt much better.'

'I was thrilled with my new job, and for the first time I was given the chance to spread my wings. I was lucky to have a supportive employer and a team who valued my knowledge. I got stuck in, and went on to write the self-evaluation form and guide their Ofsted inspection.'

'When my employers opened their new setting in Birkenhead, I moved there to pass on and continue my work. I prepared the setting for its inspection and took on the role of curriculum advisor. I was asked to evaluate the provision and begin a process of change. During this time I faced a big challenge; when moving to Birkenhead, the nursery had taken on an already established setting, plus its staff. I realised early on that implementing change was going to be tough. I had the utmost respect for the methodology that was in place and I was keen to maintain tradition and reputation. Yet I could see that this setting had needs, and I felt that I knew what to do about them.'

'In the midst of this, I began the EYPS course at Edge Hill, and was keen to get some guidance from my peers. I was fortunate to be part of a very supportive group. It was comforting to hear that the others had similar worries. We all came from different professional backgrounds, and I valued the advice I got. We always had great discussions, and I looked forward to the sessions. However, I kept thinking how difficult it seemed for others and myself to achieve EYPS when not in a managerial position. Some of the 39 standards required were tricky to evidence outside of management, and I couldn't help feeling as if I had less opportunity to implement change than a manager would. Fortunately, I had the chance to voice these concerns as my group representative at the next feedback meeting. My tutors were great and helped me to negotiate these boundaries. It became about understanding my worth and the worth of others.'

'The more I focused on my goals, the more my confidence grew in my job. I worked from an action plan I had developed and liaised closely with the staff to implement changes. The real task was keeping the benefits at the centre of change: a careful delivery of "this is what we have to do to meet standards, and this is the best way to do it"'.

'Developing the observation, assessment and planning procedures has been the most challenging aspect so far. But through dedication and cooperative teamwork I believe my setting is now on the right track.'

'At the moment I'm preparing for my setting visit. I think all EYPS students can relate to the struggle of juggling the course assessments and work commitments, whether they are in an existing job or joining a setting. I have so much respect for the students that join a setting for their practice element. Implementing changes in your job is one thing, but joining a setting temporarily to implement changes is another.'

'When I think back over the past year, I feel like I have been on a fast track course in "how to lead". When I started becoming an EYP, I struggled to see the light at the end of the tunnel. It's been extremely challenging, and at times I have felt so hopeless and frustrated. I've questioned myself so many times, wondering if I'm capable.'

'Now, it may sound clichéd, but I see my experiences on the course as something I have truly gained from. Even my experiences with my learning difficulty have given me an interest in how we teach early years mathematics.'

'My determination to achieve better outcomes for the children I work with has driven me forwards. The EYPS course helped me to realise my strengths and weaknesses, and this boosted my confidence. I was then able to recognise my role much more clearly and I became better at seeing what my colleagues could offer. I could take advantage of what I was good at, and work on my limitations. I was also able to accept those limitations; it's very easy to be hard on yourself when you're in a position of leadership.'

'I now continue to guide the care and learning at both settings, and I find that each day brings new learning opportunities. At the moment I'm guiding the QISP (Quality Improvement Support Programme), and I'm heading an international partnership between our nursery and a setting in South Africa. Through becoming an EYP I have realised that if you want to make changes, you've got to really believe in yourself and what you're doing. Becoming a leader in a situation can be terrifying, but with support and dedication, a great deal can be achieved. We, as educators of children, should know that above all.'

Case study 2 – a nursery owner describes how employing an EYP impacted upon her setting

Liz Ludden:

'I achieved my EYPS in 2007. As a qualified teacher with experience across the age ranges and a nursery owner, I was ideally placed to undertake the status within its early stages.'

'As soon as I began to gather evidence to demonstrate that I met the 39 standards I realised that this was going to have a major impact on my professional development. I was able to reflect upon my current role and analyse the balance between my practice and my leadership and support for others.'

'Collating the necessary evidence to demonstrate the standards was time-consuming; however, I felt that it validated my professional practice and gave me the opportunity to identify areas for development.'

'Although I was proud when I was notified of my accreditation, I also understood that the status meant more than a certificate to display in the setting to mark the Government's aim to have an EYP in every setting by 2009. During the accreditation process I had begun to research current good practice (I had been given access to the university library again), I had been able to work with other professionals who were also working towards accreditation and, above all, I had reawakened my enthusiasm for my work within the early years sector and reinforced my opinion that these were the most important years of a child's life.'

'I found that my enthusiasm had a positive impact upon my setting and upon my colleagues. We were questioning our everyday practice and felt confident to be able to back up any changes we made with a sound knowledge and understanding of current good practice, and the different and diverse ways that children develop and learn. This came at a time when the EYFS was being rolled out across the country and therefore settings were required to be responsive to change.'

'Throughout my career I have always been supported by headteachers and mentors who have encouraged me to continue my professional development. As the leader of my own setting I have always taken a proactive approach to staff training and development of staff. We have a very low turnover of staff and, as such, there were several members of staff who were ready either to embark on EYPS pathways or begin to work towards level 5 or 6 qualifications.'

'I trained as an EYPS mentor and the setting began to offer placements to EYPS candidates on full training pathways.'

'Suddenly, gaining EYPS was something to which a large number of the staff were aspiring, and I was in a position to be able to support and guide them towards the routes to EYPS.'

'Currently we have two full time EYPs with a further six staff who will achieve the status by 2011. We have also supported at least 15 candidates on full training to achieve the accreditation.'

'Whilst I have been criticised by some and warned that by enabling my staff to gain this qualification will mean that I will inevitably lose them as the setting cannot afford to maintain the salaries of eight EYPs, I feel that the benefits far outweigh this risk. Within our setting the status of the profession has been raised considerably. They understand how their role impacts upon the achievement and enjoyment of the children.'

'The impact upon the setting has been immense; the learning environment is no longer recognisable to what it was 5 years ago. Staff are motivated, enthusiastic and confident. I observe quality interactions between staff and children, and staff have high expectations for the children based on knowledge and understanding of child development. Above all, the children are happy and our partnerships with parents have increased considerably.'

'Myself and the staff at the setting have also been given the opportunity to be involved in practitioner-based research projects on the outdoor environment, the inclusion development programme, the block play project and Every Child a Talker, in conjunction with local universities, which will lead to MA accreditation.'

'Without a doubt I am proud to be amongst the growing number of EYPs who will continue to improve outcomes for children.'

Case study 3 – an early years development officer describes how gaining EYPS made a difference to her role

Elaine Canale:

'It was with great trepidation that I embarked on the EYPS pilot in 2007 as the study of early childhood at postgraduate level was relatively new. Pioneers in early years have been stating for many years that there needed to be a clear career structure for those who work with our youngest children and, with the early childhood studies degree and the EYP status, we finally have this.'

'Upon achieving the status I began work for a north-west local authority and my passion for the status was channelled into developing the EYP network with the support of a workforce development colleague. Funding was granted by CWDC to set up an EYP network and, in April 2008 with a membership of three, we held our first meeting. Currently in 2010 this has expanded to 17 and is still growing with the support of graduate leadership funding. As the network has grown, the members have taken it upon themselves to develop terms of reference. The terms of reference included opportunities for CPD. So the challenge began to seek appropriate speakers and opportunities to meet the needs of the network.

Members have had opportunities to attend bespoke training programmes in mentoring with EYPs from another local authority. Communication-friendly spaces training from Elizabeth Jarmin was offered jointly to EYPs and those on the home grown graduate pathway. The aim of this was to develop a support mechanism for those striving to achieve EYPS. Opportunities to attend sessions with widely published authors such as Margaret Edgington and Sue Palmer have also been arranged, and the EYPs have felt privileged to have such experiences.'

'In 2009 the numbers of EYPs across the north-west had increased significantly and there was a gap in specific training for those with the status. With this knowledge I decided to organise the first ever conference for those with EYPS in the north-west. The choice of workshops included working with babies, inclusion, outdoor learning and, with key notes from national strategies, the event was a huge success. The event was held in Chorley and evaluations were extremely positive, stating that they would like this to become an annual event. A working party of officers from across the north-west has formed and a second event took place this year. Once again this was a huge success, with capacity for 200 delegates. It is hoped that this will be replicated in future years.'

'It had been identified by the network that they would like to develop their leadership skills further. Earlier this year an opportunity arose to apply for funding from CWDC to support the CPD of EYPs. I embraced this opportunity and submitted a bid for 20 EYPs from three local authorities to attend a bespoke "leading for results" programme. The programme has been of great benefit and has given opportunity for the EYPs to gain feedback from those they work with regarding their leadership skills and use this information to support a specific project in the setting.'

'The local authority by whom I am employed in the north-west has recognised the importance of the EYPS and this is reflected in our team. We have EYPs as early years consultants to challenge and support the private, voluntary and independent sectors.'

Case study 4 – a deputy manager in a private day nursery describes her EYPS experience

Karen Howard:

'As a qualified teacher with early years as my specialism, I had spent a number of years as a teacher in nursery and reception classes. Early in 2007 I was offered the position of deputy manager in a private day nursery. I considered that the opportunity would broaden my experience of the early years sector and allow me to develop my management skills further.'

'I am afraid that I was naïve in relation to the operation of private day nurseries; from my preliminary visits to the nursery I concluded that they must not be subject to the same guidelines as school nurseries. However, my initial research enlightened me to the fact that all preschool provision had to comply with the Early Years Foundation Stage (EYFS) document (unless exempted) and, for children younger than 3, "Birth to Three Matters". The setting had been open for 7 years and appeared to have changed very little in that time. Much of current recommended good practice did not appear to be in place.'

'I spent about 3 months working with the existing system to get to know staff, ascertaining their backgrounds and strengths and gauging their readiness for change. It transpired that although staff turnover was fairly static, most staff had only ever worked in this setting, they were happy with the status quo, and had not been previously challenged to change. They reflected that guidance had changed frequently over the preceding years and felt that it was not worth investing time, effort and money in change only for it to be undermined by other new initiatives.'

'A number of items were brought out of the store cupboards each day for the children to play with. Their educational value was mapped against the six areas of the early learning goals. There was little focus on planning for individual needs or children's interests. Free play time was very limited and there was a lot of whole class adult-directed time. Access to the outdoors was timetabled to 20 minutes per session. There was an emphasis on keeping children and the setting safe, clean and tidy, which meant that access to messy activities and natural resources was very restricted; plastic toys made up the majority. In other aspects the nursery did well. It had a lovely homely feel and many of the staff were very experienced; the welfare and social aspects of children's learning were very well catered for and the staff had an excellent repertoire of circle activities, games and whole class activities which enhanced speaking and listening skills.'

'The owner of the setting was very reluctant to change as she considered that the staff and parents were happy with the existing provision. She also worried about placing extra work on an already underpaid staff.'

'The publication of the EYFS in June 2007 in preparation for its implementation in September 2008 coincided with my enrolment onto the EYPS short pathway. The setting was also due an Ofsted inspection. The combination of these gave me the leverage to begin to make changes. A cash incentive for the setting was attached to my participation on the course and this really helped. As an EYPS candidate I needed to demonstrate that I could act as an agent for change. Change was a huge requirement of the course and was definitely a primary factor in the developments that I was able to make in the setting. Initially, I audited practice against the principles of the EYFS and identified areas for change with management, staff and local early years advisers. We created a nursery improvement plan (NIP), which included long- and short-term projects and which came to be reviewed and updated annually. In meeting the 39 standards to attain EYPS I had to demonstrate competencies, which enabled me to complete or initiate many changes. Initially, I introduced continuous provision; this was followed, over the next 2½ years, by the introduction of the key worker system, effective planning based on children's individual interests and needs, sensory play, 'Sounds and Letters', continuous snack, greater involvement of parents in children's learning and continuous access to, and refurbishment of, the outdoor environment. In the process of implementing these changes I identified staff training needs, which were met by in-house or external training and support.'

'My enrolment onto the EYPS course definitely kick-started a culture of change within the setting and initiated a spirit of reflective practice. I do not claim that all change went smoothly or that I reached all of my targets – there were many disagreements and compromises along the way; however, individuals have definitely taken ownership and responsibility for identifying the need for and implementation of change. Many staff enrolled on courses to further their qualifications and now almost everyone is qualified to at least to level 3. Two members of staff have begun a foundation degree in early years and one is about to qualify as an EYP. On reflection, my becoming an EYP has had a huge impact on the setting in terms of the professional development of staff and the quality of provision for the children.'

'Since attaining EYPS other professional opportunities have opened up to me. I have supported other students towards their qualifications, joined my local EYP network which allows EYPs to have an impact on local policies and strategies, and also to address aspects such as CPD and support for EYPs in settings. The qualification definitely has the potential for giving highly qualified practitioners the status to be able to implement positive changes and drive up standards in the early years sector. However, I feel that once the status has been attained it is up to local and national government to maintain the high profile it deserves and the funding needed to enable private and voluntary sectors to meet the ever changing requirements of early years provision.'

EYPs may wish to continue their professional development by carrying out their masters degree. A master's degree typically consists of 180 credits at level 7. The 180 credits will usually be broken down by the university into modules, with each module being allocated a credit amount. There is no central place to apply for a master's degree; individuals will apply direct to the university at which they wish to study. There are many benefits to continuing on to a master's degree, including:

- Developing personal knowledge and understanding
- Potential to carry out research in a subject of interest
- Career development
- The knowledge to develop practice based on a theoretical underpinning
- The ability to analyse, be critical and consider different perspectives.

Some EYPs may decide to become involved with or carry out research. Some of the research projects currently being carried out by CWDC are:

- Analysis of local integrated workforce strategies
- Creating relevant and sustainable employment opportunities for looked after children in the north-west
- Development of occupational summary sheets
- EYPS research
- National evaluation of integrated working
- National occupational standards (NOS) usage
- Occupational and functional mapping of the children's workforce in England
- Pilot study to explore the feasibility of using occupational summary sheets to map key workforce intelligence data for CWDC's sector skills footprint in four regions
- Practitioner-led research (PLR)
- State of the children's social care workforce
- Research into the composition, needs and aspirations of the nanny workforce in England
- Review of the children's outreach workforce
- Travellers, Irish travellers, gypsies, Roma and showpeople
- Use of team around the child (TAC) model for the 11–14-year age group
- Volunteers in the children's workforce.

The full details of each research project can be sourced on the CWDC website. By reviewing these research projects, EYPs will be able to consider how they might approach their own research.

Completed projects carried out by CWDC include:

- Analysis of the e-training materials used by those in the children's workforce
- Career pathways in the learning, development and support services
- Evaluation of EYPS training (full pathway)
- Evaluation of newly qualified social worker and early professional development programmes
- Evaluation of the One Children's Workforce Framework tool
- Evaluation of the peer support pilot programme for middle managers
- Evaluation of the remodelling social work delivery pilots
- Longitudinal study of those who have achieved EYPS
- Practitioner-led research (PLR) (May 2009–May 2010)
- PLR good practice guide
- Review of current guidance and training on poverty and disadvantage to support the children's workforce
- Review of the data on the state of the children and young people's workforce
- Scoping study to assess how research on workforce issues is used to evidence practice in the field
- Understanding the children's social care workforce.

A piece of research that may be of particular interest to EYPs includes 'Evaluation of the career developments of early years professionals (EYPs)'. CWDC and the National Foundation for Educational Research (NFER) collaborated over a research project that investigated the early impact of EYPS. A sample of EYPs and their employers were interviewed, either face-to-face or over the telephone, about their experiences around 6 months after EYPS had been achieved.

The project focused on the role of the EYPS workers, and how the status has impacted on their career prospects. A number of areas, including additional responsibilities, career progression and recognition of EYPS among other professionals, were looked at closely to identify successes and to highlight areas that needed improvement. A summary report and response from CWDC are available on the CWDC website.

It is essential that, once practitioners gain EYPS, they continue on their journey of professional development and sharing good practice. Many local authorities have EYP network groups where the members identify training needs and exchange information about conferences and exhibitions. Some network members visit each other's settings to share good practice. It is a forum where the

dedication and commitment of EYPs can be recognised and a sense of belonging can be achieved. Some networks produce newsletters and invite guest
speakers to the sessions. To become a member of the network, EYPs will need
to contact their local authority as each local authority sets their own membership
regulations.

EYPs may continue on their journey by contributing to conferences and writing journal articles. Some EYPs may start this work in a group and, then as their
confidence grows, begin to approach journals and magazines for publication on
an individual basis. Some of these may include:

Early Years Educator
Nursery World
TACTYC
Practical Pre-school
Nursery Education Plus
Early Childhood Education
Early Childhood Research Quarterly
Early Years: Journal of International Research and Development
Educational Policy Making
Practical Professional Childcare.

All practitioners undertaking EYPS require a mentor as part of their programme of study. Many EYPs have become mentors to practitioners undertaking EYPS working with the training providers. Practitioners with EYPS are best
placed to undertake this role as they can relate to the anxieties that the practitioners experience and offer support and advice from their own experiences. If
becoming an EYP mentor is a role you are interested in, contact your local EYP
training provider and enquire about their processes.

Some EYPs will become members of associations or unions to keep up to
date with changes happening within the sector. Aspect is a professional association and union representing EYPs.

Aspect – The Association of Professionals in Education and Children's Trusts – is the
only professional association and trade union exclusively representing professionals
working in children's services. These professionals play a vital role in shaping and influencing the lives of millions of children and young people.   (www.aspect.org.ukl)

Many settings can access support for EYPs, and one way this is offered is
through the graduate leadership fund. The graduate leadership fund is aimed at
private, voluntary and independent settings to support training and professional

development and focuses on attainment of graduates in early years settings. Many local authorities give this money to settings to:

- Contribute to the salary costs of graduates
- Provide CPD to support retention.

Each local authority defines the terms and conditions on how they will release the money to the setting and the commitment they expect in return. This will depend on the need within the area. You will need to contact your local authority to enquire how they are using their money and the support you and your setting can access.

EYPS is a status that gives recognition to specialist knowledge and understanding of working with children from 0 to 5, and the skills of being able to lead and support other practitioners. Gaining EYPS is a tremendous achievement and the start of a journey for early years workers. We hope that the book has enabled you to deconstruct the standards and consider the implications for practice. Best of luck in your journey.

Conclusion

EYPs undertake many different roles in a wide variety of settings. However, all EYPs are aiming to achieve the same thing – to improve outcomes for children. EYPs are leaders of change and are raising the quality of experiences with which children engage. Undertaking EYPS has had a significant impact on developing practitioners' skills and practice, allowing career progression. Many employers have commented on the improvement to the staff knowledge and understanding through undertaking EYPS. Gaining EYPS gives recognition to the hard work and dedication of many early years workers.

Index